DATE DUE

SEP 2 8 1998	

GAYLORD   PRINTED IN U.S.A.

D1247236

body movement
PERSPECTIVES IN RESEARCH

body movement
PERSPECTIVES IN RESEARCH

Advisory Editor: **Martha Davis**
Hunter College

A PSYCHOLOGY OF GESTURE

by

Dr. CHARLOTTE WOLFF

ARNO PRESS

A NEW YORK TIMES COMPANY

New York • 1972

Reprint Edition 1972 by Arno Press Inc.

Reprinted by permission of Methuen & Co. Ltd.

Reprinted from a copy in The Princeton University
Library

Body Movement: Perspectives in Research
ISBN for complete set: 0-405-03140-8
See last pages of this volume for titles.

Manufactured in the United States of America

————————————

Library of Congress Cataloging in Publication Data

Wolff, Charlotte, 1897–
    A psychology of gesture.

    (Body movement: perspectives in research)
    Reprint of the 1948 ed.
    1. Gesture. 2. Hand. I. Title. II. Series.
BF935.G4W63 1972   152.3'84   72-348
ISBN 0-405-03147-5

A PSYCHOLOGY OF GESTURE

The banquet, though riotous, had been agreeable, and now the blessings of leisure—unknown to the West, which either works or idles—descended on the motley company. Civilization strays about like a ghost here, revisiting the ruins of empire, and is to be found not in great works of art or mighty deeds, but in the gestures well-bred Indians make when they sit or lie down. Fielding, who had dressed up in native costume, learnt from his excessive awkwardness in it that all his motions were makeshifts, whereas when the Nawab Bahadur stretched out his hand for food or Nureddin applauded a song, something beautiful had been accomplished which needed no development. This restfulness of gesture—it is the Peace that passeth Understanding, after all, it is the social equivalent of Yoga. When the whirring of action ceases, it becomes visible, and reveals a civilization which the West can disturb but will never acquire.

E. M. FORSTER,
A Passage to India

A PSYCHOLOGY OF GESTURE

by

Dr. CHARLOTTE WOLFF
FELLOW OF THE BRITISH PSYCHOLOGICAL SOCIETY.

Author of *The Human Hand*

Translated from the French Manuscript by
ANNE TENNANT

SECOND EDITION

METHUEN & CO. LTD. LONDON
36 Essex Street, Strand, W.C.2

TO

F. C. BIEBER

First Published   *October 11th 1945*
Second Edition   .   .   .   *1948*

CATALOGUE NO. 3697/U

PRINTED IN GREAT BRITAIN

ACKNOWLEDGMENT

I WANT to express my very best thanks to the London County Council for having permitted me to carry out research work at St. Lawrence's and at St. Bernard's Hospital.

I also want to express my gratitude to the Medical Superintendents—Dr. J. L. A. Lewis of St. Bernard's Hospital, Southall, Dr. C. J. C. Earl, now at Monyhull Colony, Birmingham, Dr. T. Lindsay of St. Lawrence's Hospital, Caterham, who have given me every facility and help for the work, on which the Clinical Study of this book is built.

I am also greatly indebted to the Nurses of the Hospitals mentioned, especially to Sister Turner, of St. Bernard's Hospital, who has assisted my research work with untiring interest and efficiency. Last but not least I want to thank my translator, Miss Anne Tennant, for her extraordinary devotion to her task and for her kindness in typing the Manuscript.

C. W.

CONTENTS

The illustrations are between pages 206 and 207

INTRODUCTION

WHILST pursuing my research on the psychology of the hand I was always aware that a supplementary study would be necessary : a study of gesture. My work so far was designed to develop a psycho-diagnostic method based on the features of the hand. I showed their correlations with constitutional tendencies—the endocrine glands in particular—temperament and mentality. In carrying out that work I realized that the dynamic aspect must be included, and for this reason I dwelt upon gesture in my last book, *The Human Hand*. In the theoretical part I explained that the gestures of the hand are largely responsible for the nature of the crease lines and indirectly for the form of the hand. I observed that certain types of hands corresponded with certain types of gestures. A correlation between hand, constitution and gesture could thus be logically assumed : but a systematic study and an adequate theory were necessary to substantiate my observations, and this task I have striven to fulfil in my research work of the last three years.

In my attempt to find a theoretic basis I owe a great debt to Professor H. Wallon with whom I had the good fortune to work in Paris for three years. Wallon gave great prominence to the psycho-motor system in his investigations on the psychology of the child, and his observations greatly helped my comprehension of the evolution of gesture.

The French school of psychology as represented by Wallon, Ribot, Borel and others is less sanguine of a statistical approach than the English and American school. Modern French psychology is based on clinical observation. In doubting the value of statistics it is in line with many of the conclusions of " Gestalt Psychology ". One of the most prominent representatives of the latter, Koffka, stressed the fact that laboratory experiments which take only achievement results into consideration have obvious limitations. Another notable Gestalt-psychologist Koehler and the psychiatrist Goldstein have made a special study of psycho-motor behaviour, based on clinical research. The theoretical conclusions of Goldstein are so important and far reaching for a psychology of gesture that I have quoted him at length in the second chapter of this book.

I have also been influenced by the work of the American psychologist Krout. Krout is noted for his studies on autistic gestures (movements directed towards the body). He embarked on a new method of experiment which differs widely from those of other American investigators who have worked on the same subject—as Luria, Allport, Vernon and others. These only carried out instrumental studies on a relatively small number of college students in the classical laboratory fashion. Krout was aware of the limitations of such an approach, namely the impossibility of getting any true emotional gesture response from the subject and the consequent failure to acquire any knowledge of the deeper layers of personality. Instrumental studies test performance behaviour which only indirectly reveals the emotional make-up. Krout was concerned to detect direct emotional response through movement. He therefore studied gestures in typical life-like situations first and then tried to establish similar experimental situations afterwards. He used the free association technique of words which Jung had adopted for diagnostic purposes and observed those expressive movements which were produced by word stimuli. Krout found that : ' Postural sets tend to coincide with verbal responses to given sets of stimuli.' Another experiment for testing psycho-motor behaviour in a life-like situation consisted in asking the students who took part to relax and to pass into a state of day-dreaming. As soon as they made gestures they had to stop and make descriptive notes. Krout admits that several of the subjects had been unable to carry out the experiment which was done at home and without any supervision. Nevertheless he found the results of this process much more significant than those of the same experiment done under class-room conditions, when the students were watched by a committee. He considered a global observation of the subjects very difficult to attain and did not trust the judges to give an impartial interpretation of gesture responses owing to a bias either of sympathy or antipathy towards the subjects. Krout was also aware of the difficulty of making conscious efforts in order to get subconscious reactions which are the essence of autistic and other involuntary gestures. Such efforts defeat their own ends as they act as inhibitive factors instead of releasing subconscious responses. Krout was able, however, to show that autistic gestures exist, as they recurred when the subjects were under the influence of hypnosis. The method of testing expressive movements under hypnosis is of course impracticable in ordinary circumstances but it is of scientific value.

The type of experiment which left the whole performance to

the student without any supervision had in a milder form the same handicap as the test situation in the laboratory, namely that the subject was overconscious of an inner process and was therefore on the lookout for certain results, while he should completely relax and leave his subconscious free to wander in any direction. Anticipation must falsify results which depend entirely on spontaneous reactions.

I have mentioned Krout's work at length for two reasons :

1. His investigations concerned the subconscious emotions and conflicts.
2. He has to a large extent abandoned the classic method of experiment of which he realized the shortcomings.

Modern psychologists (no matter of what school) have one common aspiration, namely to align psychology with natural science, physics in particular. This preoccupation has latterly become a sort of obsession with the danger of forcing methods of investigation into a wrong direction. Such an attitude has been engendered by the cold shouldering of psychology by representatives of other branches of science, particularly of medicine. These look down on psychology as a perverted creation, or at best an illegitimate child. In consequence psychologists strain every nerve to prove the legitimacy of their offspring. They have become uncertain of themselves and have developed an inferiority complex towards the other sciences, whose methods of investigation they try too eagerly to imitate. This state of affairs is mostly responsible for the overvaluation of statistics in modern psychology. By the effort of reducing man's personality into figures and formulae the true aim of investigation is badly envisaged and wrongly treated.

Nervous and emotional reactions cannot be measured in quantity nor comparisons made between individuals who are complete entities with specific functional laws. Certain individual qualities can only be compared with other qualities of the same individual with due regard to the personality as a whole. Furthermore, emotions are irrational reactions, and for this reason escape quantitative formulae, otherwise they would be rational and calculable. If statistical analysis of the emotions becomes absurd it is certainly a doubtful process in regard to mental qualities, as Chambers showed recently in a critical article in the British Journal of Medical Psychology—' Statistics in Psychology and the Limitations of the Test Method '. Chambers maintains that it is impossible to separate mental qualities from the rest of the personality. They are profoundly influenced by physical conditions, moods and preoccupations. They are also affected by the test situation and a nervous reaction towards the examiner. A state of anxiety can for example simulate an inferior intelligence, and a lack of inhibition can on the contrary simulate a superior intelligence when in reality it is only mediocre. This criticism of the statistical method is not intended as a condemnation of its value but as an indication of its possible abuse. Rightly and reasonably applied the statistical experiment has a wide scope. It is, for example, invaluable in testing the performance of skilled action in selecting persons for specific jobs, but it must not be forgotten that it is the actions themselves which are judged and classified and not the performers. The fundamental qualities of the individual cannot be judged since they are modified by irrational factors like emotions and nervous reactions. To find a code by which to interpret human personality other methods must be applied. Kretschmer, in *The Experimental Method treated as an Instrument of Psychological Investigation*, stresses the fact that :

The greatest number of medical discoveries have not been made by statistical methods but reached without experiment, the only method being that of scientific description of fine acoustic, optical and tactile distinctions.

And :

If a patient enters the room one can diagnose at once shaking palsy, and this diagnosis embraces a lot of knowledge on temperament and character as well. It is easy to see how difficult it would be to come to a similar diagnosis and knowledge of personality through seeking out the components of this shaking palsy through experiment and statistics.

The method so strongly advocated by Kretschmer has been criticized as subjective. This argument defeats itself since most of medical diagnosis is based on observation and description, and psychology according to my view, is a branch of medicine. To avoid the subjective intermediary who is the observer, psychologists use an electrical machine which registers with the faithfulness only achieved by mechanism the working of the mind. Such a mechanical registration does not unfortunately include the mechanizing of the mental process which is under investigation except in certain distinct cases of psycho-pathology. It is for this reason that the Encephalograph of Berger and Adrian has an undoubted value as it registers abnormal waves proceeding from the brain of an epileptic. In this type of a mental malady the inhibitive factor no longer counts, as the anomaly is organic and systematized, the mechanism of self-regulation being thrown out of gear.

It is evident that reliance on the machine as a scientific register of the mind has replaced reliance on the observation and judgement of the investigator. This seems to me to be a dangerous innovation which not only leads to a falsification of the results of investigation, but also to a complete negation of psychology.

For the reasons which I have given, *A Psychology of Gesture* is constructed on a system of clinical studies and medico-psychological interpretations. I have thus followed the model of the French school as represented by Wallon and to a certain extent that of the ' Gestalt ' psychology. I am convinced that the knowledge of man's personality cannot be acquired by investigations which only touch the periphery but by those which reach the centre. The functional and synthetic conception of personality which we owe to the ' Gestalt ' psychology is in line with my own ideas. It is in this direction that I have made this study on gesture—as a form of behaviour which depends in the first place on the core of personality or on the structure of the centre. By the mirror of gesture I have tried to recognize the degree of integration or disintegration of the individual, which, as Goldstein was able to show, is revealed by the predominance and quality of movements either of flexion or extension. Integration can be defined as the perfect co-ordination between perception and expression and between the conscious and the subconscious. Obviously the more an organism is evolved and complex the more difficult will be the integration of personality. Integration is easier to attain when outer and inner circumstances are favourable than when they are difficult. Integration also greatly depends on hereditary and other constitutional traits. For this reason I have given special attention to the correlation between physical type and gesture type. A knowledge of the constitutional type includes, as Kretschmer and others have shown, a knowledge of temperament. The study on gesture amplifies this knowledge in the realm of psychodynamics.

Gestures of the hand have naturally attracted my particular interest and they occupy the first place in this book. Gait and

facial gestures are only treated in correlation with hand gestures.
I have entirely omitted vocal gestures which certainly merit special
investigation but are, however, outside the scope of my work.
It is not only in view of my special branch of research that I have
placed hand gestures in the forefront but on its own merits. The
outstanding significance of hand gestures has been recognized,
amongst others, by Professor Osseretzky of Leningrad, who in
his *Psychomotorik* recommends the study of hand gestures as
follows :

It is no exaggeration to say that the whole body in its static as well
as in its dynamic state is continually adapting itself to the functions of
the hand. That is why the study of hand movements is the most
important of all. (Quotation translated from the German text.)

Osseretzky elaborated a vast scheme for testing motor patterns
of the whole body with a distinct preference for methods which
register the static and dynamic co-ordination of the hands. Unfortunately his scheme is too vast, too theoretic and too mechanized to be practicable. He has collected all the data that exist
on gestures and postures but has somehow confused the issues.
Osseretzky also designed a detailed plan for the study of the hand,
fully realizing its importance for psychology. But his suggestions
for a chirological study are so poorly substantiated by his own
experience that the scheme lacks depth and conviction. Osseretzky
is a man of vision but his reach exceeds his grasp. He has been
strongly influenced by Kretschmer and his pupils. Amongst them
Willi Enke produced a classic study on 'Die Psychomotorik der
Konstitutionstypen' (The Psycho-Motor Reactions of the Constitutional Types).

Enke describes psycho-motor behaviour as the living expression of character and maintains that therefore psycho-motor expressions constitute an essential part of the psycho-physical knowledge of personality. His material consisted of 500 subjects all
representative of pure types as indicated by Kretschmer. Enke's
investigations on the subject were concerned with the psycho-
motor tempo, the motor co-ordination of both hands, the starting
speed, the fatigability, the rhythm and the grace of movements.
For testing the psycho-motor tempo he used the 'Klopfversuch'.
The subjects were asked to hit a metallic disc with a metal pencil.
The speed of their attack differed widely in the various constitutional types. Enke observed during this experiment that certain

people always hit the disc in the same place, óthers vacillated from one place to another. The precision of movements was therefore also variable in accordance with the constitutional type. The result of Enke's experiments are well known to psychologists, but I will summarize them here :

1. The pyknic type of Kretschmer is characterized by slow starting speed with a swift adaptation to new circumstances.
2. The leptosome type adapts himself slowly to a new motor task and the co-ordination of his gross movements is imperfect. His hand movements are superior to those of the preceding type as far as delicate movements are concerned. He has more manual skill but less general motor skill (motorische Gesamtbegabung) than the pyknic type. Enke explains this by the more marked development of the frontal cortex in the leptosome type of man. It is indeed well known that intellectuals who have very often a leptosome physique, are as a rule clumsy, but frequently exhibit great grace in hand movements which are subtle and slight.
3. The athletic type is distinguished by a starting speed which is superior to that of the other constitutional types, but he tires more readily. His movements are clumsy and forceful.
4. The whole motor behaviour of the pyknic type shows more variety, spontaneity and therefore irregularity than that of the other types. The leptosome and athletic types are characterized by regular, mechanized, and stereotyped movements.
5. Simultaneous concentration on mental and physical effort is much more difficult for the pyknic person than for the leptosome and athletic types. The latter types show sudden fatigability while the pyknic person tires less and more gradually.

These conclusions of Enke have a fundamental value for a psychology of gesture, but only in so far as they prove the underlying laws governing motor behaviour in different types and not as an interpretation of personality traits, since they take no account of the variability of life-like situations and contain no reference whatever to emotional gesture responses. They are the result of mechanical and instrumental studies.

Gesture has been recognized as an indication of character from the earliest times. Many of the ancient philosophers have testified to this idea. In China, also, involuntary gestures were always considered to be a revelation of inner dispositions. In this sense the psychology of gesture is as old as the history of the oldest human culture. But in our day the intuitive understanding of character must be elevated from the instinctive sphere and placed in the realm of methodic science.

To arrive at this it is necessary to limit the field of research in order to find a sure basis and to elaborate those laws of interpretation which are substantiated by clinical observation and a sound psycho-physiological theory.

This book must be accepted as a contribution to certain laws of psycho-motor behaviour which allow for an interpretation of emotional states and of the degree of integration. A more detailed and complex estimate which would permit of an all-round understanding of personality is not yet possible and must wait for future research.

My clinical material consisted of 88 mental patients, all inmates of St. Bernard's Hospital, Southall. Sixty-three of the patients had been observed in the occupational therapy class or at meals, and twenty-five patients had been studied during the process of taking hand-prints. I had investigated before, but not systematically, the gestures of mentally defective children as well as adults in St. Lawrence's Hospital, Caterham, Surrey. All the patients mentioned had been tested by my method of hand-interpretation. This material enabled me to study hand gestures and hand forms from a direct source. I considered mental patients especially suitable for a systematic research on gesture. Their integration and identity are largely or completely broken up, and their emotions appear, as in children, without inhibition. In schizophrenics and paraphrenics I had the best opportunity to study the influence of the imagination on gesture. In this respect, too, mental patients provide an excellent material, as their imaginative life is so completely real to them and as their movements and expressions are mostly the result of their special type of images.

The reader may rightly ask if certain laws of expressive movements derived from the study of mental patients can be applied to the normal. That this is so I hope to be able to show in the course of this book.

The special place that a psychology of gesture merits is obvious.

It permits a direct knowledge of personality without any effort or misleading co-operation on the part of the subject, since it can be applied without his being aware of the fact. A psychology of gesture might find a place side by side with the best personality test known to me—the Rohrschach test. Hermann Rohrschach was a psychiatrist of Zuerich who died in 1922 at the age of 32. A year before his death he published a book on his method of interpretation of ink-stains, of which five are in grey-black, two in grey-black and red, and three multicoloured. The subject is asked what he sees in the splashes of ink, and according to whether the stains are described as a whole or in detail—with emphasis on form, colour or movement, he is classified as such and such a psychological type. Affective states, emotional preoccupations and inhibitions along with the working of the imagination and the subconscious can be interpreted from the answers.

But up to a certain point the Rohrschach test demands the co-operation of the subject, and for this reason it contains a margin of error which can, however, be greatly reduced by a repetition of the process at different times.

A psycho-diagnostic test based on gesture or the Rohrschach test should always be used in conjunction with a diagnostic method which assesses constitutional tendencies. My principal research work on the Psychology of the Hand is designed to build up such a method, and this book, *A Psychology of Gesture*, must be regarded as a complementary study to my main studies.

CHAPTER I

THE NATURE OF GESTURE

GESTURE is a pre-verbal language which starts at birth. In the first years of life it is the most important means of expression, only receding into the background as speech develops, but remaining vivid and powerful in the child up to 5 or 6 years. Children imitate gestures long before they imitate words. Their first knowledge of the world is obtained through gestures of touch. They convey by expressive movements not only what they feel but what they mean to say and what they want. This primary form of language is entirely instinctual and emotional, and it is left to speech to give expression to the typically human capacity of thought. The whole body can participate in the language of gesture, whilst verbal language is restricted to the organs of speech.

The legend of the Tower of Babel illustrates how the peoples of the earth became divided and alienated—through the spoken word. And not only are different languages barriers to communication and understanding, but even the dialects of the same language have this severing effect. But however far apart in colour, habits, manners, and religion people may be, the universal language of gesture can forge links between them. For gesture-language is practically the same in all human beings, and it follows that it must correspond to the primary level of existence, comprising instincts and emotions on the one hand and an elementary knowledge of objects on the other. It is only abstract thought which cannot be expressed in the language of gesture.

It is of the nature of emotion to find expression in movements. A Chinese woman will certainly understand a Dane when he tells her in gesture ' I love you ' ; but the Dane will find it less easy to express more matter-of-fact needs by means of gestures. Races who gesticulate freely overcome this difficulty more easily than those who are restrained by disposition or education. Those peoples and individuals in whom kinaesthetic consciousness is well developed can easily learn to make themselves understood in foreign countries of whose languages they are ignorant. It is obvious that gestures could be used as a language for travellers and one that could help to unite the different peoples of the world into one great family. The use of gesture as an international idiom is not a new idea. Sittl relates in his book *Die Gebärdensprache der Griechen und Römer* how one of Nero's satellites, the Governor of a population of mixed tribes living on the coast of the Black Sea, requested the Emperor to send him a mummer to serve as interpreter. In our days, Sittl comments, the sailors who call at Italian and Greek ports make themselves understood by gestures.

In the Seventeenth Century the English physician Dr. John Bulwer, inventor of the deaf-and-dumb language and author of *Chirologia*, or *The Natural Language of the Hand*, suggested an international language of gesture. He described the movements of the hand as being 'the only speech that is natural to man', and said 'that it may be called the tongue and general language of human nature, which, without teaching, men in all regions of the habitable world doe at first sight most easily understand' (quoted from a paper 'John Bulwer, The Chirosopher', by H. J. Norman, in *Proceedings of the Royal Soc. of Med.*, May 1943). Leibnitz had the same idea of uniting the different nations by means of a common gesture language. The deaf-and-dumb language is a conscious and systematic form of sign language, derived from involuntary expressive movements : an international language of gesture would have to be built up on the same principle. But interesting though this problem is it cannot be dealt with in this book, which is concerned only with gesture as a subconscious expression of personality. All I want to point out is the beneficial influence which the teaching of a universal language of expressive movements could have on the individual.

It would first of all exercise the capacity of translating images into movement, and so develop kinaesthetic consciousness, which is so closely allied to the feeling of identity. It is no exaggeration to say that a gesture language would develop a better centralization of personality. This is not all. Expressive movements being the natural discharge of nervous tension, gesticulation therefore eases the mind by keeping it supple and mobile, as gymnastics do for the muscles and the circulation. In helping to develop the flexibility of the mind, gesture-language encourages the flow of associations and images, increasing the power of both and also of the emotions. Emotions are freed by unrestricted movements. They become inhibited and atrophied by suppression of gesture.

To study and interpret the gestures of a people like the British, who employ so few, might appear to serve no useful purpose ;

but actually the opposite is the truth. Inhibited expression is comparable to a river blocked by a dam ; it floods the surrounding country and seeks numerous more or less tortuous outlets. When direct expression is barred the inner dynamism discovers other outlets, less obvious and more bizarre.

The movements of the hands have suffered the greatest restriction through education, which tends to condemn gesticulation as undignified. The current of emotion thus broken can, up to a point, find outlet in movements of other parts of the body, such as the face and feet, and certain types of gesture escape altogether from conscious control and appear in slight movements of the hands. The expression of the face, the gait and the involuntary gestures of the hands retain, therefore, an expressive quality, both concentrated and revealing, which provides psychology with a valuable key to the subconscious motives and reactions of a personality.

Man without movement is 'dead' and the vital concern of each individual is to find adequate expression for his inner dynamism.

As the result of education intervening to cut off the natural means of expression, the child, and especially the adolescent, models his approach to life in accordance with a conventional code. The result must be an 'emotional uniform', worn when the owner is with others, taken off when he is alone. And what does he find when he is alone ? An accentuated self-consciousness, an exaggerated ego and a mass of inhibitions. Such people are rarely at their ease and are consequently thrown back more and more on themselves. An inner condition of this kind is reflected, in the long run, in the emotional life of individuals and peoples and results in an ever-increasing introversion. The introvert rarely escapes the danger of a strong autism and his mind is coloured by anxiety. His individualism is always in conflict with his social sense, which prepares the way for the character known as the 'escapist'. The simple and natural approach to others, which is the basis of a humanitarian life, becomes falsified and gives place to extravagance : to a cruel mysticism as we find it to-day among the Germans : to a lack of social cohesion as we find it among the English. The former, being more primitive, give expression to their progressive introversion in a collective and superstitious fashion ; the latter, being more civilized and evolved, end in a refusal of social obligations and take refuge in the pleasures of an aesthetic or sporting life. These characteristics have their root in the suppression of emotional expression in the individual.

Introversion produces at opposite poles genius and imbecility. In the vast area between there are many intermediate types more or less adapted to life but never really natural or happy, and a large number who must inevitably become neurasthenic or neurotic. The ill-adjusted person suffers from a sense of inner insecurity which goes with professional and social insecurity, the true explanation of which is hidden from the victim. The introvert of every degree has more need of the understanding and co-operation of his fellow-men than the extravert, who easily creates a milieu to suit himself.

For this reason it is more important to know the man who is badly adapted than the one who is well adapted to life. The latter is easy to 'read', for his expressions are unified and direct; the former is difficult to know, because his expressions are complex and indirect and only partially correspond to exterior situations. The introvert always remains partially self-absorbed, his mind in check, and this restricts its volatility and prevents communication. It is thus clear that the gestures of the well- and the ill-adjusted types are essentially different. Those of the former are marked by ease, naturalness and spontaneity, those of the latter by discomfort, effort and hesitation.

Man reveals himself by three languages : the language of acts, the language of words, and the language of gestures.

Our acts are the complex result of a continual strife between our instinctive, aesthetic and moral needs ; in other words, between the ego and the superego. They are indications rather of the façade and polish of personality than of its basic structure. And as the fine façade of a house may hide underlying decay, so may the acts of a man conceal his true nature.

The language of words is also for the most part under the control of consciousness, and is rather an indication of intelligence and style than of personality.

It is the fleeting and scarcely tangible expressions of gestures which unmask a man. Here we have a language conveying by continual and secret messages the essence of personality.

Expressive or involuntary gestures arise from the subconscious mind without passing through the cooling temperature of the critical consciousness. It is almost a platitude to say that a man reveals himself less in the great moments of life than in the humdrum of everyday existence. For this reason it is best to observe him in ordinary circumstances without his being aware of scrutiny and to avoid too intimate or too self-conscious situations. The opportunity for such observation is not limited to the psychological laboratory but is to be found everywhere and all the time, in social contacts. It is largely the study of his involuntary gestures which reveals the man and the difficulties from which he suffers.

The word gesture comes from the Latin *gerere*, which means to comport oneself or to show oneself.

The old precept of Socrates, ' Speak that I may see you ', conveys the same idea : that it is in expressive conduct that man reveals himself with an unconscious and poignant truth.

The way in which a woman opens and shuts the door, how she walks, gives you her hand, takes a chair, remains seated, gets up, the way she lights a cigarette, tears up a letter, turns the pages of a book, arranges flowers—all these things contribute to a picture of her personality. The way a man runs after a bus and gets on and off it, his habit of looking at his nails when speaking, of rising brusquely in the middle of a sentence and striding up and down —all these gestures contribute to a portrait of his personality.

The study of involuntary gestures is an inexhaustible source of information. It shows at each instant the undercurrent of personality running through all human activities, even the most banal. Every voluntary action directs attention to the ultimate aim, a fact which places expressive movements in even higher relief. Writing is an example. It represents a crystallization of gesture of which the writer, who must concentrate on the contents of his composition, remains, as a rule, unaware.

Graphology is a specialized study of expression, a study which merits a special place in modern psychology, for writing has the advantage of constituting a permanent record of the disposition of the subject. The writing of an individual at different phases of his life can be kept and compared, allowing of an all-round study of personality. Few other forms of expression register at the same time the potential of nervous energy, moods and temperament, and the level of intelligence, education, &c.

Hand-writing is a chain of crystallized gestures shaped by an individuality of greater or less development. Dancing also is a graph of gestures. Ritual and national dances are in a class by themselves. They are a mirror of the cultural history of a people.

In them expressive movements are woven on a symbolic pattern, giving us a key to the secrets of the people's ' collective ' emotions.

In Europe dancing has become more and more an affair of the feet, but in the Orient the hands still play an equal or even superior part.   That hands and feet are the really rhythmic organs of the body, reacting by reflex to music, everyone can observe in the ball room where rhythm is communicated as if by magic even to the feet of spectators.

Gestures are either rhythmic or arrhythmic. People with rhythmic movements are those whose movements are natural and easy and who charm us with their grace and elegance. Arrhythmic gestures are halting, abrupt, and impulsive, faults of expression which pain us by their clumsiness. People suffering from motor-arrhythmy are always ' *à côté* ', and the awkwardness of their movements corresponds to the awkwardness of their minds. Harmony or disharmony is therefore one of the essential traits of movements of expression.

Rhythmic faults, when they are striking, have a psycho-pathological significance. They often reveal inner conflicts very difficult to diagnose because those afflicted by them try to conceal them. Only a highly qualified person can see through the dissimulation. But it can be done. In graphology, for example, however skilled a forger may be, his forgery can nevertheless be detected by the expert.

Directly allied to the sense of rhythm is the sense of balance and co-ordination. It is difficult to separate them, for they form a functional system in which the faults of one reflect upon the other. One thing is certain : faults of balance and co-ordination are much more obvious than lack of rhythm. They can never be disguised and are rooted in emotional, mental, and nervous disturbances.

A lack of balance or of co-ordination always produces arrhythmic movements, but the presence of the latter does not necessarily indicate that the sense of balance is deranged.

Rhythm puts, so to speak, the finishing touch to movement. It develops only after the language of gesture is acquired ; the gestures of an infant do not show a marked rhythm. Their special charm lies in their touching clumsiness. Children learn to control the language of gesture by slow degrees, commencing for the most part with those movements designed to protect the equilibrium of the body. Infants are always tumbling : a strong desire to acquire objects which are out of reach and to run towards them arises before their sense of balance and co-ordination is established.

The first gestures of man are entirely utilitarian and demonstrate two antagonistic impulses : the forward movement and the movement of withdrawal in order to protect the equilibrium.

The mental capacities of the small child are absorbed in this game of making outside contacts and at the same time maintaining his uncertain balance. His mental life remains in this primary phase up to the moment when he succeeds in becoming familiar with his own body and the outside world. Only then does he commence to develop his personality. And the play of his impulses of advance and withdrawal go a stage further. They are more and more transposed from the physical to the mental plane, finally producing the fundamental human conflict between forward drive and inhibition.

As Dr. Vaschide has explained in his book *Essai sur une psychologie de la Main* (p. 450) (translated) :

All mental processes are the result of two contradictory actions : forward movement and withdrawal. This duality is to be found at the root of all inner manifestations such as voluntary movement, passion, determination, thought. The relative predominance of forward impulse or withdrawal determines the character in man.

Inner balance and co-ordination are the means by which an adult keeps his integrity. The lack of inner co-ordination corresponds to an absence of motor co-ordination, as can be seen in the movements of imbeciles and certain other mental patients. There are, for example, few of these unfortunates who walk like normal people. But it is not only in these extreme cases but also in psychoneurosis that one can discern want of balance and co-ordination of gestures. Binet and Feré found that the gestures of hysterical people show a muscular impulsiveness : the muscles of the hand contract and relax in sympathy with the pre-occupations of the invalid.

Even a normal person in times of difficulty may suffer from a state of mind which resembles neurotic conditions and his or her gestures may betray these negative moods. A woman who is always careful of her appearance and continually visits her friends in her best get-up, every movement expressive of poise and self-esteem, may appear one day completely *distraite*. It is not her eyes that betray her ; they preserve their tranquil look.   But she drops her handkerchief or her cigarette, breaks a plate or spills her tea, and these accidental clumsinesses tell a tale of preoccupation.   Her inner rhythm and co-ordination are as disturbed as her movements.

The disintegrating influence of the subconscious effects a disturbance of expressive conduct which may be temporary or permanent.

It must be remembered that each gesture is a synthesis of many movements.   In walking, each step is the sum total of small, perfectly co-ordinated movements.   Each gesture of the hand brings different muscles into play and is also a synthesis of more or less complex motor impulses.   As Vaschide pointed out, the gesture of hand-shaking is composed of a whole series of movements which give most valuable psychological information. Sympathy, coldness, different forms of anxiety and much more can be 'read' in this one gesture.

As gestures correspond to a very complex psycho-motor mechanism they are extremely sensitive to emotional or nervous disturbance.

Under 'positive' influences of good humour, sentiment, joy, and inner peace the whole system of the flexor muscles is stimulated, whilst in all 'negative' moods of anxiety, jealousy, rage and any physical discomfort the system of the extensor muscles takes the upper hand.

It was about fifty years ago that psychologists like Muensterberg, Stoerring, and Feré demonstrated that agreeable feelings suggest movements of flexion and disagreeable feelings movements of extension.   They noted, moreover, that of all the organs of the body the hand is the quickest to react ; then the arm ; then the shoulder.   This observation has a profound bearing on the psychology of gesture.   As I shall show later, gestures of the hands have, for a special reason, the deepest psychological significance. But apart from a segmental division of the expressive organs of the body, the predominating activity either of the flexors or the extensors in positive or negative emotions is common to all the muscles of the body.   For example, negative emotions affect the face, which becomes drawn ; wrinkles on the brow and between the nose and lips become deeply graven on a pale or yellow skin, and the face is pinched and long.   All these symptoms are produced by states of discomfort such as fear or painful anticipation under the influence of an acute and destructive tension.   But when emotional relaxation produces motor relaxation the lips re-form, the cheeks become full and pink again and the wrinkles disappear.

When a woman's pride is wounded she instinctively stiffens ; the head is thrown back, the shoulders raised, the hands are held out at a distance from the body in a strained posture with the fingers separated from each other fan-wise. This muscular rigidity is the direct consequence of inner rigidity.

It is easy to recognize that this motor mechanism is of a defensive and inhibited kind. The gestures of such negative emotions have the character of self-protection, as if the wounded mind were seeking to form an armour to resist an injury which not only menaces its happiness and equilibrium but its integrity as well.

A woman who is happy in the tender looks and caresses of her lover becomes literally smaller. Real happiness eases muscular tension ; the head is lowered, the shoulders fall slightly forward, the hands and arms adopt an attitude of repose, the fingers are held close together and slightly flexed.

The anticipation of happiness, extreme joy, stimulating conversation, and artistic creation are positive stimuli and urges which are translated into ' forward ' movements. These emotions go with a feeling of identity and of an expansion of the ego, as well as with heightened *joie de vivre*.

The man who is extremely happy becomes ' round ' not only in a figurative but also in a literal sense, for his flexor muscles become rounder through the animated circulation and reinforced tone.

The inhibited man suffering from discomfort is under the influence of an impoverished nervous dynamism. The happy man is under that of an accelerated dynamism. The gestures of the former are not only rigid and defensive, but the advance movements reduced to a minimum. A man in anguish is motionless. A happy man is expansive. He makes many gestures which enlarge his sphere of influence. He gets up often, walks about the room, takes hold of things. His gestures show emphasis and are at the same time direct, decisive, round, and full, whereas those of the inhibited man are elongated and hesitant.

The language of gesture is not, on the whole, fixed on one pattern, but is flexible ; the gestures of the same person can change completely under extraordinary influences. Such changes sometimes take a spectacular form. I have myself seen how the gestures of a person's face and hands underwent a transformation into almost opposite patterns. In my own case, my hands in the course of eight years have become different and my hand gestures have completely changed. The form of the fingers is as altered as their colour and flexibility ; the muscles of the palm have become thinner. But everybody can recollect cases of this kind. I remember a man of thirty-five years of age that I had always known with a long thin face and almond-shaped eyes, oriental and melancholy. In one year his whole bearing, which had been that of an introvert, altered, and he adopted the gestures of a more extravert type. His face seemed to become shorter, fatter, coarser, his eyes appeared smaller than before and their expression cold and stern.

It is impossible to detach inner dynamism and gestures from certain physiological conditions which influence both, such as race, sex, illness and fatigue.

With advancing years a man generally becomes more and more self-protective, and his gestures are governed by the necessity for prudence and caution. Everyone knows the old man's walk, the slow, careful steps, the bent back and lowered eyes.

People who live in a metropolis like London or New York are alive to the differences which exist in the movements and expressions of other races. An attentive observer can recognize persons of different races from their walk and the way in which they hold themselves. The marked gesticulations of the Orientals and the Latins distinguish them from other people at first sight.

The influence of sex, of fatigue, and of illness on expressive behaviour is also common knowledge.

It is undeniable that the expressive conduct of small groups like families, and large groups like races, shows so great a resemblance that one can trace their kinship by their gestures. I have often wondered what was the basis of this congruity. The individuals of one group often differ widely, but a certain type of gesture is preserved and unites one with another in spite of the deviations of temperament and culture. Even if we accept the fact that individual character can never escape the mysterious influence of racial patterns persisting through the centuries, this explanation is not a satisfactory one since other groups than those of the same blood—as, for example, social and religious sects—can present a similar unity of expression.

Spiritual unity, then, produces similar results to those of blood affinity. But is there not yet a third factor—the suggestive force of gestures which are transmitted to a group by imitation ?

Small children begin early to imitate the expressions of other children and of grown-up people ; even adults do so. If some-one coughs or yawns others will do the same. The imitation of expressive movements goes still further, especially with people who have not a strong ego. The adolescent is often the victim of expressive imitation. He is possessed by hero worship and will surprise by appearing not only in the same style of dress but with the look and gesticulation of the idol. Or a young girl will greet us in the precise manner of the lady she admires. Fears can work in the same way as desires and produce similar results. The ner-vous imitate the expressive signs of the illness they most dread, and the more receptive they are the more convincing will be the imitation.

The transmission of gesture as shown by imitation presents us with a major psychological problem. It seems to be designed as a principal, subconscious channel by which to gain our know-ledge of others. It is true that we learn nearly everything by imitation ; but after the apprenticeship is complete and the age of full development reached, why does the stimulus persist ? It may be said that the apprenticeship never does end, and that with advancing years the fear that man inspires in man increases rather than diminishes. This fear begets the instinct to recapitulate and deepen what we know of one another. And how could we do that better than by imitation of gestures ?

To gain full understanding one must imitate.

The graphologist, presented with a writing of which the curves and angles are very peculiar, follows them with the finger, and will succeed by thus imitating the form of the letters in tracing the state of mind of the writer. It is a commonplace that the genius of the actor is the genius of identification and imitation.

Apart from imitation gestures are transmitted by an immediate magnetic force. Under certain conditions a person's gestures can instantaneously affect the nervous system of another person. They convey the nervous fluid from brain to brain. But in order that the ' current ' can function a positive and a negative pole are required. The former is represented by the authoritative and hypnotic personality, the latter by the receptive and suggestible personality. When two such opposite types of people meet, or when a powerful personality is juxtaposed to a group, the magnetism of gesture can function to the extent of exercising a hypnotic influence. A man who is dominated by his wife will obey her slightest gesture, and a teacher with a strong personality will control his pupils with a look or a movement of the hand. Love and fear, physical and spiritual fascination, provide the best material for this magnetism, which, of course, can also take a destructive form. In a room where two people are at variance there is a recognizable atmosphere and a sense of continual and secret struggle which creates an accumulation of nervous tension. The gestures and looks of the pair have a hypnotic force, but it is of a negative kind, leading to ' short cuts ' or nervous shocks which may finally produce a neurotic state of mind and a malady of expression.

Gestures in situations such as these take arabesque forms, since inhibition and nervous tension upset the natural balance between exterior stimulation and psycho-motor response. The gestures of such people are more and more directed towards themselves ; they are what the American psychologist Krout called autistic gestures. In difficult or intolerable situations man not only retires into his shell but becomes infantile and expresses himself in a re-gressive fashion. Krout defines autistic gestures thus :

When an individual, inhibiting his direct response to an external situation, responds to subsequent internal stimulation explicitly, we have autistic gestures. Gestures such as clearing one's throat, forced coughing, convulsive spitting, without objective stimulus, deserve attention.

It is evident that this type of gesture obeys a mechanism of emotional unbalance. Deprived of natural contact with others, the source of spontaneous expression becomes more and more atrophied and finally disappears.

Natural psycho-motor response is centrifugal, its motive being communication of thought, emotion, and sentiment. Autistic expression is centripetal and directed towards the body. This state of affairs represents a natural law which is evident in hand-writing, where it provides an established rule for interpretation. Curves directed towards the writer represent signs of egocentricity and introversion.

Meaningless grimaces, aimless fidgeting with the hands and feet, arranging a tie or fiddling with a button, all movements directed towards the body, belong to this category of autistic gestures. As all these gestures are beyond control they are in-capable of correction.

Autistic gestures reveal an autistic personality, a man who is completely self-centred and blind to his surroundings. The drastic reduction of outside contacts causes a return to impressions of an infantile pattern centred on physical sensations.

I conclude this chapter with a definition of gestures. Gestures are expressive movements of the whole body, of every degree of intensity. They range from a scarcely perceptible frown to a frenzied agitation in which the whole body may participate. Obviously those organs which are free in movement, such as the hands, the feet, and the face, are the natural organs of gesture. While the latter is restricted to expression and more static gestures, the former possess the power of transmitting psycho-dynamic impulses into space. The face is the seat of passive, the hands, and to a certain extent the feet, of active gestures. In animals the face and to a lesser degree the feet are also expressive organs. The hands as tools of expression which convey the inner world of a person to the outer world are a human evolution. When man digressed from the animal through his upright walk the hands became free for new functions—one of them being the almost unlimited power of expressive movements. The language of gesture with which the hands are endowed is therefore one of the most valuable keys to the human mind.

CHAPTER II

THE PHYSIOLOGY OF GESTURE

EXPRESSIVE movements commence at birth and only end at death. The infant enters the world with a cry, and man leaves it with a sigh.

The infant's language of gesture grows more varied in proportion to the development of the organism, the brain in particular, but it acquires the mark of individuality only when personality and character are definitely formed. The individual character of gestures is altered, however, by old age or by physical and nervous maladies when there is no longer complete control of body and mind.

As expressive movements are dependent on the organic functions of the body, I want to give, briefly and summarily, an idea of the physiological background of gesture.

THE MUSCLES

It is obvious that asthenic and hypersensitive people possess a different muscular build from those who are physically stronger and more stable ; and up-to-date knowledge has shown that physical constitution is intrinsically linked with temperament.

The outline of the muscles, be they vigorous or feeble, can change through simple or complex movements, and through the immense variety of posture and gesture, body and mind present themselves in a great variety of aspects : for the muscles serve two purposes at the same time, action and expression, and even in intentional movements the muscular outline possesses an expressive potential.

The muscles which serve primarily for action, such as those of the legs and arms, are long, and the muscles which serve primarily for expression, such as those of the face and hands, are short. But they are of the same texture and structure, and no complete differentiation in their functions exists. They possess striated fibres which are put into action by a vast number of nervous cells called neurons, which connect the nervous with the muscular system.

The striated muscles are inserted in the skeleton and are very different in form and function from the muscles of the intestines and viscera. The latter muscles, which are long and thin, act only in dilating and constricting the digestive and respiratory tubes and the blood vessels.

THE NERVOUS SYSTEM

The nerves are arranged in a similar fashion to the muscles and have the same division into two parts : the cerebro-spinal and the autonomic nervous system. The first is connected with motor activity proper, the second with the vegetative or organic activity.

In every type of human expression, and in particular in gestures, two fundamental principles are involved : an extravert impulse directed towards the outer world and an introvert impulse directed towards the ego. Of the two nervous systems the cerebo-spinal is the one designed to maintain contact between man and the outer world. The life of contacts is guaranteed by the cortical functions of the brain and the working of the sensory and central nervous systems.

THE SPINAL CORD

The spinal cord is in the form of a cylinder which occupies two-thirds of the spinal canal. The front of the cord is indented with an anterior fissure to which a more superficial posterior one corresponds. The nerves of the spinal cord are enveloped in a membrane and they have a central canal, containing the cerebro-spinal fluid, which in the skull is enlarged to form the four ventricles of the brain.

The nerves, regularly spaced, issue from the spinal cord on both sides. They have two roots, an anterior and motor, and a posterior and sensory. The nerves of the spinal cord are thus composed of the fibres of both. The anterior and posterior roots are also connected by a bar. This arrangement, which can be seen when a transverse section of the spinal cord is made, resembles the letter H. One can also observe that the sensory neurons of the posterior root arborize round the motor neurons. This describes the interior substance of the spinal cord, which is grey and represents the most simple instrument of nervous activity. The sensory neuron or ganglion operates as a receptive organ which collects the stimuli from the periphery and passes them on to the motor root, which brings the corresponding muscle into action.

The grey matter is only part of the spinal cord. It is enveloped

3

in the white matter, which is composed of ascending and descending motor and sensory nerves arranged as a two-way road, one conducting the nervous influx to the brain and the other transmitting the cerebral impulses to the muscles.

Thus the spinal cord fulfills two functions : it serves the most simple reflex actions and is a pathway to and from the brain.

THE BRAIN

The brain consists of three parts—the hind-, the mid- and the fore-brain.

(A) *The Hind-brain*

The medulla oblongata is the continuation of the spinal cord, and with the Pons Varioli and the cerebellum it forms the hind-brain. The arrangement of the nerve substance, with the grey matter in the centre and the white matter surrounding it, is broken up in this region by the decussation of the pyramids where the great tracts of nerve fibres cross from one side to the other. This is the prelude to a complete reversion of the distribution of the nerve mass in other parts of the brain where the grey matter is contained entirely in the periphery and the white matter occupies the centre.

The cerebellum is situated at the base of the skull and is suspended over the medulla oblongata and the Pons Varioli and is connected with both through the crura cerebelli.

The function of the hind-brain is of particular importance in expressive movements. The medulla oblongata can be compared to a simple telephonic centre. The main stems of the sensory axons are collected here and are relayed to the other side of the body. The mechanism is as follows. Many sensory axons which come from the spinal cord communicate in the medulla oblongata with tracts of nerve fibres of the pyramidal pathways coming from the cortex and accompany them on their way into the muscles. Other sensory axons are not returned towards the periphery of the body, but are conducted into the fore-brain.

The medulla oblongata also controls vital organic functions, such as breathing and vaso-motor reactions, which accounts for the important part it plays in emotional expression.

The principal function of the cerebellum is the maintenance of equilibrium. It also presides over voluntary and involuntary postures.

It is interesting to note that, in birds, those artists of balance, the cerebellum is very strongly developed.

The hind-brain in its entirety is devoted to the most vital functions, and controls the most elementary expressions; gestures retaining a more or less reflex character, but showing more complex movements than those controlled by the spine, are directed by the medulla oblongata.

The labyrinth of the ear is an organ of balance which is connected with the cerebellum and this link explains why sound has particular effect on the sense of equilibrium and on posture.

(B) *The Mid-brain*

The mid-brain connects the hind- and the fore-brain. It shows, like the hind-brain, a certain dispersion of the grey matter, but its principal function is to link up the medulla oblongata with the fore-brain.

(C) *The Fore-brain* (The Interbrain and the two Hemispheres)

The *ancient brain* is the centre of the whole brain. It contains, among other nervous centres, the corpus striatum and the thalamus. The former controls muscular tone which decides the vigour of movements and is the centre of motor co-ordination, controlling reflex movements which are partly under conscious control since they are associated with voluntary movements originating in the cortex. The corpus striatum also presides over reflex movements of fear and over facial expressions such as laughter and tears. It represents, therefore, one of the sources of primary emotional expressions.

But the region of the thalamus has a still more important bearing on our subject. It is closely allied to the autonomic nervous system and contains a pool of nervous impulses which come from the intestines and the respiratory and circulatory systems as well as from the duct- and ductless glands. The thalamus, or more exactly a small region beneath it, the hypothalamus, presides over the vegetative and emotional life. Nervous pathways join the hypothalamus region to the cortex and the cerebellum. These pathways between the hypothalamus and the cortex are arranged in a two-way pattern and put into action a whole nervous mechanism which links the emotional life with consciousness, rendering the emotions, on the one hand, more inhibited and less animal, and on the other, drawing from them inspiration and warmth for thought and action.

Primary physical love or maternal affection, for example, is thus given the flavour of a broader and more inspiring emotion which may result in a compassionate approach to humanity. Thought acts as a bridle on emotion but draws from it that vigour and colour without which it would be dry and lifeless. Variety of feeling and richness of thought result from the connexion between emotion and consciousness and find outlets in expressive behaviour.

The nervous pathways between the thalamus region and the cerebellum are responsible for the influence of emotion and feeling tone on physical attitudes and on the sense of balance.

Both the sympathetic and parasympathetic nerves are represented in the hypothalamus region, which accounts for the reciprocal influence of organic sensations on emotions and vice versa. Apart from this link with the autonomic nervous system there is another vitally important connexion between the hypothalamus and the pituitary gland, due to their neighbouring positions. Hypothalamus, sympathetic and parasympathetic nerves and pituitary gland form a functional system on their own with definite repercussions on emotional and sexual functions and behaviour. Modern endocrinology attributes to this gland the presiding place in endocrine function. We know that the thyroid and the adrenals are most closely related to the pituitary gland, and this interdependence is, naturally, reflected too in the functions of the hypothalamus.

Apart from the pituitary gland, the adrenals have a special bearing on emotional behaviour through their direct influence on the functioning of the sympathetic nerves. The adrenals not only possess the typical characteristics of endocrine glands but also those of nervous substance. They are like a miniature brain which is attached to the sympathetic nerves and which consists of a cortex and a medulla, the cells of which are on the pattern of nerve cells.

The hormone of the adrenals has the same effect as the activity of the sympathetic nerves. It is no exaggeration to say that the emotional type of man is ruled by his hypothalamus, which registers every change of mood and emotional tension.

The importance of this region of the brain for emotional expression is well illustrated by the following account of an illness, a calcification in the thalamus region. The patient, a woman of culture and remarkable gifts, became gradually more and more depressed and lost all interest in the things which had formerly made up her life. She could not concentrate on reading or writing nor see friends, nor even go for walks ; every small effort was payed for with disproportionate fatigue. At 59 she was a very old woman, suffering from a sort of mental and emotional atrophy. Her expression changed, the eyes, now always half closed, looked dead ; her gestures were reduced to a limited set of protective movements and anxiety reflexes. Her haggard face showed that she was continually haunted by physical and mental discomfort. She complained of all sorts of intestinal and nervous symptoms, had a craving for food, but felt ill after a meal. She lost weight rapidly and her muscles atrophied until she became the picture of emaciation. Her mind only registered impressions in the most futile way. Thought and feeling were just as impoverished as the vital bodily functions ; there was a complete atony of body and mind.

The Two Hemispheres

The two hemispheres of the brain are separated from each other by a long fissure and are only joined in the middle by a thick band of transverse fibres : the corpus callosum.

The grey matter is in the periphery and forms the cortex, that most developed and still mysterious cerebral organ, which contains in its tortuous folds in a minimum of space a maximum of nervous substance.

The white matter is situated in the interior and consists of three types of nerve fibres :

I. Projective fibres, which link up the cortex with other parts of the brain and the spinal cord.

II. Fibres of communication between the two hemispheres (corpus callosum).

III. Association fibres which distribute nervous stimuli from one part to another of the same hemisphere.

My subject does not require a detailed discussion of cortical functions, but a general survey is useful.

The cortex represents :

I. A receptive organ where sensory impressions are sifted and brought to the level of consciousness.

II. A motor organ where sensory impressions are transformed into motor-impulses.

III. A creative organ of thought and imagination.

The highest cerebral functions, those of abstract thought and judgement, are strangely 'unexpressive'. It is the imaginative thought containing some emotional flavour which is accompanied by gestures, especially, according to H. Wallon in his book *L'Enfant Turbulent*, gestures of the hands.

Expressive hand movements often precede verbal expression and correspond to a formative state of mental process. A creative effort can be traced in them. Ideas are not genuine, nor can they become clarified, without passing through the phase of imaginative effort, and it is always with a certain amount of pain that the chaotic pattern of images, tinged with emotion, is clarified into concise formulas of detached ideas. Hand gestures preceding and accompanying the verbal expression of thoughts are thus characteristic of the working of an original and imaginative mind.

Gestures are, however, less linked with strictly cortical functions than intentional movements and skilled acts, which entirely depend on them.

While expressive movements as a rule retain a more or less subconscious character in the individual, they have been used by all races as a conscious and symbolic language which replaces words. They are employed as a sign language by the deaf and dumb, for example, and by people who have lost the power of speech through a cerebral lesion. The conscious and systematic use of expressive movements finds its truest place in the arts of mime and of the dance, which, with oriental people, are largely made up of gestures of a ritual and mantic type. These gestures have nothing to do with subconscious expressions. They belong to the category of skilled acts which depend on cortical function.

THE AUTONOMIC NERVOUS SYSTEM AND THE DUCT AND DUCTLESS
      GLANDS

The knowledge of the autonomic nervous system is of fairly recent date. In the middle of the nineteenth century the famous English physiologist Charles Bell, in his book *On the Anatomy and Philosophy of Expression*, introduced into medicine the term 'sympathetic nerves'. He maintained that the emotions and passions which are the driving force of human relationships make themselves felt in the region of the heart. Phrases like 'I have a heavy heart', 'My heart's in my mouth', illustrate how and where we feel the strongest emotions.

When the heart is affected breathing is altered too. The respiratory and circulatory systems are inseparable in their functions, and a strong emotion or feeling produces immediate repercussions on the rhythm of breathing and on the voice.

Modern science has taught us, however, that the sympathetic nerves are only a fraction of the autonomic nervous system. Along with them the parasympathetic nerves function, sometimes in unison but for the most part antagonistically.

Mary Collins and James Drever, in their book *Experimental Psychology*, call the autonomic nerves 'a connective system controlling and co-ordinating in particular the activity of the involuntary muscles and glands'. Not only the blood vessels, the heart and respiratory tract, but also the organs below the diaphragm are under their control.

When the sympathetic system is stimulated, a whole set of organic activities is switched on : in the intestinal part the splanchnical nerves slow down peristaltic movements, in the breast the sympathetic system has a contracting and accelerating effect on the heart, while it causes a relaxation in the muscles of the speech organs which accounts for the deep and moving timbre of the voice when we are swayed by tender and compassionate emotions. Through the same nervous stimulus the pupils become dilated and the eyes dark and shining. The sympathetic nerves have also a dilating influence on the blood vessels. When we feel happy and elated, when we are at peace with the world and ourselves, the blood circulates freely and we have warm hands and feet.

The working of the parasympathetic system, on the contrary, throws us back on our introverted and self-conscious emotions.

Its mechanism is on the whole of an inhibitive type. It contracts the pupils of the eyes and gives them a cold and observant look. It slows down the activity of the heart and the pulse rate by contracting the blood vessels. It is responsible for the suppressed voice as well as for spastic discomforts of the intestines and the stomach.

When a depressive mood prevails the parasympathetic system goes into action and makes itself felt by an oppressive feeling in the region of the heart and in a general state of displeasure and tension, in paleness of the face, as well as by cold hands and feet and many other symptoms.

The ganglia of both sets of autonomic nerves are arranged like a chain on both sides of the spinal cord and fuse into one big ganglia below it. There are also four large ganglia on either side in the region of the medulla oblongata. Many others are dispersed among the visceral organs and the intestines.

Like a complex network of channels the autonomic nerves link up the whole of the inner organs with the spine and the brain and are of the highest importance for the origin of the emotions as well as for their expression.

The close connexion between the autonomic and cerebro-spinal nervous system is due not only to their neighbouring position but also to a direct contact between them.

The non-medulated grey fibres of the autonomic nerves penetrate into the spinal cord and into the tissues of the voluntary muscles. This accounts for a certain amount of conscious control of emotional reflexes on the one hand and for the influence of vegetative functions on the muscular tonus on the other.

Voluntary muscles have therefore a double innervation : one of the cerebro-spinal type, which provides for the skilled execution of intentional movements ; the other of the autonomic type, which provides for muscular tonus and, to a certain extent, for posture.

The intimate link between the autonomic nerves and the endocrine glands has been stressed before in the example of the adrenals, but the hormones of all endocrine glands stimulate the autonomic nervous system.

The ductless glands, taken as a separate system which releases most vital energies and works on a rhythmical pattern as do all life-giving forces, represent one of the fundamental sources of expressive movements.

Of less importance, but nevertheless of some influence on expressive behaviour, are the duct glands. The liver, pancreas and kidneys, the sweat glands and the glands which secrete the saliva and the digestive juices, all form part of the organic dynamo which drives and regulates our bodily functions. Their working is largely conditioned by the emotional state, which can key them up to capacity or slow them down into inactivity.

THE SENSES

The popular notion of the five senses has been corrected by modern physiology, which has added three more : the kinaesthetic sense, the static sense and the visceral sensations.

While the five original senses communicate the exterior world to our brain, the three others provide a cerebral registration of what is going on in our own body.

The receptor cells are essential parts of the senses and the centre of their specific reactions, while the other parts of the sense organ only modify or intensify this quality by making reception more subtle, more distinct and more precise.

The exterior world presents continual stimuli in the form of an amorphous energy to the receptor cells. These have to transform exterior energy into an interior or nervous one, through a bio-chemical process which is associated with an electric current produced by the ions of the cells.

The receptor cells of the senses are on a more or less individual pattern and react to adequate stimuli. Waves of light work on the organ of vision, and the impressions received by the sense of touch have, as a rule, no effect on the other senses. But there is no complete differentiation of the senses. Sound, for example, can produce visual images ; many musical people see colours or forms while listening to music. Tactile sensations can be involved in visual impressions.

In accordance with their position two types of receptor cells can be distinguished : exteroceptors and proprioceptors.

The exteroceptive senses possess a highly discriminative quality through their structure and function and are at the base of all our knowledge of the outer world and of all higher brain functions and achievements. Among them the eye is the most highly developed, the mouth the most sensitive to primary impressions.

The hand, in which the sense of touch is most acute, has developed in one way as an affiliation of the mouth, which in animals still serves as an organ of prehension as well as of eating. In man the former capacity has shifted to the hand ; but the ancient link between mouth and hand is still mirrored in brain—representation. The basal part of the fissure of Rolando in the cortex is occupied by the representation of the muzzle region, which is immediately followed by the zone representing the hand.

As the hand has become the foremost organ of sensibility and skill in man its gestures express emotional states as well as thought. Through their special evolution into tools of intelligence the hands have become increasingly associated with the eyes. As both thought and emotion are reflected in hand gestures, it is easy to understand that images, which in some people ceaselessly follow one another, are accompanied by scarcely perceptible movements of palm and fingers, as Wallon has indicated in his book *L'Enfant Turbulent*.

Every exteroceptive sense organ possesses a specific sphere of activity, while the field of ' influence ' of the proprioceptive senses is limited to the body. The static and kinaesthetic senses are involved in an indirect way in all manual and mental activity, and, together with the sense of touch, which is most concentrated in the hands, they are the fundamentals of spatial orientation, which is the medium of all movements and gestures. It must be remembered that movements and gestures of the hands can only be effected in the ' manual ' space (within arm's reach), which the German psychologist von Uexkull identified with ' the field of action ' (Wirkraum) in general.

The visual space is considerably larger than the manual space, and is produced by the accommodation of the eyes, which explains its deeply illusory character. One has only to alter the angle of objects, to change their distance or to move them at different speeds to perceive them as utterly different from what they were before.

W. Koehler expresses the mirage of visual perception in *Dynamics in Psychology* as follows : ' Objects work on a pattern of stroboscopic movements. For example, two visual objects shown very rapidly one after another appear to be one.'

Hand and eye, in different degrees, are dependent in their functions on light : the ear works better in darkness. A symbolic and legendary relationship has existed since the early days of mankind between light and clarity on the one hand and darkness and confusion on the other. For ' clarity ' and ' confusion ' we might substitute conscious and subconscious mind.

The eyes as organs of perception serve observation and are at the root of all functions of the intelligence : and so to a certain extent are the hands. As organs of expression the eyes reflect, more than any other part of the body, intelligence. But, as we shall see later on in this book, this is by no means their only expressive function.

Hearing and the gestures which are provoked by it are more connected with the subconscious, especially subconscious anxieties, because sounds reach us from behind and below and this gives them a frightening and uncontrollable power. The ' space of hearing ' is larger, more dispersed, less defined than the ' space of vision '.

The buccal space, the seat of the sense of smell and taste, is the narrowest of all, and the most closely connected with the essential functions of life : breathing and eating. The expressive power of this region mirrors therefore more than any other part of the body the vital feelings of pleasure and displeasure.

Mood and temperament are closely linked up with the visceral sensations, a fact which calls for no further explanation. The kinaesthetic sense determines the position of the ego in the world both physically and mentally. Kinaesthetic consciousness, because it is related to the feeling of identity, therefore plays an important part in the mental make-up. The static sense is responsible for the feeling of balance and postural behaviour.

NERVOUS ENERGY

How many people use the expression ' nervous energy ' and how few really know what it means ! Catchwords like these are the Maginot Line of psychology. They are dangerous symptoms of mental lassitude and lack of knowledge. It is therefore necessary to define scientifically what nervous energy is and how it works.

Since the experiments of Hans Berger and, more recently, of Prof. Adrian, the popular notion of brain-waves has become a scientific reality. These two scientists have shown that the undulations of the cortical cells are measurable by the electric current. This, however, does not imply that nervous energy is electric energy ; indeed many modern psychologists doubt it. They describe nervous energy in very general terms as a bio-chemical force of a more or less unknown nature. An exception is the psychologist W. Koehler, who points out that nervous energy has the same attributes as electricity.

Mental energy is, of course, only a special branch of nervous energy, and nervous energy can be translated into movement and expression as well as into thought.

In its primary form nervous energy is responsible for instinctive and emotional behaviour and is thus connected with the organic functions and the autonomic nerves. That the latter are conductors of electro-nervous energy is now an established fact.

It is also known that the process of transmitting nervous energy from its mainsprings into the effector-organs goes with the secretion of a liquid called neuro-humor. It originates at the points of contact between the nerves and either muscles or glands.

As Koehler convincingly argues, the two parts of the nervous system cannot be essentially divided from each other. It seems therefore probable that percept and thought processes are also animated and carried through on the pattern of electrical conduction. In *Dynamics in Psychology* he says : 'Percept processes show behaviour obviously analogous to electric currents. Can it be that they are actually associated with electric currents in the nervous system ? The present situation in nerve physiology makes this assumption quite plausible.' He further concludes that in the brain itself nervous energy works in the same way.

Nervous stimuli reaching the brain are also accompanied by a chemical substance, which penetrates from the end fibres of the sensory nerves into the brain tissue.

Nervous energy acts not only on the point of contact but expands in the form of an electrical field, the extension of which in the brain will depend on the intensity and frequency of the stimuli and the specific resistance of brain tissue.

I have left the description of nervous energy, as the source of expressive movements, to the end of this chapter, in spite of the fact that it represents their primary mainspring and would seem to be more correctly placed at the beginning. But to understand the meaning and functions of nervous energy it seemed advisable to introduce the subject with a survey of those systems which participate as a whole in producing gestures. None of these systems, however, would function if they were not animated by nervous energy.

For the term 'nervous energy' can be substituted 'inner dynamism', which is the basis of all inner life as well as of its visible signs such as words, postures and gestures.

Koehler goes so far as to call impulse and *élan*—which represent what I have called inner dynamism—the essence of our being. In his paper 'Les Forces Motrices du Comportement' he underlines the strictly individual nature of expressive movements and speaks of the Me as a composition of perceptive and autonomic functions. These two types of function are modified by states of mind and body, such as fatigue, joy, suspense, which are ambivalent in their nature but are equilibrated by the play of nervous tension and relaxation.

The 'Gestalt' Psychology, of which Koehler is one of the outstanding protagonists, has contributed much to a biological conception of psychology and also to a synthetic comprehension of personality. K. Goldstein, Professor of Neurology and Psychiatry at Frankfurt (before his emigration to America), went further even than the ' Gestalt ' psychologists in his conception of all the functions of man, both physical and psychological, as a centralized unit. In *Le Fonctionnement de l'Organisme, d'apres K. Goldstein*, by A. Gurwitch, one finds a very complete interpretation of the bio-psychical forces which govern expressive behaviour. According to Goldstein the entire organism reacts to a stimulus, and the stimulus produces a different situation in each individual.

Goldstein describes the nervous system as a network of nervous fibres wherein are situated the ganglions. This system is in a chronic state of average excitement to which it always returns after no matter what stimulation. This return is accomplished by means of movement, and gesture therefore serves as a regulator of nervous tension.

The effect of each exterior or interior stimulus is never local but always total. The ganglion cells prevent a too rapid spread of excitement and cause the arrest and relative localization of nervous energy.

There are thus two fields of reaction to a stimulus. The field of perception in the cortex of the brain, and the field of ' background ', which is the entire organism.

Nervous tension is naturally different in the part which is directly affected from that in the rest of the organism, because of the bio-chemical nature of the cells, which offer different degrees of resistance to the electro-nervous energy produced by stimuli. But, apart from a global reaction of the organism, the cortex itself reacts in its entirety and not only in the part directly affected. Thus it may be said that each perceptive process and each organic process affects man as a whole. For example, in brain injuries, not only are those organs affected which are in direct nerve communication with the brain, but also those which represent the loca minoris resistentiae. The healthy condition of the ' background ' (the whole organism) is one of the factors on which depend the development of what is passing in the foreground (the brain). According to Goldstein a condition opposed to the stimulus—an inhibitive process—is instantaneously produced in the ' background '.

It is by this antagonism of reactions that the phenomenon of motor perversion can be explained—for example, when someone reacts by movements of flexion instead of extension.

The failure of an organ after a lesion of a certain part of the cortex in no way proves the dependence of this organ on the cortex, for the failure might have been caused by a functional deficiency of the ' background '. In other words, when a function attached to a certain cerebral part is weakened, a functional anomaly of the ' background ' may be equally responsible.

In the subcortical regions which represent the centre of psycho-physical life the perceptive functions act on the emotional centres. Goldstein considers exterior situations which affect both not as objective instances detached from the person involved in them, but as part of his organism which fights continually to assimilate the *milieu* in order to maintain its psycho-physical integrity. The powers of assimilation brought to this task are miraculous. The transplantation of nerves, for example, has proved that a specific function of the nerves does not exist, since, if a nervous communication can be artificially created, it follows that the organism after a certain time re-establishes the state which existed before the lesion. Vicarious functions assure the integrity of the organism— the left hand can replace the right, and in hysterical blindness the patient can learn to read by gestures. But the perfection of the vicarious function depends upon the general state of health, the individual ability and the whole personality. The force of personality depends on the power of centralization or integration. Centralization is therefore the principal factor in the life of the organism. It assures balance or the return of the nervous system to a state of moderate excitement after a shock or commotion of any kind. In some nervous patients the cortical ganglia are partially destroyed, and in consequence the stimulus requires greater space in which to diffuse if it is to be efficacious, and the return to a medium state becomes more difficult. A continual excitation of the nervous system results in and is responsible for a lack of precision of movements, for perseverance and stereo-typed gestures.

This perseverance appears in lesions of the spine and of the cerebellum and leads to the prolongation of postural attitudes, gestures and perceptions, while reflex movements increase. When the living substance is damaged there is always a return to reflex activity. Instead of co-ordinated activity there is piecemeal activity. Owing to the loss of the centralizing force of the organism, movements are directed towards the originator of the reactions —the *milieu*—and man is overpowered by it and becomes the victim of the outside world. He reacts like the newly born by reflex and instinct. The effect of exterior stimuli on the nervous system is in proportion to the lack of centralization. One can measure the degree of maturity by the degree of independence of exterior stimuli. These, in the mature man, are selected according to the organism and its needs.

If from physical or psychological reasons the functions of perception (in the cortex) and the functions of 'background' (in the rest of the organism) are disproportionate, antagonistic and unstable reactions result. Abnormal fixations or fixed ideas are formed which produce nervous and emotional ambivalance and the exaggeration of global reactions. The nervous system, in a state of continual tension, cannot find repose or equilibrium, and with the lack of centralization there is no capacity for objectivity. This capacity represents, according to Goldstein, the essence of the Me as well as the power of detached thought and judgement.

All these considerations of Goldstein have a vast application for psychology in general and for gestures in particular. As he indicates, the higher functions of the cortex, such as objective thought and judgement, go with flexor movements, whilst subjective and emotional attitudes correspond to extensor movements. The predominance of the former type of gestures represents the Me, and the detachment from the *milieu*; the predominance of the latter, the empire exerted by the *milieu*.

The movements of flexion are characterized by precision and subtlety, whilst the movements of extension are gross and imprecise. The former have a special relation with the cortex and the cerebellum, the latter with the spine. Sufferers from a cerebral or cerebellar lesion cannot establish nervous equilibrium and the normal *milieu* produces nervous catastrophes. Their motor behaviour returns to a primary phase—automatism. They try to escape from upsetting reactions by stereotyped activities, and their pedantry and meticulousness are well known. Through this form of behaviour they are able to establish enough self-protection to preserve for themselves and their surroundings a façade which provides a shelter from surprising situations that might otherwise compromise their psycho-physical failings. A similar situation is to be found in the case of neurotic people who suffer from deep conflicts between the subconscious and the conscious mind. Introverted people are the most exposed to this kind of trouble ; in extreme cases one can observe in them attitudes and gestures characteristic of patients with cerebral lesions.

There are motor patterns in every individual which reveal the temperament and the personal conflicts and which give a key to what is happening in the organism.

CHAPTER III

THE EVOLUTION OF GESTURE

AMONG the vital functions of the body, growth plays the most important part in the development of gesture. At each age expressions change : the toddler uses different gestures to the baby, and the child of five makes still fuller use of expressive movements.

Since, for one reason or another, we can never escape from our childhood it is evident that the alphabet of gestures, which is formed step by step in the child, remains the basis of all the most subtle and complex expressive movements in later life.

Three types of gesture govern the scene in early life :
   I. Automatic or reflex gestures.
   II. Emotional gestures.
   III. Projective gestures.

A special state of consciousness belongs to each stage of evolution. The first, that of automatic gestures, is characterized by an absence of mental representation.

The expressive life of the infant in the first weeks after birth is conditioned by reflexes of comfort and discomfort. Between the two poles of its existence, sleep and meals, there remains only the bath to exhaust reality. But while food and sleep give complete satisfaction, the bath is already a doubtful pleasure. The infant rebels against the sudden immersion and contact with humidity but finds an immense comfort when it adopts postures which resemble those in the womb.

The extension of expressions is allied with the development of the muscles and the brain, but psycho-motor behaviour only attains maturity after the age of puberty. Psycho-analytical discoveries have shown that adults retain certain forms of expression belonging to an earlier stage of existence—to a period when inner difficulties produced a kind of emotional indigestion, often leading to neurosis.

Such repressions take revenge on our nervous system either in the form of definite neurosis or in a general nervous instability. Furthermore one cannot escape the conclusion that man's capacity for adaption remains always imperfect even in the well-balanced, and that at certain moments in his life there is a tendency to revert to infantile expressions. Confronted by a difficult or unbearable

4

situation the mechanism of control is thrown out of gear and the emotions thus disrupted defy inhibitions and become transparent.

It is at such moments of crisis that man reverts to the gestures of childhood. Nevertheless one must not confound the symbol with the meaning. The adult may use the same gestures as the infant, but in his case they give expression to a whole range of emotional experiences of which the child knows nothing.

I. *THE INSTINCTIVE PHASE* (First Stage of Evolution)

AUTOMATIC GESTURES

A. *Gestures of Equilibrium*

The effect of a sudden noise on the infant produces one of the most early gestures—the startle. But this is purely reflex, without any mental resonance, and is the result of a sudden change of pressure produced in the labyrinth of the ear, the organ which regulates equilibrium. In the adult the same gesture has an entirely different significance and is due to an emotional surcharge

That the static sense is responsible for a whole series of gestures can be seen already in the infant. In the bath it throws out its arms to preserve its balance, and when it takes its first steps it uses the same gesture. At every stage of existence movements which protect equilibrium are movements provoked by fear, since both are intimately allied. In the adult, anxiety is the reply to a state of suspense caused by an inner disturbance which he is unable to adjust. Fear consists, therefore, of a rupture of equilibrium and powerlessness to maintain psycho-motor co-ordination.

We throw out our arms like the child in the bath when we receive bad news, as if to ward off a blow by a gesture of self-protection. We retreat when menaced. But a severe physical or mental shock paralyses all movement. Fear restricts voluntary action but cannot suppress reflex movements. At first the gestures remain intentional, but control is quickly lost and the gestures become awkward and either fall short of or overreach their aim. Anxiety in the first stage makes a person hesitate or jump, but it may culminate in a syncope of consciousness, causing either paralysis of movement or fainting fits.

The mechanism which produces these reactions is due to an irregularity of balance for which the static sense in the labyrinth of the ear and the cerebellum are responsible.

Often the remedy comes from the same source as the malady. The static sense, which from infancy onwards causes so much trouble, provides on the other hand many soothing and agreeable sensations. One has only to rock a crying child to quieten it and send it to sleep. The rocking-cradle, now out of fashion, is not only a symbol of infant contentment but also an instrument of education for the sense of balance, which is so delicate in the child.

While brusque movements produce sensations of suspense and fear, rhythmic movements have the effect of a soothing drug. Perfect alternating balance between tension and relaxation, between expectation and its immediate fulfilment, provides the nervous system with a hypnotic gratification. The appeal to the static sense by agreeable sensations, like the rhythm of rocking, develops in the child its powers of adjustment and makes it better prepared to cope with disagreeable sensations. Perhaps it is through an educative and formative instinct that children never tire of rhythmical games, at first passively, and later actively.

That the static sense is related to hearing is already apparent in the infant. He begins at an early age to make rocking movements a pleasure which is enhanced by sound. Many children amuse themselves by making sounds and drumming with their fingers on their lips at the same time. Sounds and rhythmic movements are linked together and form, at every age, an inexhaustible source of pleasure. The ' Ride a Cock-Horse ' on its mother's knee has the same effect on the child as dancing has on the adult.

B. Gestures of the Mouth

The expressions of the mouth are the true mirror of the first phase of life. They are born of organic needs and reflect primary instincts. For the infant the mouth is the source of life itself and is the instrument of the first vocal gesture—the cry—soon followed by its counterpart—the smile. Sucking gestures express the desire for nourishment and the tongue is the favourite plaything of the baby. In adults it is especially expressive of animal instincts : of greed and erotic pleasures ; developing a new significance, it plays, with the lips, a part in sexual excitation.

Involuntary tongue movements are frequent in hysterical persons and are common in schizophrenic patients, both types reverting to the expressions of early childhood. Sucking the thumb and biting the nails when found in grown-ups reveals a fixation on a very early period of existence. Such a regression often goes with mental deficiency or different types of neurosis.

The muzzle region is also the primary region of touch and the first source of knowledge of environment. The infant puts everything into its mouth, including its own feet and hands.

C. Gestures of the Hand

The first gesture of the hand is the grasping reflex. A two days' old infant, the imprint of whose hands I wanted to take, hindered my efforts by such a strong flexion of the fingers that I had the greatest difficulty in opening them and withdrawing my own finger.

Before children develop an active sense of touch they react by grasping objects with which they come in contact, a proof that prehensile gestures are more ancient than tactile gestures.

The latter develop along with the intelligence. Wallon and others have observed that reflex movements are earlier and better established in the right hand than in the left.

It is only after the fourth month that these reflex movements undergo a certain cortical control which renders them purposeful and that at the same time the eye begins to guide the activities of the hand.

II. THE EMOTIONAL PHASE (Second Stage of Evolution)

There is no abrupt transition in nature. In the emotional stage many gestures remain which are purely reflex, while in the instinctive phase already certain emotional gestures can be observed. It is thus difficult to determine the end of the first phase and the commencement of the second.

The first emotions appear, according to some psychologists, as early as the second or third week after birth, but are expressed in a global fashion showing no differentiation. The sixth month is definitely marked by a great enrichment of gesture corresponding to an enrichment of the primary reactions.

Valentine classifies the earliest emotional reactions or feelings as follows :

    I. Resistance—later becoming anger.
    II. Content—later becoming joy.
    III. Startle—later becoming fear.
    IV. Gloom—later becoming sorrow.

It is nevertheless doubtful whether these earliest reactions are

really emotional and not merely instinctive.   Valentine maintains
that the first sympathetic contacts also appear as early as the third
month, since the baby, as he says, takes pleasure in the company of
adults.   He smiles when they approach, he cries when they leave.
These signs of gregariousness are, however, in my opinion, misleading, they are no proof of real contact but only signs of an instinctive
desire to learn.   The child's perception of the adult is at first incomplete.   He sees only colours and vague forms in the enormous
person in front of him.

There is a utilitarian purpose in this gregarious interest, namely
to develop the senses and the brain.

We know that the perceptive functions develop slowly.   As
long as they are in the first stage, contact with others does not
exist ; when they are a little better established, but still fragile,
contact with others frightens the child.   A stranger approaching
a seven-months old child will, as a rule, be received with cries,
grimaces and defensive gestures.   I know a little boy who from
this age up to five years always covered his face with a cloth in
the presence of strangers.

The contentment of a small baby in his mother's presence, a
pleasure which easily extends to other members of the family, is
entirely animal and comes solely from the instinct of self-preservation.   Having been an integral part of his mother he accepts her
entourage, and both signify for his subconscious a wall of protection
against the world which he is incapable of grasping either by
emotion or consciousness.   This state of affairs is so fundamental
that it rarely disappears altogether even in the adult ; an element
of fear of others remains a source of inhibition through the whole
of life.   How many of us ever lose the protection of family life
without paying the price of a profound inner insecurity ?

As far as the infant is concerned it is only when contentment
is transformed into joy, displeasure into rage, and boredom into
sorrow that he reaches the emotional stage.

DIFFERENTIATION OF INSTINCT AND EMOTION

Instinct and emotion have one thing in common : both are
accompanied by physical sensations.   But what differentiates them
is the utilitarian nature of the former and the irrational nature of
the latter.   Instinct arouses an immediate need whose satisfaction
is final.   Emotion accumulates slowly until it reaches the expressive stage but is not satisfied by immediate outlets ; on the con-

trary, it increases the more it is exteriorized. Urged by a dynamic force which seems to be inexhaustible, particularly in the child, emotion takes control of the muscles and spreads until the whole body is in a frenzy.

NATURE OF EMOTION

While the nature of instinct is clear and simple, that of the emotions is complex and obscure. Emotion originates from suspense and conflict. It does not function when an inner situation finds a direct and satisfactory solution. Thus, even in an agreeable form like joy and affection, it contains a certain element of pain and nostalgia.

Emotion is a kind of malady which by its inner pressure produces in man agitation and irresolution. It is the want of direction and certainty and the conflict between inner tension and adequate expression which makes strong emotions resemble madness. Their irrational and incalculable character is responsible for expressions and gestures which lack system and often seem to us completely futile and absurd. Most of all in children emotion reveals its ambivalence and incalculability. With them, smiles and tears follow each other as sun and shower in April. As suddenly as emotion invades the muscles it retreats, leaving them in a state of fatigue or weakness.

Obviously man as an emotional being, at every age, is in a helpless position, victim at the same time of his physical reactions and his imagination. The former are out of control in proportion to the strength of the emotion. The latter only produces haphazard images related to the physical reactions and to a completely subjective perception of the outside world. Such a restriction can produce a complete dissociation of thought which, in children, so often results in the lack of a sense of reality and in untruthfulness.

A subjective consciousness is attached to the emotional state in both child and adult and this subjectivism remains throughout life the weakness of highly emotional people.

How deeply images of an emotional type are connected with physical sensations and moods and how uncontrollable they are, the reader will see exemplified in the following passage from *Mlle. de Lespinasse*, by the Marquis de Ségur (Chap. VI, p. 169) :

I left you unwell and I would fain believe you free of the excessive pain that weakens your character and aggravates other pains dangerously attractive to your imagination. You fear to find yourself well and you reject the consolations and distractions of time and your own nature. . . . I know well enough how you will treat my remarks or my counsels, but I will not hide a very frequent thought of mine—You are falling into a habit of sad ideas and lamentable imaginings, and the consequences frighten me. You will not answer to the voices of nature and of friendship. But what profits it to say ' Be of good cheer ' ? Unhappiness means the mastery of notions stronger than reason, for reason points the way of cheerfulness.

The emotional stage is a transitional period between the instinctive and the objective phase. Emotion has thus a definite rôle : it opens out a path for thought by enlarging consciousness. Every functional development follows a utilitarian design imposed by nature and in irrational emotional whims can be discerned the acquirement of knowledge of the self and of the world. It is only through subjectivism that the child becomes gradually familiar with both.

To acquire knowledge of self and of the world is a tremendous task. It is in fact the final goal of wisdom, which is rarely achieved. It is difficult to grasp that in the first rudimentary forms of consciousness we should recognize the root of our most subtle and illuminating capacities.

It may be asked why, if emotion belongs to a transitional phase, we are so enslaved by it throughout life. One cannot escape the conclusion that man, even when he has developed the most complex faculties of thought and judgement, does not know how to become adult. In spite of this fact a fundamental difference exists between the subjective consciousness in infancy and in maturity. In the infant it represents a step forward in development : in riper years, a step backward. The adult reverts to subjectivism in spite of his reasoning powers and experience ; for him, subjective thought is a regression which distorts reality. For the child the images evoked by an emotion have a completely real significance. This difference gives quite different meanings to the gestures and expressions of the child and the adult. In the latter expressive behaviour is also more difficult to decipher because of the much greater variety and complexity of his emotions and the lasting power of past impressions.

Observation of the infant teaches us that extravert interests and the knowledge of objects are an antidote to the inevitable subjectivism of emotion. Already between the ages of five and six years the child becomes less emotional and more interested in objects. It suffers less than in the preceding phase, which is nevertheless the most important for the formation of character and the development of the imagination. The vulnerability of the child reaches its culminating point in this period and a surcharge of strong impressions can easily destroy its physical and mental equilibrium.

Psycho-analysts have shown that most of the neurotic disturbances experienced in later life date from this epoch. The fight and the suffering entailed by this emotional phase coincides with the first creative efforts, which are expressed by children in games and in drawing and painting. Towards the age of six years, when they become more rational, a new form of consciousness comes into being, as Wallon points out in his book *L'Enfant Turbulent*. The interest displayed by children, particularly boys, in the handling of objects is a sign of the third phase of development, that of the objective consciousness. Children gain experience of objects mostly by touch, which thus has a primary influence on the development of objective imagery and reasoning. The fact that the interest in objects is more marked in boys than in girls reveals the more emotional nature of the latter and their fundamental subjectivism.

The objective consciousness develops strength of personality and stabilizes relations with the world.

Cortical functions which govern adaptive faculties are to a certain extent antagonistic to a flow of emotion, whose cerebral counterpart is situated in the hypothalamus region of the brain. The cortical activity puts a check on the expressive extravagances of emotional reactions and controls them by a system of inhibitions.

CLASSIFICATION OF EMOTIONS

Emotions are determined by temperament and are accompanied, according to their nature, by muscular and vascular tension or relaxation.

One can speak of sthenic (strong), asthenic (weak) and hypersthenic (very strong) people in describing the development of their muscles, and a similar classification has been devised for the emotions. Féré, for example, speaks of hyper- and hyposthenic emotions. Wundt recognizes the principle of tension and relaxation as the dominant factor of emotions and stresses the fact that the four temperaments recognized by the Greeks are based on this idea, since ' they are the resulting combinations in a two-dimensional scale of emotional reaction types :

	Strong	*Weak*
Quick :	Choleric	Sanguine
Slow :	Melancholic	Phlegmatic.'

This tabulation has been applied by Pavlov (*Lectures on Conditioned Reflexes*) to the psychology of animals. He discovered in his famous experiments on conditioned reflexes that dogs showed emotional reactions similar to those of human beings and that the four ancient temperaments, choleric, sanguine, melancholic, and phlegmatic, applied also to them. He observed that sanguine and phlegmatic dogs, those with a hyposthenic emotional make-up, resisted shocks better than the others. Pavlov was convinced that the difference between emotional behaviour in man and in the higher animals was negligible, and he noted the importance of emotional inhibition in both, Hypersthenic emotions in man and dog tend primarily to overcome inhibitions whilst hyposthenic emotions are under its control from the start, resulting in a slowing down, both in speed and intensity, of emotional reactions. Hypersthenic emotions such as rage and exuberant joy release agitated and emphatic gestures because of their impulsive nature, and they go with vascular hypertone, which causes hyperaemia of the brain. Thus the region of the hypothalamus and the cortex receive more and more powerful stimuli in proportion to the force of the emotion.

The terms hyper- and hyposthenic emotions refer to muscular tone only and not to vascular tension, which, however, is also affected by emotional states. Both muscular and vascular tone depend on the autonomic innervation in co-operation with endocrine functions, those of the adrenals in particular.

Adrenalin, which is freely poured into the blood under the influence of emotion, is the hormone of the medulla of the adrenal glands. Adrenalin elevates the blood-pressure and at the same time inhibits the action of the intestinal muscles, &c. It has a physiological resemblance to sympathin, which is the neuro-humoral product of the sympathetic nerves. This liquid, as well as adrenalin, dilates the blood vessels and is thus responsible for a rush of blood to the head. Its opposite is parasympathin, the neuro-humoral product of the parasympathetic nerves, which has a special influence on the myocard (the heart muscle) and also on the blood vessels, which it compresses. Its earlier name was inhibitin, since it inhibits the action of the heart, slows down the pulse rate and reduces the blood pressure. By inhibiting the influx of blood to the muscles, parasympathin can in the end produce a state of muscular flabbiness and atony.

It is possible that the parasympathetic part of the autonomic nervous system has a special relationship to the pituitary gland, which also plays a dominant part both in the regulation of blood pressure and in emotional expression because of its proximity to the hypothalamus region. It would therefore be better to speak of the sympathetic or relaxing emotions and the parasympathetic or inhibitive emotions. The former correspond roughly to the hypersthenic and the latter to hyposthenic emotions ; but it must not be forgotten that the functions of the two portions of the autonomic nerves overlap. The emotion of rage, for example, has, at first, the aspect of a relaxing emotion, but finishes with inhibitive symptoms ; while fear, a parasympathetic emotion, often shows in the final stage symptoms resembling rage. When the paralysing reactions of fear have passed a vasomotor relaxation under the influence of the sympathetic nerves takes place, and this may show itself in a change of countenance and a heightened colour.

K. Bridges defines emotion as a mixture of vasomotor and glandular reactions with motor traits, and she underlines the fact that the former change with growth but are also individually different.

It is difficult to diagnose an emotion from vasomotor symptoms alone, a fact which was recognized by Stratton as equally true for the infant as for the adult. Fear and rage according to him can manifest themselves by the same expressive symptoms. The two writers distinguish agreeable and disagreeable emotions and point out that the former are under the control of the sympathetic nerves while the latter are dominated by the parasympathetic nerves.

Although vasomotor signs alone are not sufficient material for psychological diagnosis, together with motor reactions they convey sufficient diagnostic evidence. Rage is expressed by a tendency towards agitation, whilst fear tends towards immobility, and this type of reaction does not vary in individuals of opposite temperaments. But the cycloid man will give way to violent anger more easily than the schizoid man, who, faced with the same situation, will probably succumb to fear, since he is not capable of such a strong and healthy reaction as rage. If when, urged by some overwhelming excitement, he does give way to it, there will remain an undercurrent of fear.

The emotional development of the child has a special place in psychology. I shall give here the names of only some of the authors who have made remarkable contributions to the subject, like H. Wallon in France, A. Gsell in America, Susan Isaacs, K. Bridges and Valentine in Great Britain. K. Bridges made a special investigation on the differentiation of the emotions and their expressions according to age in ' The Development of the Emotions in the Young Child '.

Her material consisted of 63 children between the ages of 13 weeks and 5 years. Her study gives in a concentrated form an exact idea of what happens in the emotional life of the very young. One of her tables, which I reproduce here, indicates the evolution of the two types of emotion—the disagreeable and the agreeable.

Suffering	Delight (3 months)
Fear Disgust Anger	Delight (6 months)
Fear Disgust Anger	Joy Affection (12 months)
Fear Disgust Anger Jealousy	Joy Affection (24 months) :
	A, for adults ;
	B, for children.

The two groups of emotion have no rigid boundaries but are fused one with the other. Delight is transformed into fatigue and prostration when the nervous energy is spent, and suffering is diminished when the nervous tension which sustained it is discharged. Ambivalence is the most characteristic feature of emotion and can be explained by the functioning of the autonomic nervous system, which changes from one reaction type to the other after a certain limit of excitement has been exceeded.

In the newly born there is no emotional differentiation : hence one can say that the newly born has no emotions. Towards the age of three months there are only two emotional tendencies, those of suffering and delight. After six months the emotional life proper begins with the disagreeable emotions predominating. Suffering, in fact, up to the age of two years is the outstanding feature of life and is more easily differentiated than delight through the reactions of fear, disgust, and rage.

The expressions of suffering are not essentially different in the infant and the child of 5 years, but suffering is most acute between the ages of 2 and 3 years. Fear is a reaction of defence against new and overpowering situations ; rage, a protest against deprivation ; disgust, a reaction to disappointment which, even in the child, is essentially a disappointment in himself.

Suffering in both the child and the adult goes with muscular tension, a change of respiration, inhibition of movement, arrest of speech and laughter, paleness or heightened colour, and digestive upsets.

Joy produces a greatly increased activity and speed of movement with a slight lack of co-ordination in subtle movements. It goes with a heightened tone of voice, a rapid modulation of vaso-motor expressions, such as laughter, and heightened colour.

Delight is occasioned by gentle stimuli, especially those of touch, in the young child.

EMOTIONAL GESTURES

A.   Gestures of Rage

Rage is a direct continuation of the most primary reaction—agitation. It is essentially an autistic emotion and more primary than fear, which is based on a psycho-nervous conflict produced by contacts with the outside world. Rage demonstrates egoism pure and simple, with a tendency to aggressiveness. Expressions are thus autistic on the one hand and aggressive on the other. The visceral and tonic functions are especially involved with a tendency to vascular and muscular hypertony. The vasomotor symptoms are characterized by a heightened colour of the face, quickened and deep respiration and a protrusion of the eyes and lips.

In the primary emotions three phases can be discerned : the initial phase, the climax, and the final phase, manifested by different types of expression and gesture.

The emotional reactions of the infant are intimately connected with the mouth region, which is the source of all its interests. In the initial stage, whether of rage or fear, it is the muscles of the mouth which react. The lips tremble : they are drawn down in fear and pushed out in rage. Children, and adults too, when in a temper cry and protest in an uncontrolled and spastic or staccato speech. Children put their tongues out, which is an involuntary gesture of hypertension.

In the second phase of rage the muscular hypertonus is more marked than the vascular hypertonus and results in unrestrained and brusque movements of hands and feet. The first show to start with aimless agitation, expressed by opening and closing the fists, but soon aggressiveness predominates, and children, and often adults as well, throw things about or hit objects. Simultaneously they kick out at all those who come within range.

In the final phase of rage the autistic element is expressed by violent gestures of the hand towards the body. One sees children and even adults hitting their chests, and in particular children, whose gestures are less localized, proceeding at the same time to make movements in a half circle similar to those made by sufferers from St. Vitus's dance, or throwing themselves on the ground. Angry children hit and bite themselves, being unable to vent their wrath on the offending adult or child.

These gestures of auto-aggression reveal a profound frustration. Gestures of rage, because of their autistic element, are centripetal and, owing to their aggressive nature, emphatic.

In the last stage of the final phase the vascular and muscular tone is increased to such an extent that the face becomes tense and the muscles absolutely rigid, putting an end to motor activity. There is a resemblance or even identity of expression, particularly in the first and final phases, between rage and fear.

B. Gestures of Fear

Fear is allied to shock, to which the infant reacts by the startle and tears. Later on fear is provoked by adults and older children and shows two tendencies : the effort to maintain equilibrium on the one hand and to conciliate the originator of the fear on the other, an attitude containing an element of submission which may amount to loss of self-respect.

Gestures of fear are therefore either reflexes of self-protection or movements of appeal. The latter contain, even in early childhood and certainly in the adult, an element of self-consciousness.

As a rule gestures of appeal are made to impress an audience. From this it is evident that grown-up people who are hypersensitive and easily frightened have a tendency to self-consciousness and exaggeration.

It is mainly through the perceptions of hearing and sight that fear, which is a negative contact with the outside world, is induced.

The functions of the parasympathetic nerves determine the expressive behaviour of the frightened person. In the initial phase there is anaemia of the brain instead of hyperaemia, as in rage. Instead of augmentation and acceleration of movement there is a slowing down and impoverishment of gesture. The face is not red as in fury but pale or drained of all colour. In place of a torrent of insulting words there are only sharp cries or inarticulate words.

Fear is a parasympathetic emotion *par excellence*, and vagatonic reactions are produced in different parts of the organism. In the cardiac zone anguish causes a feeling of oppression which may take the form of an angina pectoris, and the intestinal symptoms of fear, in the child as well as the grown-up, are well known.

In the initial phase expression is conveyed primarily by the face and is concentrated to start with in the region of the mouth, the muscles of which contract, producing a tightening of the lips. But they can also tremble in fear as well as rage.

The eyes, which in rage have an aggressive expression, are fixed and startled both in the child and in the adult. The fixed regard remains throughout life a visible sign of anguish when other manifestations of fear have disappeared.

The regard is fixed on the originator of fear, and staring represents an attempt to maintain control over the situation. The nervous and muscular tension accumulated by such an effort must be discharged and this is achieved by the opposite reflex : the fluttering of the eyelids. This gesture often survives infancy and is always a sign of a hypersensitive personality with an anxiety complex.

Owing to the fact that the eyes and ears are the organs which register the impressions which arouse fear, hiding gestures of the face are very frequent in the initial stage, especially at an early age. To cover the eyes or the ears with the hands are automatic movements. The child as a rule hides completely behind an older person. In the case of the adult, hiding gestures are performed in a more subtle and hypocritical fashion and are often unrecognizable : for example, the gesture of covering the profile with the hand and at the same time turning away, is a movement simulating fatigue which is often resorted to by nervous people in trying and uncomfortable situations.

Motor activity in the initial phase consists in movements of recoil and in hypo- and hypermetric gestures of the hand. Whilst the feet move backwards the hands make a forward movement to maintain equilibrium. These gestures are designed to maintain not only the physical but also the mental balance.

The climax of fear goes with a more or less complete motor inhibition. This may develop into a reflex of immobilization comparable to a hypnotic state. With complete loss of control goes a loss of peripheric sensitivity, which produces a state of aura as before a fainting fit.

In the final stage, when the nervous system has slightly recovered from the shock, autistic gestures accompany the return to life, and adults as well as children can be seen scratching themselves, plucking hair or eyebrows, biting the nails and gnawing the fingers. After the loss of self in a state of paralysation the urgency of reconciliation with the originator of the fear supervenes and results in imploring gestures. For example, the child, menaced by punishment, having recovered from the overpowering reaction of terror, runs to the adult with open arms and with every sign of affection. The adult, on the other hand, tries to conciliate the originator of fear by words and gestures of appeal or only by a forced smile.

But in extreme cases the final phase of fear produces quite another effect : that of complete powerlessness, resembling the final stages of fury.

Thus the nervous paralysis of the climax is accentuated by complete muscular rigidity, a feeling of suffocation and sometimes a loss of consciousness.

Expressions of fear are evident in the infant of 7 months but develop, according to K. Bridges, into real storms towards 14 months.

Gestures of the hand in Fear

Already in infancy gestures of the hand play an important rôle in expressions of fear. The anguished child puts its hand into its mouth, bites its nails or gnaws its fingers. Hand and mouth in these gestures discover their primary alliance. In the adult, gestures of the hand are particularly revealing in spite of the fact that they are more subtle and hypocritical than in the infant. Wringing and interlocking the hands are the most common manifestations of a state of fear and anxiety. But there are also more delicate and more discreet hand gestures which reveal the same state of mind : tapping with the fingers on the mouth or on the furniture or only the pressure of one hand on the other. Often one hand, generally the left, clasps the other by the wrist.

Movements of the hand towards the head are also more frequent in the adult than in the infant : stroking gestures of the face, and hair, touching the nose, &c. All these gestures serve to discharge nervous tension, but they are mainly designed to revive the peripheric sensibility.

C. Gestures of Disgust

Reactions of disgust commence when the infant is about five months old. They are chiefly localized in the region of the mouth, the most instinctive and primary zone of expression, and they correspond to the impressions of the most primitive senses—taste and smell. It is the mouth which in the first place reacts by expressive movements to situations which arouse disgust. The corners go down and the lips tauten, producing an acid expression. Movements of the nostrils, especially in adults, accompany the muscular tension of the lips. The child's disgust over physical dirt is sublimated in the adult to moral disgust. In the latter, the muzzle region develops an increasingly expressive and symbolic value. Moral disgust is an emotion of refusal. It brings to the fore more than any other emotion disappointment at the insufficiency of others and also of oneself.

In the child emotional reactions are more global and violent and less inhibited than in adults. The child often points to the dirt and says 'Ugh !' 'Nasty !' &c. But it must be remembered that physical dirt, especially its own excretions, have a certain fascination before they cause repugnance.

It is only as a result of education that children feel disgust for things which are usually repugnant to adults.

An instinctive reaction of disgust towards nourishment which disagrees with the child is nevertheless fairly early developed. The instinct of self-protection produces gastric reflexes and expressive movements of refusal. Otherwise disgust may be considered as an emotion canalized by education. This fact enables us to understand how in certain cases of psycho-neurosis there is a regressive fascination for filthiness.

Perhaps the cult of ugliness and repugnant objects favoured by some surrealist painters is such a regressive fascination mixed with a protest against the corrective methods of education.

D. Gestures of Jealousy

Jealousy only develops after the second year as a counterpart to affection. K. T. Bridges describes jealousy as ' an emotion compounded of anger and fear '. Gestures of jealousy, therefore, combine expressive movements characteristic of both. They exhibit two tendencies : aggressiveness, which goes with the sense of possession and self-assertion ; and submissiveness, which goes with the sense of resignation. This combination of sadistic and masochistic reactions creates pandemonium, causing intolerable suffering. The confusion of expressive conduct in jealousy is as abrupt as it is contradictory.

It reveals an ambivalance of emotions in the most clear and visible way. In the adult the gestures of jealousy are, except in certain cases of extreme crisis, more subtle and hypocritical and are therefore more difficult to decipher. For this reason emotional gestures can be very deceptive, if the individual make-up of the subject and his emotional history are not taken into account.

An emotional stimulus leads to quite different expressions according to whether it is experienced for the first time or has been registered over and over again. Also temperament, the degree of nervous resistance, age, the actual state of health, &c., are factors which modify emotional gestures.

E. Gestures of Joy

Joy develops from delight and is shown in two ways : a passive and an active form. In small children it is closely allied to the sense of touch and may be considered as the first sign of sensual reaction. In its initial phase it is a relaxing emotion which develops contact with the outer world and confidence in the environment.

In this sense it is the exact opposite of fear, which is also an emotion of contact, but a negative one developing introversion and mistrust. But passive joy and fear have one thing in common : the predominance of psycho-motor reactions over visceral reactions.

Passive joy is mirrored at first in the face, which becomes radiant, the mouth relaxed and half open. Laughter and gurgling and in the climax shrieks of joy accompany rhythmic movements of the whole body, the hands and feet in particular. All these reactions appear in the infant of 6 months. The gestures of the hands already at this early age show great variety. The opening and closing of the fists, which is characteristic of a state of general excitement, is very common in young children when emotion has reached a climax.

Exuberant joy is an active form of delight. It is only apparent towards the age of 1 year. Active joy goes with heightened vitality and increased muscular and vascular tone. The nervous dynamism is accelerated. Thus both the organic and expressive functions are stimulated.

Joy is the sympathetic emotion *par excellence* and the one which is at the base of social contacts in infancy as well as in later years. But as exuberant joy is the expression of a forceful ego it always contains an element of self-assertiveness. The desire of the happy person is to impose his happiness on his surroundings. That is why joy possesses a suggestive force which is at the same time infectious and social. Passive joy goes with a submissive attitude to the outer world, exuberant joy with a certain amount of under-lying aggressiveness.

Gestures of Exuberant Joy

Gestures of exuberant joy are characterized by three qualities : acceleration, extension in space, and rhythm. The lack of inhibition which goes with joy causes an acceleration of movements, sometimes to such an extent that perfect co-ordination suffers. All the movements tend to raise the body from the ground and the spatial frame of gestures is extended upwards as well as in a horizontal direction.

The dynamism of elation is transmitted mostly to the feet of the child, who runs to and fro, makes dancing movements or hops from one leg to the other. When about two years old, children make rhythmic movements with laughter and cries of joy. They invite others to share in these pleasures, dancing round them with open arms. Later on they give expression to exuberant joy by climbing on the backs of chairs, rolling on the floor like a ball or sliding down banisters.

Those adults who are not restrained by convention also perform dances of joy, and in certain countries, as, for example, the Tyrol and Switzerland, yodel and throw their caps into the air to give further expression to their enchantment. There is a superabundance of gestures in moments of elation which often produces acrobatic movements.

In the final phase, when the nervous energy is spent, vagatonic reactions set in and produce fatigue or exhaustion, together with irritability. The child's exuberance ends with tears and a pale face with dark shadows under the eyes, until sleep brings refreshment and renewed vitality.

F. Gestures of Affection

When the child develops affection for both adults and other children he enters into a new world. Once he starts to choose his objects of affection he has left the first phase of purely autistic feelings. It is through sympathy and affection that human beings find complete contact with others in a process of identification. The first feelings of affection develop in the child the first sense of a group consciousness.

The fact that, after the age of 2, affection is shown in a submissive form for adults and in a protective form towards other children, shows that it represents the first form of a true collective existence. Through our submissive feeling we learn not only to love but to obey. Through our protective feelings we learn not only to protect the feeble but also to take responsibility and to enjoy giving pleasure to others.

The child's gestures of affection are at first gestures of tenderness and the desire to please. The former are expressed by caresses, kisses and the satisfaction of being embraced.

The desire to please develops coquetry and an urge to show off. Affection is not an emotion like delight, from which it originates, but an emotional state of mind, and it introduces a new element into the life of the child : a continuity of contacts and a distinct emotional memory. Through affection the child gives out what he has experienced more or less subconsciously, caresses, kisses, smiles, stroking and touching gestures of tenderness, &c. The child makes use of the whole scale of expressive movements characteristic of both passive and exuberant joy with a single aim, namely to attract the interest of the object of affection and to make it happy. There is a subconscious identification with one of the parents in the love of the child for those younger than himself, an identification which gives him a sense of power as well as the pleasure of passing on what he himself has enjoyed. In protective affection tenderness has a 'tactile' quality, expressed chiefly by cautious and subtle gestures of the hands which satisfy both the pleasure of contact and an unconscious physical curiosity. By touching the object of affection the child gains his first emotional and sensuous knowledge of others.

The paternal or maternal rôle in this type of affection often involves a complete imitation of attitudes and words, especially at a more advanced age, between 4 and 6 years.

G. *Autistic Gestures*

The first autistic gestures are the result of a kinaesthetic feeling (awareness of the body proper) and are, as the name indicates, directed towards the body. The feeling of identity is based on an early narcissism and on a contact with the body which every human being has to experience. Kinaesthesia is constantly changing throughout life. It is the basis of consciousness of self, and remains always the exact opposite of the awareness of other people.

Kinaesthetic feeling begins to develop about 18 weeks after birth. At this age the child looks at his fingers and not at the object placed in his hand. At 23 weeks, according to Wallon, his interest is in suspense and is divided between his hand and the object which he holds. At 33 weeks he examines his body in the bath and touches and pats himself. In this phase of his life his body and his limbs are still detached objects for him and not sensitive parts of himself. In the 62nd week he tries to pull out his fingers as if they were playthings. Kinaesthesia, according to Wallon, is only fully established after the age of one year.

The first awareness of the body is gained through the hands and it is by them that the child discovers himself, bit by bit, by a process of continual repetition. By patting himself all over—on the chest, the abdomen, the sexual organs—he begins to understand that all these parts are himself. This discovery goes with an emotion of joy which develops the love of self and prepares the centralization of the personality, on the solidity of which depends, later on, the capacity to assimilate exterior impressions which are a continual potential or real threat to nervous and moral balance.

In the first stage of infancy exterior impressions are predominantly negative and produce reflexes of tension. In the second stage, when a half emotional and half sensitive consciousness is formed, gestures of relaxation—flexor movements—predominate.

The interior life of the infant and the adult swings between two poles : the effect of the world on the Me and the effect of the Me on the world. Perfect co-operation between the two, which is guaranteed solely by a strong centre of personality and a fine perception of the outside world, is the basis of nervous and moral health.

The natural narcissism of the child imposes an especial task on education. The child is not completely satisfied by repeatedly touching his body, though this gives him mental and physical pleasure ; he likes to share the pleasure with adults or other children and gain reassurance for his discovery. He seeks attention and admiration for his body. To give him too much renders him autistic for his whole life, to give him too little makes him uncertain of himself. Wallon denies that the first sensations induced by touching the genital organs are of a sexual order, but explains them as the simple delight in the discovery of self. To interfere with this type of gesture renders the child self-conscious, upsets his feeling of identity and arrests the natural evolution of the sexual emotions by fixing them in the narcissistic phase.

The opposite approach, that of giving him too much admiration, has a similar effect. It fixes them in infantilism and sexual exhibitionism.

Autistic gestures are exhibitionist by nature. The child has to repeat them constantly until he can outgrow this kind of experience of himself. If the experience remains incomplete it will be revived at a later phase of life in a neurotic form.

Autistic gestures are not only provoked by kinaesthetic stimuli, but are soon made in response to other causes. When the child receives a present or listens to a funny or exciting story he expresses his pleasure by patting and touching himself or by rhythmic movements.

It is natural that, since the body has become a source of pleasure and at the same time the first means of realizing the Me, practically all impressions of enchantment should be expressed by autistic gestures.

Affection for others, especially for smaller children, is the first antidote to this egocentricity, when emotional awareness of others develops the realization of the ' Thou '.

It is obvious that narcissism in the adult is a regressive tendency. Autistic gestures at a mature age may reveal narcissistic tendencies, but they also occur in conditions which go with the loss of identity and an abnormal kinaesthesia.

A megalomaniac who identifies himself with a symbol of power has lost his own personality, and a catatonic schizophrenic who can keep his limbs for hours in the most uncomfortable postures has also lost his personality.

These patients resort to autistic gestures, probably in a vain attempt to memorize former feelings of themselves which are no longer present in their consciousness. In a much milder form one finds a similar process in neurotic people, particularly those suffering from anxiety neurosis. Anguish leads to an enfeeblement of identity and the anxious person subconsciously restores self-assurance by touching his body.

The autistic gestures of the child and the adult have entirely different meanings. In the former they build up the ego and release feelings of satisfaction and elation. In the latter they demonstrate either a weak or disrupted ego and unmask subconscious conflicts which generally go with depression and a feeling of frustration.

H.   Gestures of Imitation

For the child and, up to a certain point, for the adult, imitation is the most important means of learning about life. Imitation, in the shape of simple reflexes, begins as early as the age of 2 months. The first gestures of imitation are those of the mouth, which for the infant is the centre of existence. It smiles when others smile, it cries when others cry. After 6 months, in the transition stage between the purely instinctive and the emotional phase, the child imitates gross movements, using its arms and hands.

The true age of imitation is between 18 and 30 months. In this period two principal tendencies, sympathetic imitation and imitation of movements, take definite form. Imitation is an innate function like speech, but with more global and profound repercussions than those of language. Even with adults, it is dependent on a more or less subconscious mechanism and thus betrays two essential characteristics : suggestibility and a lack of conscious control.

Suggestibility can be described as a state of nervous and emotional receptivity working on the two nervous systems : the central and the autonomic. It goes with a special awareness of the outside world, and with submission to the influence of another personality. In infancy this submission is a natural state, necessary to the completion of the child's apprenticeship. In the adult it is a potential or real danger, since it renders him too susceptible to exterior impressions and makes him dependent on contacts. Normally, suggestibility diminishes with the development of intelligence and judgement, as L. Reyment and A. Kohn have shown in a paper ' An Objective Investigation of Suggestibility '. The infant, as a suggestible being, is part of his surroundings, on which he depends and in which he believes. A decisive separation between the Me and the Thou does not exist either for the child or the suggestible adult. Suggestibility, which produces imitation of words and actions, is the basis of the mental development of the child.

There are two different types of imitation : a motor-ideo and an ideo-motor imitation. The imitativeness of the child proceeds gradually from the former type to the latter. It imitates movements and gestures without comprehending the process behind the expression.

Motor-ideo imitation works from the periphery to the centre. The corresponding gestures are, as a rule, unconsciously performed. ' Responsive imitation ', as Valentine calls it, is completely uncontrolled and unconscious ; it belongs to the instinctive phase of childhood but remains the most primitive form of collective expression in adults.

In every situation where individuality is suppressed, as in group emotion, responsive imitation takes the place of criticism and judgement. This type of imitation is due to an influence similar to the effect of hypnosis. It takes place independently of consciousness and will-power, both of which are paralysed. Sympathetic imitation is a direct continuation of responsive imitation, and has the same compulsive quality, but the former extends with age further into the realms of the more subtle emotions.

Sympathetic imitation commences very early, at about the age of 6 months. From this age onwards the child cries when another child cries and laughs when another child laughs. As a rule he is more susceptible to the emotions of other children than to those of adults, with the exception perhaps of its parents. A very young child is influenced in its moods by the moods of its mother, and can put on the same dejected air or burst into tears when he sees her depressed or crying. But he is not suggestible all the time nor susceptible to all the emotions. He responds only to those which are in accordance with his nervous state, his phase of development, his personality and temperament. One day he will imitate certain expressions, another day he will be indifferent. This can be explained by varying day to day moods, physical conditions or special preoccupations.

Sympathetic imitation, owing to its emotional nature, touches only the primary level of subjective consciousness. Imitative gestures of this kind, which are more or less automatic, are therefore shallow and are thus quite different from the gestures of real emotions.

The grown-up individual who is too suggestible and imitative, has a tendency to neurosis and hysteria.

In the child sympathetic imitation develops his gregarious instincts, which at a later stage of development are transformed into a social interest and human sympathy. The child exhibits all the virtues of a true sympathetic participation, which makes it by nature a group member. But sympathetic attitudes must be reinforced in early childhood by real affections if they are to have substance and reality.

The child's imitation of acts and words has a special significance, for it develops later on the knowledge of objects and practical activities on the one hand and the power of thought and verbal expression on the other. This form of imitation contributes to the development of the objective consciousness. It is based on a mixture of mental and emotional suggestibility which is especially characteristic of the age of puberty, the first traces of which can, however, be found in the child of two years.

Docile imitation, as this approach might be called, is developed in a distinct and cumulative fashion between the ages of 3 and 4 years. At this age the child likes to copy the grown-up in everything : brush the carpet, dust the furniture, iron the washing, and so on. The child performs these tasks with an intensity of feeling which shows that with him, even more than with the adult, everything that depends on suggestibility is tinged with emotion.

The emotional element of docility is transformed, later on in life, into hero worship.

When the child has intuitively grasped, by imitative gestures, the inner processes on which they are based, he is capable of making use of another type of imitation by comprehending images to begin with and translating them into movement afterwards. This is the ideo-motor imitation which is the actor's province. Having understood the make-up of the character he represents the actor works, so to speak, from the centre to the periphery by realizing all the expressions and gestures which are suggested to him by the character portrayed. If he only tried to express the living essence of the character by words the true substance and individuality would be lacking. By embodying them in gestures he makes them living and real.

Ideo-motor imitation does not preclude creative discrimination, and every fine and intelligent actor knows the value of choosing the most characteristic and impressive gestures and omitting those which confuse the essential structure. These powers of deduction and interpretation reveal the great actor, whilst the second-rate artist, in his efforts to be exact in every detail, produces only a dull and lifeless portrait.

The actor must not be confounded with the mimic, whose talents are based on quite another gift : a motor-ideo imitation which can only reproduce what has been seen or heard and requires no subtle intelligence or psychological comprehension.

To compare the finished actor with the child actor is beside the point, since the child is lacking in the conscious art and the superior intelligence which inspires the creations of the theatre. But he possesses all the ingredients of the actor without being capable, except in the case of the infant prodigy, of incorporating them in a conscious work of art. These ingredients appear in children's games, which represent an ideo-motor imitation of a primitive kind. The gestures, words, and symbols which they use are gross, false and primitive, because they have not the capacity to correct or model them by intelligence and experience ; but it seems probable that an acting talent is allied to certain faculties which are the natural property of the child's mentality rather than of the adult's. I do not hesitate to admit this and to stress the fact that all the arts, except literature, which to a great extent makes use of abstract thoughts, are based on ideo-motor thought, and in this way the child is seen to be in fact not only a natural actor but also a natural artist. It may be asked—and this question was put to me by the well-known actor Michael Redgrave—if the actor's nature always retains certain traits which are characteristic of extremely suggestible children, and if, in consequence, his ego is weak and his emotions superficial and unstable. Within limits I am prepared to admit this. There are certain actors who possess strong identity and a stable temperament, but I think they are exceptions.

Ideo-motor imitation, which is the real element of the actor, necessitates the predominance of certain subcortical functions which make him what he is, an emotional and intuitive being, with the virtues and shortcomings which that implies.

I. Stereotyped gestures

Whilst imitative gestures bring a variety of contacts to the inner life of the child, particularly between the ages of two and four years, stereotyped gestures, which belong to a more advanced stage, throw him back again on himself. They are the consequence of brain development, especially of the cerebellum, which is the centre of equilibrium. They therefore give expression to a postural sensitivity which goes with a highly developed kinaesthetic consciousness, and this period of development represents, according to Wallon, the first link between the purely emotional and the mental phase. Kinaesthetic consciousness develops the 'motor imagination', a term coined by William James. Some children at this period perform frightening acrobatics with their fingers to such an extent as to dislocate the joints.

These gymnastics are characteristic of many backward people and certain lunatics, who, deprived of the possibility of abstract and concrete thought, make use of stereotyped gesture to express a kinaesthetic fancy, the characteristic traits of which are constant repetition and meticulous execution. This gives them relaxation and satisfaction.

The whole body, but especially the hands, play a part in these exhibitions, as for example when children stretch in the bath and on the floor, roll and twist like serpents, balance on a narrow ledge or slide down the banisters. Others make use of stereotyped movements by stepping only on certain boards of the floor or certain paving stones in the street, or missing out certain steps of the staircase. Some children make designs on the pavement or in the sand and content themselves with touching the outline. Or they amuse themselves by hopping on one leg, simulating lameness or passing a turning with a special posture of the head.

At a more advanced age these stereotyped gestures may be charged with superstition. I can remember certain games in which these gestures were treated as oracles and a wish was supposed to come true when these motor-conditions were fulfilled. Such practices develop in the child the feeling of motor power as well as a self-created refuge of a superstitious kind. This latter characteristic remains the same in the adult, in whom stereotyped gestures express otherwise quite different emotional and mental processes.

One must remember that all expressive movements which are natural to a given phase of development are constructive and enlarge the power of the mind, whilst they become negative when they appear out of their natural phase.

In the adult stereotyped gestures must be considered as regressive. They go with perseverance of images and indicate both an obsessional frame of mind and a lack of supple adaptation to circumstances. They are crutches for the mind, by the help of which a poor inner balance and a weak ego try to keep going. In this respect they are akin to autistic gestures but with one essential difference : autistic gestures are allied to the awareness of the body and its form, while stereotyped gestures, especially in the acrobatic form, are allied to the sense of movement. Their narcissism is, so to speak, of a more subtle and complex type. It is the perfect execution of movements which counts and gives the desired satisfaction, and this kinaesthetic pleasure goes with a strong rhythmic feeling and often a sense of elevation.

This is particularly noticeable in children, who derive, on the whole, great pleasure from stereotyped gestures. A radiant look of joy and pride lights up the faces of boys and girls amusing themselves by bicycling without touching the handle bars or balancing themselves precariously in other ways. A certain type of adult who retains narcissistic features throughout life retains also the feeling of elation derived from stereotyped gestures. This is the case only in a certain psycho-physical make-up which can as a rule be diagnosed in early youth. Children of an asthenic constitution, with slender bones, who are exceedingly mobile and move gracefully, are kinaesthetic types and gifted for kinaesthetic arts. They are often highly strung and hyper-sensitive and show inconsistency of expression and a general nervous instability. They frequently develop a taste for decoration and dress, and, in the case of boys, enjoy dressing up in female attire. These children rarely develop a superior intelligence.

There is a correlation, as I have pointed out, between acrobatic gestures and mannerisms which are characteristic of people with obsessional traits and a disintegrated personality. This personality type more readily obeys impulses of a subcortical than a cortical type.

III. THE HALF EMOTIONAL, HALF OBJECTIVE PHASE
(Intermediate Stage of Evolution between Emotional and Objective Consciousness)

PROJECTIVE GESTURES

Emotional gestures correspond to a subjective consciousness, which is the foundation on which the child gradually builds up an objective consciousness. But even when this has been achieved, the intervening stages of development are never discarded but remain incorporated in the psycho-physical organism throughout life. The emotionally formed expressions of the child can be transformed or absorbed in new mental activities, but only when the process of development has taken a normal and undisturbed course. Otherwise the emotions and expressions of earlier phases continue to exist unabsorbed, and damage the development of body and mind. The sixth year is the crucial age of transition from the emotional to the objective phase. This age is marked by the centralization of the cerebral faculties, both perceptive and expressive, which from now on work in unison. A normally developed child of this age is a mental and emotional entity. It possesses a certain stock of emotional experience and certain practical aptitudes as well as some knowledge of objects. The subcortical impulses are already inhibited and transformed by the imagination and a code of behaviour, the whole revealing a distinct personality and one which will remain fundamentally the same throughout life. By personality must be understood the raw material of character, the individuality of temperament and intelligence. By character must be understood the result of a co-operation between personality and educational influences. The latter may come from the authoritative education of School, Church and State or from the involuntary education of life itself. The child of 6 has certainly more personality than character. But one faculty is still lacking : abstract and detached thought. For this reason the apprenticeship of the young is full of mistakes and suffering. The child is liable to relapse into emotionalism and give way to violent impulses, and his expressions lack complete assurance. His whole knowledge of the outside world is still bound up with the ego and therefore lacks depth and continuity. In fact up to the age of puberty he is in a transition period which, as Wallon describes it, is somewhat vague and blurred in outline.

It was Wallon who also stressed the fact that this state of mind resembles the mentality of epileptics. The epileptic has no final or intentional outlook on life. He thinks and acts on a purely projective pattern by identifying himself with his surroundings. The normal child has to pass through a phase closely resembling that of an epileptic. He wants to draw attention to himself, to complain, to demand an explanation of the actions and reactions of others and to interfere with them in order to exhibit his sense of power. He only recognizes himself in relation to others. Projective gestures, which correspond to this state of mental development are, in short, gestures of intervention : movements of appeal, acclamation, consolation, &c. The result of such a domineering participation in the life of the *milieu* is a kind of latent impulsiveness which is discharged by incalculable and brusque movements. The affections are already strong in this period, but are still attached to the physical presence of the loved person, symbolization and sublimation being feeble or non-existent. With gestures of intervention go gestures of tenderness, affection and curiosity, aroused by the awakening of the sexual instinct. At the same time the interest in the mechanism of objects is steadily growing. Whilst affection and sexual interest stimulate the emotional imagination and emotion itself, the interest in objects quenches this subjectivism. Matter-of-fact thought therefore gradually detaches the child from dependence on his surroundings by giving him faith in himself. The interest in objects and rational thought encourage extravert tendencies ; the development of the imagination encourages introvert tendencies.

It may be asked how these contradictory attitudes of mind can exist at the same time, and in reply it must be said that every process of development is the outcome of opposites which create the necessary tension by which a new synthesis is formed. The simultaneity of divergent tendencies is natural since it is the natural incentive of mental and physical growth.

It is true that inner divergencies exist also in the adult and even more so in the adolescent. It is hardly necessary to stress the fact that inner processes of development continue throughout life, but certain phases, such as childhood, puberty, and the change of life, produce more inner conflict and complexity than others.

IV. THE OBJECTIVE PHASE

THOUGHT AND GESTURE

It is only when man is capable of abstract thought that his mentality is mature. In this the child differs from the adult : he is only capable of concrete thought. Abstraction can be compared with the process of distillation. It throws off the inessential and retains the essence. This is the real foundation of reasoning and logic.

Concrete thought by its peculiar nature contains a motor potential which tends to discharge in movements of the hands.

' Les gestes spatiaux ', as Wallon calls them, constitute therefore a part of thought itself. Dynamometric experiments have shown that mental activity goes with a muscular tension in proportion to the mental effort. A new idea and a spontaneous thought cause greater muscular tension and use more nervous energy than an old idea or a purely imitative thought. Creative thought, as one may call a spontaneous mental process, especially in the initial stage, is chaotic and emotional until it finds the thread of Ariadne to guide it through the labyrinth of images and associations into the daylight. Thus it produces an acute muscular tension which is discharged in movements of the hands and a vascular tension which takes refuge in facial expression.

The gestures of spontaneous or creative thought give an outline in space of what is passing through the mind. The hands guide the groping thought and are always slightly in advance of consciousness, anticipating by a fraction of time the image they are depicting. By this mechanism the gestures of the hand are a means of simplification and clarification.

The imagination and the subconscious are always evoked in spontaneous thought and the descriptive gestures which accompany it are involuntary. Apart from hand movements, which form a dynamic design of thought in space, the vascular and muscular tension is often so marked that accessory contractions of the feet and head are produced in order to maintain nervous equilibrium. In the search for clarity of thought there are always moments of suspense and pause, and these are not translated by gesture but in the expression of the face and in postures. If the expression of the face takes the place of gesture in moments of repose and relaxation, it is evident that facial expression and hand gestures compensate each other to a certain extent, which proves that the different organs of expression have different functions. Those of the face contain a clue to the more passive mental processes : those of the hands to the more active ones.

The face can be considered as the mirror of the two poles of the inner life : primary emotion and lucid intelligence. The wide field between the two—the greater part of personality—is more obviously expressed in other regions of the body but primarily by the hands.

Of course there is no rigid differentiation of expressive zones, for muscular and vascular tension affect the whole body in different degrees.

Small children gesticulate with the whole body when they talk of an exciting subject. It is only later that gesticulation is limited to the hands. The type and quality of gesticulation differ considerably amongst different races, but they are probably equally influenced by conventional and individual customs. It is the latter which interest us here. Doubtless the subcortical type of man, with a feeble sense of identity and a lack of nervous resistance, is more inclined to gesticulate, in order to give his words more weight and assurance, than is the man who is well integrated. The same applies to the orator who makes a more or less conscious use of persuasive gestures to impress an audience. Since the orator wishes to convince he appeals by a method of suggestion. In order to grip the imagination of his audience he tries to focus the interest on images and their emotional content rather than on abstract theories and critical judgement. Besides the expressive tricks of the orator used for effect, and the expressive movements of weak personalities unconsciously used for self-assurance, there is a form of natural gesticulation devoid of conscious or subconscious ulterior motive. This disinterested form of expression is ' l'art pour l'art ', which has its mainspring in a strong kinaesthetic imagination and a strong feeling of identity. It is possible to speak of the kinaesthetic aura of a person, containing the potential of all his postures and gestures.

The existence of a postural scheme is well known through the work of Head ; but it is outside the frame of this book to enter into the details of his extremely interesting theory. Head's kinaesthetic scheme is built up on postural images. These, being extremely flexible, can adapt the organism instantaneously to new situations, assisted by a kinaesthetic memory and presence of mind. When these are impaired by illness or fatigue, postural conduct and the execution of gestures are injured. The feeling of self or sense of identity is closely allied to this postural scheme, which by its adaptive function maintains the nervous and also the moral equilibrium. I am convinced that the rôle of the kinaesthetic scheme is not only protective but is the principal form of self-expression.

Kinaesthetic expression more than any abstract realization enables us to be aware of ourselves.

In all gesticulation which is not consciously or unconsciously utilitarian or persuasive, two tendencies must be differentiated : one which expresses thought and the other which expresses the self. These two tendencies strengthen each other and work in unison. Negroes, for instance, have a more complete and perfect kinaesthetic expression than Europeans. And amongst the latter the Latin races are in this respect superior to the Nordic. Their feeling of identity is realized in the first place by an extraordinary variety of postures and gestures, whereas in the case of peoples and individuals whose education has partially eliminated the kinaesthetic expression of self, gesticulation plays an inferior part or has no place at all.

Teachers should make a special study of this fact. The acquisition of knowledge and the teaching of logic on the one hand and physical culture (as carried out by sport-loving peoples) on the other are not sufficient to develop the individuality as a whole, but only touch certain parts of personality. The natural growth of the kinaesthetic imagination and ideo-motor expressions contribute to the self-assurance and integration of an individual as well as to his happiness and to the originality of all his expressions.

CHAPTER IV

IMAGINATION AND GESTURE

GESTURES have been described by Koehler and Goldstein as adaptive acts released by exterior situations. This definition is obviously too limited, since gestures also occur without outward provocation, solely as responses to imaginative situations. The most poignant proof of the latter type are the gestures of the insane. As the imagination has the same power as reality of unleashing expressive movements, it is of paramount interest to know if there is any difference between the psycho-motor reactions provoked by reality and those induced by fantasy. The faculty of imagining is linked with the emotional make-up. Even mental images of an objective type always have a pleasant or unpleasant character and are therefore tinged with emotion or feeling. I am particularly concerned to show the influence of the emotional images on gesture as these more than 'objective' images are apt to reveal the fundamental nature of men.

THE NATURE OF EMOTIONAL IMAGES

In emotion the visceral and tonic functions have a strong influence on the perceptive faculties and a greater effect on the consciousness than exterior situations. Thus emotional images are to a great extent affected by organic impressions which they reproduce in a more or less vague and vacillating fashion.

The exterior world nevertheless plays a part in emotional imagination, but in an illogical and haphazard way. Exterior impressions are robbed of their proper proportions and separated from their objective context. A strong emotion impairs the faculty of perception or even eliminates it, but at the same time we know that the subconscious registers a great deal of the exterior world independent of proper sensory function. It is evident that this para-perception is purely subjective. It tends to falsify and exaggerate situations according to the temperament of the person concerned. The imprecise is a stimulus to the imagination as a poor achievement may be to action. Urged by an inherent sense of harmony and synthesis the consciousness tries to reconstruct the real situation, but having only insufficient material to work on fails in its aim. Emotional obscurity is in consequence represented in the consciousness an reproduced in emotional expression and gestures. It is easy to see that the imagination represents a refuge from emotional conflicts which cannot be adequately expressed in movement. But this refuge easily becomes a cage when emotions produce fixed images and fixed ideas. This is often the case in young people when their emotional situations are so painful that they threaten the nervous resistance of the personality and its integrity. The suppression of the real situation leads to obsessional images which torment the mind with their implacable rigidity. They represent an emotional substitute which is painful enough but less soul-destroying than the underlying emotional reality. Fixed ideas and images are a form of escape, and they are apt to disguise the emotional shocks from which they originate. This condition is the essence of every type of neurosis. Psychotherapy uses the regulating force of the imagination in such cases by exposing false images and by reviving the picture of the suppressed situation at an age when the person is able to understand and to accept both.

While especially disagreeable emotions tend to produce obsessional fixation by damming the flow of associations, agreeable emotions fill the mind with vacillating and flexible images, a process known as day-dreaming.

Apart from this subjectivism of emotional imagination we must remember that the creative power of the mind is built on emotion and imagination. An intrinsic bond connects the two. One has only to observe a child listening to a fairy tale to realize that emotion and imagination are interdependent, the latter having a sublimating influence on the former. What the fairy tales do for the child, literature and the arts do for the adult. Through their influence he experiences a widening of his ego as well as detachment from it by identifying himself with the joys and sufferings of others and thus creating a way of escape from his own problems. For the adult, naturally, expressions in art take on a symbolic significance which is foreign to the child.

The communication between imagination and emotion is by a two-way road. Images can revive and even produce emotions and corresponding emotional expressions. The mere remembrance of an embarrassing situation can make us blush and the recollection or anticipation of danger may paralyse our movements, while the picture of a pleasurable event, be it past or future, makes us gay and active. Thus emotional images have a direct influence on the organism. It is well known that anxiety about examinations can upset digestion, and examples of how emotions affect organic functions can be multiplied *ad infinitum*. Wallon clarifies the link which exists between the latter and emotional images. The subjective consciousness, he says, occupies a cortical region which is closest to the subcortical sphere.

The influence of emotional imagination on living matter has numberless consequences which are vital for the individual and of primary importance for medical and psychological therapy. Aldous Huxley indicates in his book *The Art of Seeing* a therapy of many diseases of the eye which is based on the idea that emotional images and motor function are intrinsically linked. It is by images which are agreeable that a maladjusted function of the eye can improve and even be completely cured. Huxley explains how images influence at the same time circulation and muscular tension and how certain movements of the eye, provoked by these images, provide the eye with that vitality and flexibility which is necessary for its proper functioning.

In psychotherapy suggestion by hypnosis profits entirely by the nature of emotional images and shows their extraordinary power over body and mind. In hypnosis the image, the autonomic nervous system and the subconscious form an unbroken chain, working in complete accord and divorced from the conscious mind. It is this proud conscious personality, allied to judgement and reason, to observation and logic, which is under the domination of the subconscious in a hypnotic trance, when man makes gestures and fulfils tasks of which he would never have been capable by his own will. Hypnosis demonstrates best the link which exists between the autonomic functions and emotional images and the osmotic contact between these two and the subconscious mind.

Emotional images are the guardians at the threshold of the subjective consciousness, the doorway which leads into two spheres : into symbolic consciousness, which is a superior form of the subjective consciousness, and into oblivion, but an oblivion which is not quite complete, since small occurrences like a scent, a vague resemblance to a scene, a face, a tone of voice can evoke long forgotten images and reproduce an emotional situation which is no longer present to the mind.

Emotional memory is passive and fluctuating and inclined to forgetfulness, except when the emotion is so strong that it absorbs the mind. In such a case of emotional preoccupation the objective memory suffers or is completely suppressed and other cortical functions are impaired.

Emotional imagination exercises an almost limitless power over man and in the end produces more definite repercussions on the organism than emotion itself. The power of the emotion decreases when it is adequately expressed through movement, while the images work on the mind with the inevitability of the Fates. To the eye of the person with strong emotional pre-occupations the exterior world undergoes a metamorphosis. Objects and situations can become charged with a hidden meaning which is purely subjective. By projecting his inner state on exterior reality, the outside world assumes an imminence and a power at once attractive and frightening which keeps man in continual suspense and expectation. If he has a sanguinic temperament his stimulus for life and his *joie de vivre* are likely to be strong and to encourage agreeable images. He will always hope for something pleasant or miraculous to happen, something which will bring· the realization of the sentiments and pleasures of which he dreams ; for him, the world holds infinite promise. For the melancholic the world contains only the anticipation of deception and defeat to justify his innate pessimism.

According to the emotional make-up images are coloured either with joy or sorrow, with pleasure or disgust, and the two, temperament and imagination, influence our taste for life or the contrary and in consequence the quality of our expressions and gestures. The fundamental influence of temperament on expression is already apparent in the more or less ' unconscious ' age before the first year of life, but becomes distinct in the emotional phase, and especially so between the second and fifth years. It is evident that his emotional nature exposes man continually to the wounds which life inflicts, and this danger is responsible for the superstitious conception of the world which is particularly marked in highly strung and imaginative people. With natives, who remain permanently in the emotional phase of childhood, superstition rules both their individual and their community life.

This state of mind is caused by a profound attachment to life, which goes with a lack of reason and judgement. Like the child, the superstitious man lacks detachment. This accounts for his inability to learn from experience. In order to learn ' by heart' the lessons which life teaches it is necessary to detach oneself from one's experiences by means of objective thought and judgement. Both are lacking in varying degrees in the emotional person and that is why throughout life he repeats the same mistakes and succumbs to the same temptations. Yet always he approaches the world with a freshness and spontaneity unknown to the detached person.

Superstitious individuals and peoples, by their fatalistic conception of destiny, are always harassed, even in moments of happiness, by an undercurrent of fear or even anticipation of disaster, and many of the religious rites of the natives and many of the proverbs, acclamations and gestures surviving in civilized nations reflect this awe-inspiring quality. They are infantile appeals by which man tries to conciliate God and counterbalance the fear of annihilation.

Everyone knows how deeply superstition penetrates everyday life. Small incidents can become for the superstitious person signs and portents of good luck or misfortune : the red rose in his path is a promise of success in the day's enterprise ; a passing funeral an augury of disaster ; the postman he meets indicates the arrival of an anxiously expected letter ; and so on. This presentiment of good and evil has a profound influence on expressions, since it produces a state of mind which keeps the autonomic nervous system in continual suspense.

It is the passive nature of the emotional consciousness which renders it so open to suggestion. Images are evoked with the same inevitability as physical symptoms, and mind and body react in the form of a conditioned reflex, a fact which Pavlov discovered in his researches on dogs.

The dossiers of psycho-analysts are full of these compulsive and irrational reactions which constitute the core of their patients' sufferings.

One of my patients suffered such an acute anguish during thunderstorms that she cried like a child, trembling in every limb and finally reaching a state of mental and physical collapse. This abnormal reaction could be traced to an incident in her childhood, when a streak of lightning struck a tree near her parents' house. A friend of mine was reduced to a state of melancholy accompanied by sickness whenever the church bells rang on Sunday morning. She had the feeling that something terrible was about to happen. She was unconsciously reproducing an emotional situation which she had experienced while her mother was dying one Sunday morning many years before. In these two cases extremely painful emotional reactions were revived in situations which resembled the outer circumstances of shock experiences, although the cause of the emotion had ceased to exist. As with the dogs of Pavlov, the conditioned reflex is set in motion in man when the same situation occurs that was present during the experience which produced the emotion. An unconditioned reflex is an involuntary reaction independent of thought and imagination. As long as the nervous system functions normally the reflexes always respond in the same way to stimuli.

The conditioned reflex is produced by the intervention of an image and is always unstable and temporary. It can be created at a certain moment, and disappear for good equally suddenly. In his book *Lectures on Conditioned Reflexes* Pavlov explains this in the following way :

These new reflexes are the function of the highest structure of the nervous system of the animal, and they must be explained on the following basis. First they represent the most complicated phenomena among nervous functions, and consequently they must be connected with the highest part of the nervous system. Reasoning further from animal experiments with various poisonings or with total or partial extirpation of the cerebral hemispheres, we can conclude that the conditioned reflex demands for its formation the assistance of the hemispheres.

The reflexes are temporary and conditional, and these qualities characterize and separate them from the old simple reflexes with which physiology has concerned itself in the past. Their temporary character manifests itself in two ways : they can be formed when they did not previously exist, and they may disappear again for ever ; besides this, when they exist they often fluctuate in degree even to vanishing, either for a short time or, under certain circumstances, permanently. As we have seen, their formation and extinction are determined by (one or several) coincidences in time of stimulation of the lower-lying reflex centres, which govern some functioning organ, with the stimulating of different points of the cerebral hemispheres through the corresponding centripetal nerves. If the stimulation of these two centres coincides many times, then the paths leading from the higher to the lower centres become more and more passable, and the conduction of the excitations along them becomes easier and easier. When these coincidences occur more rarely, or cease altogether, the paths again become less permeable, and finally impassable.

The conditioned reflex of Pavlov explains many phenomena in human psychology, for example the abnormal psycho-motor responses that appear after shock experiences and in neurosis.

In human beings conditioned reflexes are not only restricted to pathological situations but are also part of a normal psychophysical mechanism. The image of a good meal to a hungry man affects his reflexes. Saliva is readily secreted in his mouth by the stimulus of the picture of food and makes him lick his lips, and in pleasurable anticipation he rubs his stomach like a child.

This interdependence between emotional image and involuntary reactions has a frightening quality, since it places man in a painful situation through a want of control over his expressions. If man were completely at the mercy of his involuntary reactions and expressions he would become the victim of superstitions and shocks. But his objective consciousness and detached thought come to his rescue. They are the only antidote against his physical and mental slavery. A slavery which would ultimately destroy man both as an individual and as a member of a group, especially in an epoch which has outgrown the primitive social framework.

The life of natives is arranged to harmonize with an emotional and superstitious make-up, while our communal life, which is conditioned by objective consciousness and scientific thought, has little place for the infantile expressions of humanity. In spite of this progress in thought which has given us modern culture and civilization one must admit that man himself is still fettered by the emotional phase of evolution and that he is incapable of keeping step with the demands of a superior development of thought and social organization. The tragedy of modern man lies in this incongruity between objective thought and subjectivism. The two are at variance as long as emotion is stronger than the capacity for detachment and the acceptance of a synthetic view of life. The gulf which exists between the knowledge of his developed brain and the emotions of his infantile Self keeps man in perpetual conflict : a conflict which can only be solved with the help of a new type of individual and collective education. The isolated life of the individualist can offer so many mental and aesthetic facilities without providing constructive channels for the emotions, which in consequence are easily wasted in decadent eccentricities. Modern man suffers from a divided consciousness which arrests his development. There is in consequence a progressive disintegration of the individual and of society which has its repercussions on moral conduct as well as on expressive behaviour. When man has once understood his true place as an individual and as a member of a group in modern culture, his acts and his gestures will automatically change.

To eliminate emotion is impossible and undesirable. It only becomes a danger when it remains infantile and when it is badly directed. Properly expressed and directed emotion stimulates and fertilizes contacts between individuals and with the community. Further, it is an indispensable source of creative imagination and thought, however abstract and scientific the latter may be.

No society can live and develop without the constructive emotions of its members ; they are the foundation of sympathy and humanitarian feeling. It is only through emotion that we can participate fully in the destiny of our family, our friends, our country and of all humanity. Emotion unifies all human beings however different in character and race. Through its link with the imagination it enlarges our sympathy beyond the bounds of reality and unites us with the world of art through the warmth of true participation, without which aesthetic perceptions would leave no imprint on our minds. Through the link between emotion and aesthetic consciousness the mind is capable of a symbolic interpretation of both life and art. Symbolic images have an extraordinary creative power. According to Freud and Jung, who have made us familiar with the ' collective subconscious ', certain types of symbolic images, called archaic images, are as old as the world and are transmitted from one generation to another by the imprints of an inherited symbolic memory. They are proof of the continuity of a collective spirit which resists all exterior and interior changes experienced by man through the centuries. These archaic images emerge more easily from the subconscious in the neurotic than in the normal person. In the neurotic, who is apt to relapse into emotional regression, the archaic images may take entire control of his imagination and expressions. He is ruled, without knowing it, by the strange taboos which govern the lives of natives : and such a state of autohypnosis has often an infectious influence on others. This fact accounts for the dangerous gift of some modern neurotics to evoke primary emotions and archaic images in others and to lead them against their better judgement.

It is the collective subconscious which corresponds to group emotion. In their pure essence the primary collective emotions are only to be found in natives, with their religious rites, war dances, sexual orgies, and superstitious symbols and gestures.

These expressions, which in primitive man are innocent, become vicious in civilized people. The transformation from innocence to vice started in the Middle Ages, when man tried to attain super-human power by the practices of black magic and occult science. In our time, even more so than in the Middle Ages, the appeal to primitive emotions and archaic images is a crime, since it denies all the achievements of objective thought and ethics. If the man of the twentieth century starts to practise black magic and to imitate the war dances of the natives, if he allows himself to be guided by superstitious taboos and mystic trances, he renders homage to a demon who should have been buried centuries ago. Such gestures and practices are an insult to man as well as to God. In possession of a religious ethic and a knowledge illuminated by science, a regression to the primitive stage of group emotion results in a rupture of personality, a splitting of consciousness.

Such a state of mind has been admirably described by Shirer in his book *Last Train from Berlin,* where he tells of a young Nazi who was most friendly and human while in mufti but whose personality completely changed when he was in uniform. His face took on the appearance of a mask, his words and gestures lost their naturalness and became those of an automaton blindly pursuing a distant chimera.

The creator of this modern black magic evokes in his followers certain archaic images which have the effect of a drug abolishing objective consciousness and producing frenzied ecstasies. Their eyes see neither earth nor sky ; they are fixed on the distance. They have an expression of anguish mixed with cruelty. The hands and feet of these human robots move as one man, so entirely is the rhythm absorbed in the rhythm of the human machine. These people march through life with expressions and gestures which are at the same time aggressive and frightened, menacing and servile, like those of paranoiacs who are relegated by sane people to mental hospitals.

This description of a mental aberration should not be taken as an argument that every form of collective emotion represents a dangerous regression. That is not the case. As philosophy developed from occultism, chemistry from alchemy, a new type of collective emotion should develop from its primitive precedent :

a type which absorbs the archaic images but gives them a new sense and a new expression. Replacing the image of Christ by the image of Wotan is a moral and mental regression, since we only progress in accordance with the enlargement of our consciousness and the sublimation of our emotions.

ARCHAIC IMAGES AND GROUP EXPRESSIONS

The example of the young Nazi shows a dissociation of consciousness and personality which is manifested in paradoxical expressions. Man as a primitive collective being is subject to hypnotic influences since he is at the mercy of his subconscious and his emotions. A kind of mediumism which is at the root of group emotion works on the mind and produces manifestations similar to the automatic writings produced by some mediums in trance. Such irrational and uncontrolled reactions and expressions are to us, who have learned to follow ethical principles rather than demoniac impulses, an inferior form of collective life. This does not hold good in the case of native tribes. In their culture, produced entirely by the magic of the emotions and the subconscious, expressions are not at variance with consciousness but correspond to the completely psychic make-up. In his book *Stone Men of Malkula*, Layard gives striking examples of the hypnotic influence of archaic images and emotions on primitive man. They affect every aspect of his religious, collective and personal life. Ceremonies and tomtoms regulate the initiation into manhood, marriage, warfare and medicine. The primitive mind, which has not yet developed objective thought and judgement, can call upon many powers which civilized man has lost. Above all on the power of ecstasy, which is at the same time unselfconscious and invincible : unselfconscious since ecstasy is outside ego-consciousness and can utterly abolish the instinct of self-preservation : invincible, since the man who is possessed by ecstasy and blind faith has fear neither of defeat nor death. No wonder that modern demagogues should have sought to revive primary collective emotions and archaic images by a new form of occultism.

As Layard and others have shown, natives frame their group expressions in rites accompanied by the exciting music of gongs and by incantations. These make an irresistible appeal to the musical and rhythmic sense which is so strongly developed in the native. This primitive music sets all the nerves vibrating, producing frenzied gestures, particularly in the dance. To illustrate the effect of music on natives I will quote the following passage from Layard's book :

When to the already complicated rhythms of the gongs are added the further counter-rhythm of the dance-steps and of the accompanying songs, the effect is one of indescribable excitement, stirring emotions that the concerts of Europe never touch, but that the natives can call forth at will through their unrivalled sense of rhythm.

Layard also mentions that the communal dances of the natives of Malekula are organized in different forms : dances in line, serpentine dances, and round dances. They are arranged according to a religious and social plan and reflect a symbolism which betrays the taboos and idiosyncrasies of the natives. In these communal dances, and even more in the individual dances, where the erotic element predominates, the whole body takes part in rhythmic creation : arms, hands, head, as well as feet and trunk are set in motion.

It is obvious that group emotions, where they are to be found in their original state as with natives and to a certain degree with children, are expressed by ecstatic, infectious, and rhythmic movements. Through a complete co-operation between all the parts of the body they produce a complete unity of expression. They also show a remarkable dramatic sense which always goes with a certain exhibitionism. These are characteristics which we can all observe in children's games.

EMOTIONAL IMAGES AND INDIVIDUAL EXPRESSION

Group emotion is very different from individual emotion in spite of the fact that they are both at the mercy of the subjective consciousness and the subconscious. Group emotion takes a visible form in the framework of religious and superstitious rites. However irrational their expressions may be they conform as a rule to an exterior discipline and for this reason are almost calculable.

The imagination plays quite another rôle in the expression of personal emotion, where prescribed channels do not exist and must be created by the person himself. But how should he proceed to find avenues for emotional discharge ? He cannot be guided by imitative conduct modelled on an ideal person, since few people are closely similar in their emotions and means of expression, the power of which is strictly individual, as also are the emotional images, which are never identical in two brains. Further, these emotional images possess a meaning which is relative and incomparable, depending on the individual temperament and mentality and the sum total of personal experience.

No one can have exactly the same feelings as another person because of these individual factors. Since the door into the imagination of other people remains always half-shut, it is difficult to give specific interpretations of expressive movements which are the product of images. One can, however, discern general tendencies ; one can know, for example, if someone is preoccupied with disagreeable or agreeable images, those of jealousy and disgust, or those of peace of mind, affection, and happiness. It is also possible to get an idea of the part played by the imagination in the ensemble of the personality and of the amount of power which it exerts on body and mind. As Wallon explains in his book *L'Enfant Turbulent*, emotional imagination begins to function when the direct expression of emotion is barred. As the imagination represents a refuge from an inner tension otherwise intolerable, it is a form of expression in itself. From the fact that emotional imagination develops in proportion to emotional frustration it is evident that images engender, if at all, only passive and indeterminate gestures. As the real aim of the emotion, which is its communication, cannot be achieved, emotional images go with an expressive introversion, and the gestures resulting from this process are withdrawn from the surroundings and directed towards the body. From this one can conclude that the following qualities of expression characterize people dominated by emotional imagination :

1. Autistic gestures.
2. Predominance of reflex movements.
3. Contemplative postures.
4. Vaso-motor reactions like trembling, change of colour, &c.

It is obvious that the image of an emotion has another effect on psycho-motor function than direct experience. Emotional reality evokes a visible response which is based on the contact with others, a contact which may be agreeable or disagreeable, positive or negative, and which may even extend to animals and objects. In the latter cases emotional reality is already half imaginative ; from animals man cannot receive an adequate emotional response, while from inanimate objects he can receive no response whatever. In an emotional experience man reacts to his surroundings and his gestures are designed to protect his nervous balance. They are the instruments of adaptation to circumstances and in consequence functional and utilitarian. Each encounter with reality demands of man an attitude of defence, since he is in continual danger of becoming a prey to his surroundings. For this reason adaptive gestures protect at the same time his nervous balance and his moral integrity. The instinct of self-preservation evoked in emotional situations brings the functions of the senses into play. Sight, hearing, touch, enable a man, unless he is unhealthily emotional and neurotic, to fight for the maintenance of control and avoid being submerged by his surroundings and his own impulses. These conditions do not exist in an imaginative situation. The man who is absorbed by his images has no need to adapt himself to his surroundings and to control his gestures. Expressive movements that go with emotional images lack direct urgency and functional purpose, for they are unchecked by reality; they follow, on the contrary, the arabesque and irrational patterns of phantasy nourished by the subconscious, while at the same time vigilance and perceptive functions are more or less numbed, since they have no *raison d'être*. Thus all cortical activity which registers outside impressions and voluntary movements is quenched.

The cortical functions are designed to maintain the integrity of personality. Emotional imagination being under the control of the subcortical functions has a disintegrating effect. When communication with the outside world is blocked the autonomic nervous system takes the place of the central nervous system. Under such bio-psychological conditions a nucleus of controlled activity does not exist, and gestures and expressions are purely passive and involuntary. By emotional imagination must be understood a sort of day-dreaming. As I have already explained, the emotional imagination partly replaces expressive movements, or, as Ribot has said in his book *Problèmes de la Psychologie Affective* : ' Ce qui se dépense en mouvements ne se dépense pas en conscience et inversement.' This, however, is only partly true, for passive gestures and facial expression survive the process of absorption of emotion into consciousness. There is an essential difference between active and passive gestures. With the latter the body remains more or less stationary : with active gestures it changes its place and position in order to respond to the exigencies of the moment.

Emotional images are either visual or phonetic, but can also produce impressions of smell. In most people visual images play, however, the predominant rôle, affecting first the head, the forehead and particularly the eyes ; but, as Wallon observed, they are also reflected in the region of the spine, as in shrugging the shoulders and tossing the head, and these remain, according to him, one of the most common ways of showing mental dispositions. Wallon also noted that mental effort augments the dynamometric force and tends to equalize it in both the right and left hand. The hands follow each state of consciousness by movements of hardly visible contractions or postures. Emotional imagination cannot, however, be wholly identified with mental effort but goes according to the nature of the images, either with mental relaxation or with mental tension. In a state of agreeable and happy reverie the whole body becomes relaxed, the face calm, and the hands almost still. Under the influence of images which cause strong tension, such as fear and humiliation, opposite expressive responses occur.

The more that symbolic and objective thought creeps into images and emotions, the more subtle become the images and emotions, and the more segmentary and limited in number become the expressive movements. In a sensitive and cultured personality they are more varied and rich in quality the more they are restrained and reduced in quantity. From this one can appreciate the expressive power of great actors, who make use of a minimum of gestures to express a maximum of sentiment.

In the main, expressive functions are under the control of the autonomic nervous system, which affects the blood vessels, the muscles and the sweat glands. The expression of the face depends particularly on vaso-motor reactions which go with primary and entirely uncontrollable emotions. They are reflected in the colour, temperature and tension of the skin of the face and particularly in the expression of the eyes. Moved by a strong emotion the blood vessels dilate, a condition which causes the eyes to protrude, whilst in a state of fatigue and lack of vascular tension they appear to be smaller. The lips respond in a similar way, becoming fuller under an image of animation and pleasure, and pinched when the nervous energy is spent. In very strong or shattering emotions the whole body submits to the influence of the autonomic nervous system. The hands and knees as well as the lips can tremble as the result of an image of profound anguish. Under these conditions physical reactions are more dispersed, which is especially so in the case of the sweat glands. Those of the axillas and of the palms of the hands react quicker than those of the face.

Emotional images can release an expressive mechanism similar to that caused by real impressions. An image of disgust, for example, causes us to make the same movements of the lips as when we eat something unpalatable, a fact which proves that the expressive apparatus coincides with the perceptive apparatus. Four of the senses are concentrated in the face—seeing, hearing, smelling, and tasting—which makes the head the region *par excellence* of emotional expression. This explains why, since the days of Piderit in the nineteenth century, the scientific study of emotional expression was centred on facial expression. The fact that the imagination has the same effect on, for example, the ocular muscles as real objects has recently been attested by Aldous Huxley, as I have already mentioned. Huxley gives examples of a re-education of the visual apparatus through images. The expression of the eyes is determined by images and the more lively and varied the latter are the more varied are the movements of the eyes. The great advantage of functional re-education through images is that these can be chosen at will. When one pictures oneself playing on a sunny day in the garden with a young dog which leaps and runs to and fro, the muscular apparatus of the eyes registers the up-and-down and to-and-fro movements. The pleasure and animation which one feels in imagining such a situation results in an improved circulation of the eye and in a refreshing humidity of the conjunctivae which goes with a feeling of ease and relaxation. Mental relaxation causes muscular relaxation as mental tension causes muscular tension. An image of sorrow and anguish causes certain ocular muscles to contract and the pupils to enlarge, and if such a depressive condition is prolonged the eyesight becomes affected. The muscles get overstrained and the adaptive power of the lens suffers in consequence, with the final result of chronic eye-strain and long-sightedness. The theory which A. Huxley has expounded for medical therapy is supported by the psychologist Jacobson (quoted in *Studies in Expressive Movements* by Allport and Vernon), who found that—' all mental effort is accompanied by contractions of muscle groups, e.g. visual imagery involves the activation of the ocular muscles '. The fact that any form of concentration goes with a general increase of muscular tension has been assessed by dynamometrical measurements by the psychologist Bills, who states that 'increased muscular tension accompanies increased efficiency in almost any kind of learning'. That muscular tension is not only associated with mental effort (cortical activity), but also with emotional reactions (subcortical activity) has been stressed by Duffy, who found 'a very high correlation of +52,15 between average tension and ratings of excitability and emotionality'.

The latter finding shows the effect of the temperament on nervous and muscular tension. The highly strung person, whose nervous tension is continually keyed up, will be inclined to more diffused and vehement psycho-motor reactions than a person of a placid temperament. As the hands are especially designed to discharge nervous tension originating either in the central or in the autonomic nervous system, they react to both mental effort and emotional activity. When the tonic and visceral functions predominate, as in day-dreaming, hand gestures become autistic, as in early childhood before the cortical functions are properly developed. As I have pointed out before, the hands are very rarely in repose ; continually they reflect by minute gestures and slight changes of posture the processes of the mind. It is they more than any other part of the body which are allied to all states of consciousness from the most subjective to the most objective.

It is well known that pleasant emotions set the flexor muscles of the hand in motion, while unpleasant emotions bring the extensor muscles into operation. The preference for one type of emotion rather than the other is largely determined by the temperament, which influences imagery as well.

The extravert type of man has a natural tendency towards agreeable representations, the introvert towards tormenting ones. The hand of the first is large and broad, that of the latter long and thin. The introvert type of man always has difficulty in adapting himself to his surroundings. His make-up therefore encourages images of suspense, nostalgia and frustration, all of which produce movements of the extensor muscles. Goldstein points out that, if reflex activity is markedly increased in a grown-up individual, there is a tendency towards disintegration of the personality ; that is to say, towards the succumbing of the personality to both the exterior world and his imaginative impulses. From this it is easy to understand that the form and crease-lines of the hand are largely dependent on the make-up of the personality. Innumerable repetitions of extensor movements produce a longish, flat hand with many accessory crease-lines. Hands of such a type are generally rigid. The man who makes movements predominantly of flexion is apt to develop a broad, fleshy hand with a small number of accessory crease-lines.

According to Goldstein, movements of extension indicate predominant activity of the subcortical functions, whereas the movements of flexion are by nature cortical. Precise actions are always the result of flexor activity, ungainly actions of extensor activity. Objectivism corresponds, as Goldstein rightly points out, to movements of flexion, subjectivism to movements of extension. In other words, the man who has a preference for flexor movements makes on the whole few involuntary or reflex gestures. The man of action, whom one may call the cortical type, does not indulge for long in emotional imagery but resolves his nervous tension by contacts or action, and when he dreams it will be of agreeable impressions and visions, which stimulate his forward impulses.

POSTURES

Postures are not included in the scope of this book, but since they are essentially allied to gestures and play an important part in the expression of imaginative situations, I must add a few words on them.

Postures are physical attitudes which serve as a sort of platform from which expressive movements take their departure. They are under the control of the postural and tonic systems which regulate the equilibrium of the body and muscular tone. The centre of postural behaviour is situated in the cerebellum. From here communicating nerve fibres run in three directions : towards the hypothalamus, towards the spine, and towards the cortex ; which explains why we adopt both involuntary and voluntary postures. The former are the more frequent and the more important for our subject, since they play so marked a rôle in emotional imagery.

Postures, in their dependence on muscular tone, its vigour or lassitude, are subject to autonomic innervation, a fact which also reveals their link with the emotional life. Each individual has characteristic attitudes which, as Goldstein has indicated (see A. Gurwitch, *Le Fonctionnement de l'Organisme*), betray 'his motor and nervous disposition'. In other words favourite postures are the mirror of emotional reactions and nervous resistance. Everyone adopts the postures in which he finds most ease and comfort and in which he can best avoid nervous strain.

The best illustration of habitual postures is the well-known Buddha posture adopted by Mongolian imbeciles. In the case of these unfortunates this Oriental attitude, which they have never seen or learnt, denotes an innate psycho-physical character which is part of their whole make-up. The posture is induced by the extraordinary flexibility of their articulations and their weak muscular tonus, and in it they experience the maximum of comfort. This example serves, moreover, to show that favourite attitudes are already established in infancy.

Postures vary according to whether we are alone or with others. They are certainly less voluntary and more natural when we are alone and free from the effort of reacting to our surroundings. In emotional imagery postural attitudes are entirely involuntary and change with the waves of tension and relaxation produced by images.

CHAPTER V

THE PATHOLOGY OF GESTURE
(CLINICAL STUDY)

General Observations

THE anomalies of gestures and expressions in mental maladies are well known. They are classified as mannerisms, signifying that they are unnecessary and excessive movements, and are considered to be a kind of esoteric language for which no adequate interpretation exists. No observer, so far as I know, has attempted to throw light on these pathological expressions or to compare them with more normal psycho-motor behaviour. The expressive conduct of mental patients, especially of schizophrenics, the patients who exhibit the greatest anomalies, is shrouded in mystery. But the more I observed the behaviour of the insane the more sure I felt that there is no absolute and insurmountable wall between them and ordinary human beings, and that therefore the study of their mannerisms might be most helpful not only for the understanding of mental illness but for the understanding of expressive behaviour in general.

Accordingly, during the last six years I have carried out special research work amongst mental patients, trying always to establish contact with them by talking to them, and attempting to interest them in the process of my investigations. I strove to understand their reactions, and often myself imitated their gestures and postures as a means of realizing their states of mind. I believe that the best way to grasp the meaning of phenomena of this kind, which defy direct comprehension, is to make oneself receptive and suggestible and to apply the motor-ideo type of imitation, as children do when they try to comprehend the behaviour of others. To get at the root of their illness I tried to identify myself with the patients by imitating their gestures. The second phase of my research consisted in methodically studying the gestures of mental patients under conditions resembling as closely as possible those of ordinary life. To this end I chose to investigate expressive conduct (1) at work, (2) at meals. The advantage of this approach is obvious. Absorbed in their activities, the patients were as little self-conscious as possible and had no idea that they were being observed. Over a period of eight months I visited regularly the professional therapy classes of male and female patients at St. Bernard's Hospital, Southall, observing the patients at their different occupations. A certain number of them were easily approachable and I talked to them and made them talk to me. In this way I was able to find out a certain amount about their preoccupations, phobias, and obsessions.

I was conscious of a special atmosphere in the society of these 'working' patients. I realized the seriousness with which they worked and the satisfaction they derived from their occupations. Many of them had greatly benefited from this form of therapy. Apart from the fact that it helped them to regain their self-esteem, manual work has the effect of a sedative without the bad effects of drugs.

The patients were inclined, I noticed, to attach themselves always to the same groups at the same tables and in the same attitudes. This stereotyped habit seems to me to be characteristic and the expression of a need for stability and security. The same need is exhibited by normal people in such habits as that of occupying always the same table in a restaurant. There were a certain number of solitary individuals who chose to remain always apart from the cliques in one special place in the class. These were paranoiacs, suffering from depression and avoiding contact with others with an inflexible resistance. I noted seven patients of this kind in the female class. They were seated near the window with their backs to the class. Sometimes they would look outside with a tense immobility but they never so much as glanced at another patient. The melancholics tried to hide in corners. One of them was a halfcast and I had been advised by the teacher on no account to ask her where she was born as she had a persecution complex about her colour. Another, who especially interested me, a woman of 43 years of age, suffered from religious mania. She was a case of paraphrenia, with ideas of persecution which, as so often with psychotics, were concentrated on sexual preoccupations. This patient, seated in front of a window as far as possible from the rest of the class, seemed to be very alive to the impressions of nature and told me that she watched the changes of the seasons while waiting for the day of liberation. She continued her needlework throughout our long conversations. She quoted the Bible to me at length ; she discussed politics ; and in fact, except for a certain mental intolerance, there was no sign of a real abnormality either in word, expression, or gesture. I could not understand why she was so sociable with me and so completely negative in her attitude towards the staff and the other patients. But one day when we had become still more intimate her obsessions found expression and I discovered the clue to her need for isolation. She suspected the patients and the staff of being in the pay of Scotland Yard in order to watch her movements and to keep her a prisoner in the hospital. All this, so she said, was due to the intrigues of a jealous woman who resented her love for a man who, in fact, she had never met in the flesh. She had been taken by his voice, which she heard every day on the radio. Later, as she imagined, she had made his acquaintance and had decided to save him from the bad woman who was now persecuting her. While telling me this story all her expressions and gestures changed. Her eyes were wide open and staring, her voice became high and pinched, and she made constant gestures with her hands. Her needlework she now dropped, though previously during our conversations when she was calm and composed she had carried on with it. She made centrifugal movements—emphatic and menacing gestures directed against her imaginary adversary, all of them extensor movements. Her fingers were splayed out fan-like and the index finger raised. From time to time these gestures were interrupted by the infantile gesture of opening and clenching the fists, revealing impatience and general excitement. All these psycho-motor reactions were the outcome of vividness of images, produced by an inner situation which had no relation to reality.

Besides the isolated individuals near the window I noticed three women who were quite incapable of choosing any place for themselves. Each time I observed them they were standing on the threshold which separates the two rooms of the therapy class. No one could persuade them to sit down. There they remained for more than an hour as if paralysed, the head thrown back, the face tense, and from time to time they muttered to themselves or gave vent to inarticulate sounds. The hands were tightly clasped on the chest, the thumbs hidden in the palm—a gesture characteristic of depression. But all at once, on their own initiative, they began in a hesitating manner to move, with small, slow steps, and sat down on the nearest chair, but thereafter remained in a state of apathy without touching their work for at least another half an hour. After this interval they started on their mechanical occupation with a lugubrious expression, saying nothing. They often interrupted their work by putting the duster they were knitting into their mouths or letting it fall while looking into the distance and muttering to themselves.

The other patients in groups were employed in different kinds of work : making hook rugs, jumpers, shawls or weaving linen. Others made slippers, dolls, animal toys, &c., or mended clothes. Several were quite silent, others chatted, smoked or sang. There were a certain number who were very restless and ran from one end of the class to the other, either to look for material for their work, to talk to the nurses and the patients, or only to attract attention or to follow a sudden impulse of agitation. Some of them quarrelled or even went for one another. Others drew nearer together to communicate their special preoccupations, their histories of real or imaginary experiences. A certain number approached me regularly during each visit, asking me about their symptoms, but also questioning me on the subject of my work and my life.

The atmosphere was noticeably different in the male classroom. I do not consider the realization of something so intangible as atmosphere as a fortuitous impression, though many psychologists might question it. The reality of the perceptible emanation of a group cannot be proved, but its existence in this case was shown by the fact that different people of different temperaments, culture, and sensibility were all affected by it. I asked three nurses and a teacher if female and male patients behaved alike in their ways, manners, and approach to their occupations—and all four of them gave me practically identical answers which corresponded with my own impressions and conclusions. The male patients had naturally less variety in their occupations. They were employed in different crafts, such as bookbinding, shoe-making and mechanics. There was one table of twelve apathetic and depressed old men who made rugs. They were the only ones with a more or less feminine occupation. Some other patients were remarkably skilful : they made dolls'-houses and other wooden toys, sometimes of first rate quality. There were fewer isolated members than in the female class ; I noted three. One of them was making paintings on the wall of a small room beside the general classroom ; the second had a workshop of his own in another room ; the third, a morose and apathetic man, was employed in ceaselessly tidying a heap of newspapers, folding them neatly into bundles. Immediately he had finished, he upset the bundles and began afresh. He was a schizophrenic and this form of stereotyped and repetitive activity is characteristic of the malady. There was much less stir among the men than among the women, less agitation and less emotional display. It must be mentioned that the male class was smaller than the female (38 men as compared with 65 women), for many of the men who were fit for such occupation worked in the garden. There were fewer cliques, apart from the large work-table of twelve ; each man worked by himself and payed little attention to his surroundings. Not one of them tried to sit near a window or to become absorbed in contemplation as was the case with some of the women. Only one of the men took any notice of me. He asked me questions and recounted his troubles and preoccupations. His case was analogous to that of the woman of whom I have spoken at length, and like her he suffered from religious mania with ideas of persecution and sexual preoccupations. He talked ceaselessly with a tense and fanatical facial expression. At the same time his hands moved continually in emphatic gestures, the demonstrative gesture of the schoolmaster with the index finger raised appearing frequently, as well as menacing movements directed against an imaginary enemy. From time to time he jumped forwards and backwards, gesticulating wildly.

The patients who visited the occupational therapy classes were specially chosen and did not include the most difficult and unapproachable cases. For this reason the study of eating gestures furnished more variety, since many of those excluded from the class were capable of eating at table. The study of eating gestures had also the advantage that the act releases primary instincts and emotions, especially in certain mental patients. The return to a spoon-fed infancy is a well-known symptom in melancholics, mental defectives and others who are ' lifeless ' and mute. I also observed distressing cases of patients who had to be fed by nurses in separate rooms, either because they refused to eat or because of those crises of aggressiveness or self-mutilation which appear in agitated melancholics.

I. GESTURES DURING WORK

DETAILED OBSERVATIONS

The object of this study was the investigation of the gestures of the insane with the aim of obtaining knowledge of their emotional pathology and of the expressive symptoms of disintegration. Mental illness is devoid of any true link with exterior situations and is therefore under the control of imaginative processes. It seemed therefore reasonable to hope for a clearer understanding of the influence of images on the psycho-motor system from the study of the expressive movements of mental patients. Schizophrenics, in whom the dissociation of personality is complete, are, I believe, the best subjects for a research into the relation between disintegration and gesture, a problem which has far-reaching consequences for the psychology of the normal.

THE MATERIAL OF STUDY

The material consisted of 28 patients, 24 female and 4 male, whose ages ranged from 17 to 69 years, the average being 39. The following table shows the classification of the patients according to sex and illness :

    1. Schizophrenia :
        Female 11   Male 2
    2. Manic-Depressive Psychosis :
        Female 4   Male 1
    3. Paraphrenia :
        Female 7   Male 1
    4. Hysteria :
        Female 2   Male 0

THE METHOD OF STUDY

I observed the patients on several occasions. I studied their attitude towards work, their social attitudes and their expressive movements. I noted, as characteristic of the malady and of the individual concerned, only those gestures which were repeated at each observation. I first described these gestures in a synthetic form, without comment of any kind. Owing to the fact that I had previously investigated the hands of all the subjects I was in a position to compare their expressive movements with a diagnosis made by my special method of hand-interpretation. In addition I had at my disposal the diagnoses in the case-papers of the Hospital. Thus I was able to compare—

    1. Gestures.
    2. Hand-test.
    3. Clinical Diagnosis.

At the end of each observation I added a psycho-biological interpretation of psycho-motor behaviour.

THE CASE STUDIES
A. 13 CASES OF SCHIZOPHRENIC PSYCHOSIS

Case I. A woman of 30 years of age who, when I had studied her hands some months before, had been mute. With two other patients she was making a rug. She never talked but was approachable, reacted when addressed by her name, and carried out simple orders, like fetching some material, &c. She was extremely slow but neat in her work.

FACIAL EXPRESSION

The face was never calm for a moment. She coughed, laughed, sniffed, and made continual mouth and tongue movements which kept the whole mouth region in permanent distortion.

HAND GESTURES

Her work was continually interrupted by an extraordinary motor unrest, especially of her hands. At rhythmic intervals of about 30 seconds she stroked the left side of her head with the left hand, the fingers slightly splayed in a stiff posture of extension. She touched her hair with a swift anxious movement as if afraid of the contact. The gestures recalled the mechanical movements of marionettes. Her hands moved directly towards her head while she was at work, but not when she was unoccupied. Then she would stop short mid-way and make some abrupt movement, describing an ellipsoid or an imperfect circle. This abnormality was especially striking when she was eating. Every time she took something from her plate she stopped half-way and made several of these brusque, stereotyped, dynamic arabesques before putting the morsel into her mouth. The right hand was by no means passive, but the gestures of the left predominated.

Besides the 'hair gestures' she would stroke one hand with the other when not working, always in this abrupt, swift and profoundly inhibited way, with gestures of an extensor type. It was very difficult to make her get up from her chair and walk. She seemed to be paralysed. But once started an extraordinary motor unrest invaded the whole body. While walking she passed her hands continually over her body, tapping her chest and then going over her thighs towards the legs and up again. She walked with very abrupt steps in an erect and stiff posture, continually interrupting her advance to perform her peculiar hand gestures.

HAND FEATURES

I had investigated the hands of Case I three months before I saw her in the occupational therapy class. At that time she was absolutely negativistic and unresponsive, and it was most difficult to take her hand-prints. Indeed I succeeded only with the right hand, the left she kept so cramped that all my efforts were frustrated. She continually used this hand for hair and face gestures. At that time she not only stroked her head but alternated from head to mouth and ears.

HAND SHAPE

Measurements

Length of the Hands [1]

Right, 17·4 cm. Left, 17·5 cm.

Width of the Hands

Right, 7·1 cm. Left, 7·0 cm.

Height of the Patient

5 ft. 4 in.

The measurements show that the hands are of the small sensitive type of the narrow variety.[2] The fingers are of an elementary type, short and thick and furnished with overdeveloped bumps of sensitivity. The fifth finger overreaches the articulation of the tip of the fourth finger and is therefore too long. The thumb, on the contrary, is abnormally short and pointed.

Physical Qualities

The hands are very stiff and cold and distinctly reddish-blue in colour.

Crease-Lines

The crease-lines are of the most primary type, only the four principal lines being present, of which the long longitudinal line is very fine, imperfectly drawn and broken at three points. Accessory creases are entirely lacking, which is a very unusual feature in a hand of the sensitive type.

Papillary Ridges

No abnormalities.

PERSONALITY DIAGNOSIS FROM HAND-FEATURES

The shape of the fingers and the peculiarity of the crease-lines

[1] The length-measurement of the hand includes the wrist in all cases.
[2] Cf. Charlotte Wolff, *The Human Hand.*

are typical of mental defectives. The small sensitive type of hand with a too-long fifth finger is frequent in schizophrenic psychotics.[1]

Diagnosis : Schizophrenic psychosis superimposed on mental deficiency.

CLINICAL DIAGNOSIS

Schizophrenia superimposed on Mental Deficiency.

Notes from the case paper :

' Ill for 12 years. Suffered from a breakdown with ideas of persecution and at that time started to neglect herself. Completely deteriorated in the last two years. Hardly speaks but can now keep clean and feed herself.'

INTERPRETATION OF GESTURES

Physiological Aspect

Gestures have been described by other writers as adaptive responses to exterior situations designed to balance nervous tension produced by nervous stimuli. This definition must be enlarged, for gestures in schizophrenics, for example, are mostly adaptive movements in response to purely inner situations.

It is known that the abnormality of postural behaviour in schizophrenics is due to abnormal functioning of the subcortical regions and to cerebellar deficiency (see H. Wallon, *L'Enfant Turbulent*), and that the nervous pathways between the cortex and the cerebellum are usually affected. Muscular tone and postures are intrinsically related to each other and are mainly controlled by the cerebellum. In schizophrenics postural behaviour is no longer in harmony with mental images, and the result is a dissociated mobility with the impossibility of controlling, among other things, facial expression, the disability affecting either the mouth or the eye-region or both. The deviations of postural reactions and muscular tone go with an abnormal feeling tone, pointing to a dysfunction of the hypothalamus region. The latter can be described as the seat of emotional behaviour. In the same part of the brain are represented both the parasympathetic and sympathetic nerves, and this situation is responsible for the vagotonic and symphatico-tonic reactions which accompany emotional disturbances in mental patients as well as in normal people.

[1] Cf. A. Friedemann, *Handbau und Psychosis*, and C. Wolff, *The Human Hand*.

To sum up the syndrome of abnormal brain function in schizophrenics, one finds :

1. Abnormal sense of equilibrium and abnormal postural behaviour.
2. Abnormality of muscular tone.
3. Abnormality of emotional behaviour and feeling tone and of the functions of the autonomic nervous system.
4. The functions of the hind-brain and the basal ganglia seem to be disconnected from those of the cortex, with the result of an expressive autonomy without relation to mental images.

In Case I one finds an expressive behaviour recalling the syndrome of athetosis, which F. Walshe describes as ' irregular accesses of hypertone into the musculature which gives rise to slow writhing movements and curious postures of the hands. In the congenital form of athetosis, which is frequent in mental defectives, movements of the face and tongue are disordered'. This description tallies largely with the psycho-motor symptoms of this patient.

Psychological Aspect

The psycho-motor reactions of Case I can be summarized as follows :

1. Reflex movements of an extensor type.
2. Stereotyped movements.
3. Perseverance of gestures.
4. Non-emphatic or fugacious gestures.
5. Autistic gestures.
6. Arrhythmic gestures.
7. Involuntary mouth and tongue movements.
8. Excessive motor-unrest.
9. Fast motor speed.

A gesture pattern which is exclusively composed of reflex movements goes naturally with an extreme restriction of voluntary and conscious activity, and is an expression of the lowest level of the inner life. Such a condition is a complete disintegration of personality. The stereotyped character of the hand gestures and their perseverance also proved that there was absolutely no spontaneous impulse and that the mind worked on a purely mechanical pattern for which any other outlet than movement was barred.

The hand gestures of the patient may be understood as a form of kinaesthetic thought which witnessed to the decay of mental capacities.

As all the expressive movements of Case I were autistic, her obsessional psycho-motor behaviour might be deemed to be a proof of her desire for continual reassurance that something of her Self still persisted. This reassurance could only be gained by motor activity, for the capacity to form mental associations and to express herself in words had practically gone. The hand gestures of Case I revealed therefore a continual feeling of catastrophe necessitating continual movements of reassurance, in order to restore the disturbed feeling of identity. The stereotyped repetition of the hand gestures served as a psycho-physical shock-absorber. Thus the motor-unrest of the patient was at the same time the consequence of profound disturbance and an effort towards healing by reducing nervous tension through movement. In touching her body remnants of her feeling of identity were preserved. The swiftness and superficiality of her gestures towards her face and head were indicative of the extreme fear typical of schizophrenics. This fear extended to everything which concerned her Self and her relation to the outside world.

The continuous mouth and tongue movements were, as I have already mentioned, part of the syndrome of athetosis, but they had also a psychological significance, namely the regression to most infantile sensations. The same regression is also found in cases of hysteria, where the same compulsive tongue and mouth movements can be observed but in a less accentuated way.

For reasons of space I have to be more concise in the following case studies.

Case II. A woman of 48 years of age. On entering the room this patient at once went to a corner without looking at any one or speaking a word to the other patients or the staff. She could not work in a group but was much absorbed in her own occupation, which was one that needed a certain skill—weaving linen in a pattern containing different colours. Though very slow at taking in the instructions of the teacher and at proceeding with her work, she did it very neatly and conscientiously. Her paranoiac make-up was revealed in her preference for isolation and her fear of others, which she expressed by making hiding gestures (covering her profile with her hand) when anyone came near her. Her face was motionless like that of a ' dead ' person.

HAND GESTURES

While she was working she exhibited only one obvious abnormality of hand movements : extreme slowness and caution. She continually halted in order to reassure herself that she had done the work in the right way. This hesitation was apparently psychological, for the co-ordination of her hand movements was faultless. There seemed, however, to be a lack of co-ordination in her mental images. She was unable to repeat the same pattern of colour and form when placed on the other side of the weaving table. No explanation from the teacher made any difference ; she repeated the same asymmetry. Such irregularity showed an obsessional trend of thought further displayed in certain recurrent hand gestures : every time this patient paused in her occupation, or after finishing for the day, she would go on making the forward and backward movements of weaving in the air. She performed this kinaesthetic perseverance only with her left hand, and it lasted for one or two minutes before she turned to another activity.

I also observed that after taking out her handkerchief from under her blouse she would tap her breast repeatedly. The same type of autistic gesture reappeared when she was walking. She took short and careful steps, her head raised, while the body moved forward like a stiff machine, the eyes looking blank and refusing to meet any one else's eyes.

It is interesting to note that the kinaesthetic monotony of her hand gestures was carried out with the left hand only.

HAND FEATURES

Measurements

Length of Hands :
Right, 20·7 cm.   Left, 21·0 cm.
Length of the Medius Finger
Right, 13·0 cm.   Left, 13·0 cm.
Width of Hands
Right, 7·0 cm.   Left, 7·0 cm.
Height of the Patient
5 ft. 4 in.

Hand Shape

As the measurements indicate, this is an extremely long and narrow hand with unusually long fingers, a rare example of a pure hand-type : the long sensitive. The palm possesses an elongated hypothenar eminence. The digital formula is 3 : 2 : 4 : 5 : 1 : with the index and middle fingers of almost equal length. The latter feature seems to be characteristic of the hands of schizophrenics, in whom I found this trait in 26 per cent of 200 patients. The finger-tips are tapered, with the exception of the fourth finger, which is spatulate.

Physical Qualities

Cyanotic colour ; high flexibility ; cold to touch.

Crease-Lines

The crease-line system looks like a spider's web, but the principal creases are well differentiated from the accessory ones. The lower transverse line is simian-like and very faulty in both hands. The other principal crease-lines are badly drawn and show every kind of fault.

PERSONALITY DIAGNOSIS FROM HAND FEATURES

This is an asthenic, devitalized and introverted person with atrophied instincts. She is highly strung and has a very low nervous resistance. She suffers possibly from psychosis either of a schizophrenic or paraphrenic reaction type, with ideas of persecution.

CLINICAL DIAGNOSIS

Ideas of persecution and delusions over a period of 15 years. Several times tried to commit suicide.
Schizophrenia ? Paraphrenia ?

INTERPRETATION OF GESTURES

Physiological Aspect

Every form of her expressive movements resembled a syndrome of nervous disease which goes with muscular hypertone approaching a state of spastic rigidity : paralysis agitans. The mask-like expression of the face recalled also the typical expression of this illness. The release of voluntary movements is always inhibited by an abnormally high muscular tone, which restricts spontaneity and accounts for the perseverance and stereotyped character of the gestures.

Psychological Aspect

The gestures of Case II can be summarized as follows :

1. Reflex movements predominant.
2. Stereotyped.
3. Persevering.
4. Non-emphatic or fugacious.
5. Very slow motor speed.
6. Partly autistic, partly centrifugal.

The psycho-dynamic pattern of Case II was in several respects similar to that of Case I, but in others it differed widely. In respect of frequency of movements and motor speed, and of the fact that she showed practically no facial movements, Case II was directly the reverse of Case I. Undoubtedly Case I was a more severe case of mental and expressive deterioration than Case II. Both suffered from obsessions and very poor mental capacities. Case II was slightly better mentally equipped than Case I, but her capacity was restricted to an entirely mechanical level.

The advanced disintegration of personality of Case II was shown by the fact that her expressive conduct was limited to persevering and stereotyped movements. The recurrent asymmetry of her associations revealed the incapacity to retain a visual image and to reproduce it under slightly altered spatial conditions. The slow motor speed and the continual interruption of forward movements witnessed to a deep-rooted inhibitive mechanism, to a marked feeling of insecurity and to profound depression.

The fear of contact with the outside world and urge for isolation seemed to be the primary cause of the inner situation from which the patient suffered. It is not merely conjecture to say that the whole mental abnormality with its repercussions on the psycho-motor system had been brought about by a paralysing shock, either real or imaginary, for the case history supported this view, the patient having suffered from ideas of persecution and delusions over a period of fifteen years. Such fundamental fears, maintained for a long time, must affect the ' feeling tone ' and the functioning of the autonomic nervous system as well as of the motor system. Fear and melancholy are often combined ; the feeling of being powerless and victimized encourages abnormal sadness and loss of initiative. That is why this woman's face had the mask-like expression of a dead person. Emotional shock, constantly reproduced, leads to such an overcharge of the emotional centres in the brain that an emotional rigidity becomes habitual. The mistrust of the world and herself was mirrored in the abnormal muscular rigidity and psycho-motor inhibition.

This type of expressive conduct is not confined to mental illness. It may be found among normal persons as well, but only temporarily and to a minor degree after severe shock experiences. Such expressive symptoms appear, however, to be linked with a certain make-up that is prone to subcortical disturbances.

Case III. A woman of 46 years of age. She was almost mute and one of those patients who were always standing and sitting in corners and had to be taken by the hand and placed in a seat. She was only able to perform the most simple mechanical work, such as knitting dusters. She was very slow in her work, which she often interrupted to stare into the distance with a completely blank expression or to make typical gestures—stroking movements starting from the mouth region and leading up to the hair. She, too, used only the left hand, but her gestures, unlike those of the previous patient, were definite and emphatic and amounted at times to scratching movements.

HAND FEATURES

Measurements

Length of the Hands
Left, 17·5 cm. Right, 17·4 cm.
Length of the Medius Finger
Left, 7·5 cm. Right, 7·5 cm.
Width of the Hands
Left, 7·9 cm. Right, 8·0 cm.
Height of the Patient
4 ft. 10 in.

Hand Shape

As the measurements indicate, this is the small sensitive type of hand. The fingers are abnormally short and the basal phalanxes enlarged. The fifth finger is pointed and abnormally short, while the others are square. The thumb and the fifth finger recall the hand of the Mongolian imbecile. The palm has an outstandingly long hypothenar eminence.

8

Physical Qualities

Normal colour ; cold and dry ; very stiff.

Crease-Line System

The lines are much fewer in number and broader than one would expect in a hand of this type. There is a strongly marked hypothenar line. The lower transverse line is abnormally short and very faulty, and so is the long longitudinal line. The general impression of all creases is that of clumsiness and lack of *élan*, qualities which are true to type in the hands of mental defectives.

PERSONALITY DIAGNOSIS FROM HAND FEATURES

This is a typical ' endocrine ' hand, characteristic of primary thyroic and secondary gonadic underfunctioning. The patient is an infantile person of low intelligence. She has a weak ego, is lacking in initiative, and shows traits of nervous degeneracy. Schizophrenic psychosis of the paranoiac reaction type.

CLINICAL DIAGNOSIS

Schizophrenia and poor intelligence.
Some notes from the case papers are interesting :

Patient is an illegitimate child, whose mother is an undesirable subject. She has apparently been badly treated by her mother. Patient has been ill since 1937. At that time she threatened her foster father with a knife, got strange ideas, was seclusive, and did not want to have meals with her parents. She lost her job. At the same time she started to neglect herself and did not wash for months. Her behaviour was explained through shock with a man whom she had picked up.
She is sometimes impulsive and uses bad language.

INTERPRETATION OF GESTURES

Physiological Aspect

The release of voluntary movements is greatly impaired and mental initiative is lost. There are, however, no gross postural abnormalities. A general state of muscular hypertone can be concluded from the expressionless face. The stereotyped and inhibited nature of her involuntary hand movements are possibly designed to relieve a state of hypertension.

Psychological Aspect

The gestures of Case III can be summarized as follows :

1. Involuntary hand gestures of a reflex type.
2. Stereotyped.
3. Persevering.
4. Emphatic.
5. Entirely centripetal or autistic.
6. Slow motor speed.

One finds here the same fundamental psycho-motor pattern as in the previous cases in so far as abnormality of muscular tone and inhibition of voluntary movements are concerned. These features go with stereotyped gestures and perseverance and show an over-charge of the extrapyramidal system, and an inner life on the lowest level, with consequent disintegration of personality.

The strange hair gestures reappeared in this patient but in a much more normal manner than in Case I. It was also noteworthy that they were performed mainly with the left hand, which seems to have a much greater expressive significance than the right. This finding tallies largely with results which I have described in *The Human Hand* about the significance of right hand and left : the first being the executive and ' conscious ' hand, the latter translating more subconscious states and impulses.

The autistic hand gestures of Case III seemed to be designed to achieve a continual kinaesthetic reassurance ; they constitute an attempt to counteract the feeling of being completely lost. Such a state of mind occurs after severe shock experience (see case notes).

The fact that the gestures were emphatic and that there was not the same spastic idiosyncrasy of touch as in the first patient, shows a less severe case of disintegration. This woman still maintained some grip on herself. As her stroking gestures amounted some-times to scratching movements, they were designed to revive the peripheric sensibility, which, as I have mentioned before, is in a state of anaesthesia under the influence of paralysing fear.

The stereotyped repetition of movements witnessed to an obsessional pattern of thought and emotion.

The loss of mental and motor-initiative is due to the same complex, enhanced by a constitutionally low intelligence.

In this patient there was a somewhat stronger mechanism of self-defence than in the previous ones, a fact which the case history confirmed in recording her sudden impulsive outbursts and her use of bad language.

Case IV. A woman of 36 years of age who always wore a hat.

She had shown signs of increasing mental deterioration for the last 5 years, and at the time of my observation was practically without any initiative and unable to keep herself clean. She walked with slow dragging footsteps in the manner of those suffering from locomotor-ataxy.

She was able to perform only the most mechanical type of work such as knitting dusters, and even at that she was very clumsy and constantly dropped the needles. She was sitting in a group of other women with whom she never made any contact and whom she completely ignored. Contact with her surroundings did not exist even in a negative form.

She had a very special obsessional complex which was revealed by her expressive conduct. She continually smelt her work, after which she would lean straight back in her chair with an expression of rapture, making sniffing noises at the same time. She interrupted her work in this way every few minutes.

HAND FEATURES

Hand Shape

Length of the Hands
Right, 18·0 cm. Left, 18·7 cm.
Length of the Medius Finger
Right, 10·0 cm. Left, 10·1 cm.
Width of the Hands
Right, 8·0 cm. Left, 7·8 cm.
Height of the Patient
5 ft. 2 in.

As the measurements indicate, this is a bony motor type of hand. The finger-tips are long and almost all of them spatulate, a typical feature in this hand type.

The fifth finger is abnormally long. The second finger is longer than the fourth.

Physical Qualities

Cyanotic colour; cold and moist; medium flexibility.

Crease-Lines

The crease-lines, of which the accessory ones are numerous,

show no deviation from the normal. They are well drawn, and there are no conspicuous faults in the principal creases.

Papillary Ridges

Strongly developed bumps of sensitivity with no regressive or abnormal patterns either on palm or finger-tips.

PERSONALITY DIAGNOSIS FROM HAND FEATURES

This is a highly-developed hand such as generally belongs to intelligent people, gifted for light sports and possessing manual skill.

A constitutional tendency to psychosis could be detected, but the diagnosis of schizophrenia would not be possible from hand features alone.

CLINICAL DIAGNOSIS

Schizophrenia.

Some notes of the case paper are interesting for the understanding of the expressive movements of the patient.

She had been a very intelligent girl who went to the University and was trained as a dispenser. She was an accomplished tennis player and pianist. She fell ill 10 years ago, when she started to show obsessional traits and delusions. She used to drink her own urine and did not want to part with her excretions. She was extremely afraid of microbes.

INTERPRETATION OF GESTURES

Physiological Aspect

Her abnormal way of walking, amounting to motor-ataxy, pointed to cerebellar dysfunction.

Psychological Aspect

In this case expressive abnormality was most concentrated in the region of the head and face while the hand gestures were free of obvious peculiarities. The most active part of the face was the muzzle region, the nose in particular. This corresponded to the obsessional complex from which this patient suffered. She was inclined to smell everything, probably urged by a fear of poisoning. When she had satisfied herself that the dangerous objects were uncontaminated she seemed to enjoy the feeling of relief. The alternate forward and backward movements of anxiety and relief can be regarded as a form of balancing or 'healing' mechanism.

Such obsessions, centred round primary instincts, are likely to have a definite repercussion on the emotional and reflex activity and the autonomic nervous system. Her regressive complex had, in the long run, sapped all her nervous energy, leading to complete mental deterioration and loss of voluntary activity.

It is interesting to note in this connexion that similar expressive idiosyncrasies can be found in other cases of mental illness and also in states of abnormal depression, when there is a tendency towards regression to such infantile preoccupations as keeping back excretions, smelling them, &c.

Case V. A young woman of 25 years of age.

She was making a rug at a table with three other patients. Slow in her work, she did it completely mechanically without showing any marked lack of co-ordination of hand movements, but I observed her at meals dropping food on her clothes. Her working movements were, however, arrhythmic as well as abnormally slow, and her facial expression revealed her lack of concentration on the work in hand. She had the same blank expression as I have previously described in Case II, except for the mouth region, which was distorted by compulsive movements of the lips which she performed without a pause.

From time to time she shut her eyes and made strange gestures with both hands, but preferably the left. When using the left hand she went over her face with stroking movements. She repeatedly raised one hand or the other with the index finger pointed and remained motionless in this attitude for some minutes.

All her gestures were carried out with a markedly slow motor speed, and this, as well as the perseverance of the index posture, indicated a strong catatonic element.

HAND FEATURES

Measurements

Length of the Hands
Right, 19·0 cm. Left, 19·0 cm.
Length of the Medius Finger
Right, 10·9 cm. Left, 11·0 cm.
Length of the Index Finger
Right, 9·4 cm. Left, 9·0 cm.
Width of the Hands
Right, 7·2 cm. Left, 7·6 cm.
Height of the Patient
5 ft. 2 in.

Hand Shape

The hand is well proportioned in relation to body size, but on the long side. There is an interesting abnormality in finger length, the medius being especially long and the left index finger unusually short with a difference of 2 cm. It is also noteworthy that the fifth fingers are abnormally short and that the basal phalanxes of the fingers are sausage-shaped. The tips are square, with the exception of the fifth finger, which is tapered.

Physical Qualities

Pale, hyperflexible, dry. The finger-tips can easily be bent backwards.

Crease-Lines

Numerous accessory lines true to type in the 'sensitive' hand (see *The Human Hand*). The main creases are very superficially drawn and faulty, the lower transverse line closely resembles the simian line.

Papillary Ridges

No abnormalities, either on the finger-tips or on the strongly developed thenar and hypothenar eminences.

PERSONALITY DIAGNOSIS FROM HAND FEATURES

Hypothyroidism with emotional instability. There is a striking difference in finger length such as is frequently found in the hands of abnormal people and conspicuously in those of schizophrenics.

CLINICAL DIAGNOSIS

Schizophrenia

Notes from the case papers :

Father is a typical introvert, mother is bad-tempered. Patient was an intelligent dressmaker and good at her job. She always broke off friendships with men after a short time. But got engaged 5 years ago and kept the engagement for three years. Then she gave it up because she got irritated with her fiancé. She had always been very clean, tidy and liked order and good appearance. She took after her father on the whole but was inclined to be quick-tempered like her mother. She was affectionate and generous. At the onset of the illness she showed restlessness, obsessional behaviour and agoraphobia. Sat at table far away, made strange remarks and dropped food on her clothes. She uttered suicidal ideas.

INTERPRETATION OF GESTURES

Physiological Aspect

This is a case of abnormal muscular hypertension and of postural abnormality, the latter pointing to defective cerebellar function. The expressive syndrome of this patient can be largely explained on the lines of Wallon's ' *insuffisance cerebelleuse* ', which goes with abnormal postural behaviour, unilateral ' obsessional ' hand movements and facial tics either of the buccal, the eye region, or both. That the basal ganglia were also involved was shown in the muscular hypertone and in the sad and mask-like expression of the face, which was especially noticeable in the rare moments of absolute calm.

Psychological Aspect

The gestures were reflex movements of a stereotyped and persevering type, mostly autistic and of slow motor speed, revealing fundamentally obsessional features, loss of identity and profound depression.

The habitual posture of the hand, with the index finger pointed, might express a desire to explain something or to deny some fictitious accusation. This habit, in spite of the fact that it revealed a catatonic element which, by its very nature, is dissociated from mental images, seemed to have an underlying psychological meaning. One might read in this mannerism a desire to justify herself.

The stroking gestures towards the face revealed a perpetual state of anxiety with an attempt to revive the peripheric sensibility in order to make sure that she was still ' alive '.

Again one finds the predominant rôle of the left hand in involuntary gesture responses.

Case VI. A woman of 39 years of age, only very recently admitted to the hospital.

She represented a border line case of psycho-neurosis and psychosis, the diagnosis of schizophrenia not having been definitely made. I have classed her nevertheless in the group of psychotics, for her hands suggest mental illness and her pattern of gestures was especially interesting in comparison with the previous cases described. Unlike those other patients she was approachable and very talkative. Every time she could get hold of me she talked freely and always complained of a number of ailments. She confessed to being scared of people and to having a feeling of panic in the ward.

She was certainly conscious of the fact that she was not normal, and was very unhappy about it. All her symptoms had appeared only a year ago after the death of her sister, to whom she was said to be devoted.

She had a very tense face and facial tics (eye and mouth), and her head shook as in paralysis agitans. She often held her head in both hands. She was sitting in a small group of especially well-behaved and intelligent patients, all doing different and individual work. She was the only one among them who was doing a very mechanical job. She was very unequal in her motor speed, working extremely slowly for a time and then hurrying up in a sort of panic. Her working movements showed marked impulsivity accompanied by ambivalence of facial expression.

From time to time she seemed to be subject to an attack of claustrophobia and ran away from the class, without giving any reason, and breathing heavily. After some minutes she would come back and start to work again.

Her hand gestures did not deviate widely from the normal. She often covered her face with her hands and stroked it, especially in the region of the mouth or eyebrows, which, like many subjects of anxiety neurosis, she frequently plucked.

HAND FEATURES

Measurements

Length of the Hands
Right, 17·2 cm.   Left, 17·3 cm.
Length of the Medius Finger
Right, 8·9 cm.   Left, 8·6 cm.
Width of the Hands
Right 7·4 cm.   Left, 8·0 cm.
Height of the Patient
5 ft. 1 in.

The patient is left-handed.

Hand Shape

The hand is too small in relation to body size and can be classified as belonging to the elementary regressive type (Cf. *The Human Hand*) for the following reasons :

The palm is of the broad elementary shape with few crease-lines in the left hand. The long longitudinal line is lacking. The few accessory creases are in both hands concentrated on the hypothenar eminences. All principal creases are very badly and clumsily drawn ; the lower transverse lines are abnormally short. The fingers are of normal length, but the thumb is abnormally short and possesses a broadened terminal phalanx often found in the hands of Mongolian imbeciles.

Other degenerative features are triangular-arc patterns of the papillary ridges on the index fingers and whorl patterns on the left hypothenar eminence.

PERSONALITY DIAGNOSIS FROM HAND FEATURES

Degenerate subject of subnormal intelligence and emotional instability. Likely to suffer from schizophrenic or paraphrenic psychosis.

CLINICAL DIAGNOSIS

Had not been decided upon. Differential diagnosis balanced between feeble-mindedness and anxiety neurosis or schizophrenia. Marked hypochondriacal features.

INTERPRETATION OF GESTURES

Physiological Aspect

There were symptoms which recall those found in paralysis agitans and were probably due to abnormal muscular tone, which points to abnormal functioning in the region of the basal ganglia.

Psychological Aspect

The gestures of this patient can be described as : arrhythmical, stereotyped, autistic, impulsive and of highly ambivalent motor speed. All psychological diagnosis is a matter of assessing the *degree* of a deficiency and not the deficiency alone. In this case, for example, the degree in which stereotyped movements were incorporated in the whole gesture pattern was different and much slighter than in previous cases, and seemed to be typical of a person suffering from anxiety neurosis. Obsessional and tormenting preoccupations produce stereotyped and arrhythmical movements. The impulsiveness of her gestures and the ambivalence in motor speed were also the mirror of the patient's inner state : a mixture of fear and aggressiveness.

The hiding gestures towards her face, which seemed to be designed to support the aching head, were a symbol of the desire to get away from outside impressions because the world produced only painful reactions in her.

Case VII. A woman of 32 years of age who had been ill for 12 years.

She did not answer when spoken to, but was able to do simple work. She was one of those making a rug in a group of patients. She had a quiet, rather stupidly happy facial expression which contradicted her frequent impulsive hand movements, and a series of idiosyncratic gestures similar to those which I have described in Case I. She giggled often and burst into sudden loud laughter at times, made sniffing noises every two or three minutes and smelt her blouse.

Her impulsive movements consisted in tapping with the rug hook on the table or introducing it with a swift and abrupt movement into her ear. Her idiosyncratic gestures consisted of writhing movements with the hook in the air. It looked as if she were writing something of a violent and emotional kind. This mannerism was repeated at regular short intervals of about three minutes. Hair gestures were also frequent and were carried out as in the previous cases, mostly with the left hand.

HAND FEATURES

Measurements

Length of the Hands
Right, 17·0 cm. Left, 17·1 cm.
Length of the Medius Finger
Right, 7·0 cm. Left, 7·2 cm.
Width of the Hands
Right, 7·8 cm. Left, 7·5 cm.
Height of the Patient
5 ft. 1 in.

Hand Shape

The hand is too short in relation to body size, the fingers are tapered and of extreme flexibility. They are too short in proportion to the length of the palm. This is a small sensitive type of hand of the broad variety.

Crease-Lines

The creases correspond to the hand type in regard to the quantity of accessory crease-lines and to their general design. But both hands possess a simian line which is unusual in the small sensitive type of hand.

Papillary Ridges

These must be specially mentioned as there are primary arc-triangle patterns on all the finger-tips, this being a hand trait of rather rare occurrence. As a rule the condition is limited to one, two or three fingers.

PERSONALITY DIAGNOSIS FROM HAND FEATURES

Infantile person with endocrine deficiency as well as mental deficiency. A mentally and physically degenerate subject given to instability, impulsiveness, and uncontrolled behaviour. As the hand is almost a case of acromicry, psychosis can be suspected as being superimposed on mental deficiency.

CLINICAL DIAGNOSIS

Schizophrenia with mental deficiency.

From the case papers : ' At the onset of the illness the patient had acute depression, neglected herself and had to be spoon fed. She now keeps herself clean under supervision and is able to feed herself.'

INTERPRETATION OF GESTURES

Physiological Aspect

There seemed to be a very complete functional abnormality of the extrapyramidal systems which recalls the syndrome of ' mobile spasm ', a term coined by Gowers (see Walshe " *Diseases of the Nervous System* "), because of the writhing movements as well as the impulsive gestures.

Psychological Aspect

While the expression of the face was characteristic of mental deficiency and lack of emotion the hand gestures seemed to express a psychological residue of preoccupations which belonged to the emotional past. For example, the obsessional smelling and sniffing might be attributed to past hypochondriacal fears of microbes and to a consequent regression into primary autistic emotions which are predominantly expressed in the muzzle region.

The meaning of the recurrent hand movements towards the hair has been described already in connexion with other cases ; a similar interpretation might be given of the ' poking into the ear ' movement. These gestures, as well as the writhing movements, were of an emphatic, impulsive type, which I attribute to an underlying obsessional pattern, a mixture of fear and aggressiveness, which was no longer present in the conscious mind but still led a dissociated kinaesthetic existence, expressing traces of the emotional past.

Case VIII. A woman of 32 years of age who was weaving a scarf in a lovely pattern of different colours.

I was struck by her taste, for she chose the colours entirely by herself. She was absorbed in her work, which she did with perfect co-ordination of hand movements but in a slow motor speed, often interrupting it in order to make sure that she had made no mistake. Her facial expression was that of an intelligent woman but showed a profound tension. In her case the most expressive region of the face was the eyes, which had the staring look of anxiety. From time to time she performed rolling-eye movements such as are known to occur after severe shock, while the mouth region was perfectly calm. She did not talk spontaneously, but answered when spoken to in a staccato voice with a slight stammer. Her answers were quite intelligent. While she was not working I noticed a tremor of her hands, which she was continually wringing. At the same time I observed fairly frequent jerky movements of her right leg and foot.

Her spontaneous activities were extremely limited. She never addressed any of the patients or the staff and only moved from her seat in the class in order to fetch material, but hesitated to leave the place on her own initiative when the work hours were over.

HAND FEATURES

Measurements

Length of the Hands
Right, 17·5 cm. Left, 17·0 cm.
Length of the Medius Finger
Right, 8·5 cm. Left, 8·5 cm.
Width of the Hands
Right, 7·1 cm. Left, 7·0 cm.
Height of the Patient
4 ft. 11 in.

Hand Shape

The hands are a perfect example of the small sensitive type. The fingers are very straight and beautifully shaped, with long tips which can easily be bent backwards. The fifth finger is markedly overlong and the thumb broader and stronger than one would expect in this hand type. Its terminal phalanx is both broad and bulbous.

Physical Qualities

Very flexible ; pale ; moist.

Crease-Lines

Apart from the presence of the simian line on the left palm, all creases are well drawn and even show a certain *élan*. The main creases are more pronounced than the much finer and more numerous accessory lines, which are especially concentrated on the long and deep-seated hypothenar eminences.

PERSONALITY DIAGNOSIS FROM HAND FEATURES

A person of good intelligence, manual skill and marked aesthetic sense. Profoundly schizoid and showing a tendency to quick temper. Highly imaginative and highly strung, both traits easily leading to states of anxiety and disintegration.

CLINICAL DIAGNOSIS

Schizophrenia with hysterical elements.
From the case papers :

The patient has been ill since 1935. She had been a good pianist and a Civil Servant. She has never been fond of boys and has always been odd. She was incapable of being punctual at her job or for a train even when she had plenty of time. She took a great fancy, amounting to a mania, to a married man before her first breakdown. At that time she squandered a lot of money and became fretful and melancholy. She had hallucinations and thought she was pregnant. She has a harsh father and a gentle mother. She came to the hospital in 1935 and was discharged after insulin treatment in 1937. She was perfectly well and earned her living in a highly responsible ' intellectual ' job from 1940–2, until her recent breakdown, which started with emotional instability and anxiety.

INTERPRETATION OF GESTURES

In this and the following cases I shall not treat specially the physiological aspect.

Psychologically the rolling-eye movements refer to anxiety due to shock, and may reveal a constitutional weakness of cerebellar functions, enhanced by negative emotions like fear.

Fear, as is well known, and repeatedly stressed in this book, affects the sense of balance, which is controlled by the cerebellum.

The gestures of the hand are typical of both agitated depression and fear, and the stammer may be explained by a general state of inhibition and abnormal inner tension. The staccato voice is typical of epileptics and one of the symptoms of their lack of motor-co-ordination. The patient has never had epileptic fits, but she is possibly a potential epileptic. The jerks of feet and legs are nervous reflexes which one finds in neurasthenic persons as well as in mental patients, revealing a high degree of nervous tension concentrated in the lower motor-neurons. They might, however, also be the expression of a subconscious aggressiveness which belongs more to the emotional past.

Case IX. A woman of 30 years of age.

An excellent needleworker, she copied needlework patterns but always enlarged them. She was also very good at drawing from her imagination. She produced with extraordinary speed pencil sketches of young men and women of the kind produced by rather cheap fashion journals. When asked to depict a landscape she always drew the same small house and fields. That she took great pleasure in these occupations was obvious by the happy expression of her face while she was working. When asked whom the portraits represented she explained that they were famous film stars. She had a special verbal obsession and in the middle of her needlework she stitched the word ' Hydrophobia '.

I watched her once for more than an hour and during that time she did not change her sitting posture by the slightest movement. Apart from this perseverance of posture, there was another noticeable tendency. She used to keep her left hand on her right shoulder when she was unoccupied and only altered this posture when spoken to.

HAND FEATURES

Hand Shape

The hands closely resemble those of the previous patient in shape. They are beautiful hands, well proportioned in themselves but too small in relation to body size. But there is a striking abnormality in the digital formula : the index, middle, and ring fingers are of almost equal length, and the fifth finger is 0·8 cm. longer than normal.

Physical Qualities

Hyperflexible finger-tips ; stiff palm.

Crease-Lines

The crease-lines show a striking abnormality. In this hand type one would expect them to be numerous and superficially drawn, but they are scanty and broad, especially in the right palm. Here the thenar-and upper transverse line alone are well developed. The lower transverse line is abnormally short, ending just beneath the third finger, and the long longitudinal line only faintly indicated between the two main transverse creases. No accessory lines except a few on the thenar eminence. On the left palm the four principal creases are all strongly marked and well drawn and there are a certain number of accessory lines on the ulnar edge.

Papillary Ridges

Triangle arc patterns on the tips of index and middle fingers of the right hand and loop pattern on the left hypothenar eminence.

PERSONALITY DIAGNOSIS FROM HAND FEATURES

Both the emptiness of the palm (unusual in this type of hand) and the abnormality in finger length can be attributed to schizophrenic psychosis of the catatonic reaction type (as I was able to show in a statistical study of the hands of mental patients).

Judging by her hand features the patient is an imaginative and highly strung person with little or no will-power and a rather low intelligence. She is not good at any practically useful work but has manual skill and a certain aesthetic sense.

CLINICAL DIAGNOSIS

Schizophrenia.

INTERPRETATION OF GESTURES

In spite of the fact that her artistic skill had been preserved while she was on the whole mentally deteriorating, her drawings were only an expression of certain obsessional preoccupations and served as a safety-valve, taking the place of expressive gestures, which were almost absent.

The perseverance of her postural behaviour showed a marked catatonic element and gave expression to her lack of initiative and complete introversion.

Case X. A girl of 17 years of age.

Lacking all concentration or interest in her work, she was continually distracted, went to other tables, and behaved on the whole like a child of about 10 years old.

Her hand movements were slow, badly co-ordinated and very clumsy. When she was not watched she frequently put the needle into her finger instead of the material, but seemed to be insensitive to pain. She appeared to be in a stupor. Her face was very drawn and had a frightened expression, with rolling eye-and-mouth movements which occurred frequently. She used to put her thumb into her mouth like a baby.

On several occasions she threw her needlework on the floor and beat with her fist repeatedly on the table, tapping on the ground with her left foot at the same time.

It was also interesting to note the very different motor speed and expressive quality of her gait. In spite of her heavily built body and strong legs she walked in a light tiptoe manner as if she were a smart chorus girl.

HAND FEATURES

I am shortening the description of hand traits in a certain number of the following cases for reasons of space, only mentioning those hand features which are most relevant for diagnosis.

Case X possessed a pair of the most abnormal hands of my collection in regard to finer length, the thumb being freakish in its oversized heavy shape and broad and bulbous terminal phalanx. It measures 8 cm. and is the same length as the index finger. The latter is equal in length to the third and fourth fingers, while the fifth finger is markedly too short.

The fingers have spatulated tips except for the little finger, which is tapered, and the basal phalanxes are enlarged and sausage shaped.

9

Physical Qualities

Hyperflexible ; cold and white.   The palmar surface is dry and the dorsal skin puffy, a condition characteristic of hypothyroidism.

Crease-Lines

Only the four principal crease-lines are present, all of them narrow and superficial.   There are practically no accessory crease-lines except for a few on the thenar eminences.

PERSONALITY DIAGNOSIS FROM HAND FEATURES

These are the hands of a hypothyroic subject with mental deficiency and an impulsive temper.   Schizophrenia of a catatonic reaction type is superimposed on mental deficiency.

CLINICAL DIAGNOSIS

Catatonic schizophrenia with mental deficiency.   Has been very noisy and excited but has now settled down.

INTERPRETATION OF GESTURES

The clumsiness of the hand movements together with the tic-like eye and mouth movements suggest cerebellar insufficiency.

The presence of obsessional fears and aggressive reactions can be interpreted from the facial expression on the one hand and the sudden and impulsive gestures on the other,   The slow motor speed and the bad co-ordination of her hand movements were typical of a psychotic as well as a mentally defective subject.

The same applies to her insensibility to pain.   The thumb-sucking was an autistic gesture revealing fixation on the earliest satisfactions.   The gait, with its attributes of lightness and physical charm completely alien to the personality, may have been an unconscious identification with some idol from the stage or screen. At the same time the gait expressed the desire to attract, and exhibited a strongly developed sexual instinct, which is frequently found in schizophrenic patients of the hebephrenic reaction type.

The girl told me she liked dancing, and I found out from the nurses that dance music excited her.

Case XI.   A woman of 27 years of age, very neatly dressed and using make-up.

She was making a doll and apparently took great pleasure in her work, which she did with *élan*, swiftness, and precision of movements. She had an euphoric expression on her face and sang while she worked, with a lovely voice, music-hall songs and extracts from Ravel's Bolero. She made contact with every one and talked freely and sensibly. There were no special gestures which could indicate any obsessional preoccupation or any dysfunction of the subcortical systems. The only hand gestures which I observed were frequent stroking movements over her hair, but those seemed to have a purely decorative purpose.

This woman was a case of schizophrenia which had been cured, temporarily anyway, by Electrical Shock Treatment, and she was supposed to be leaving the Hospital shortly.

HAND FEATURES

Hand Shape

Hands very large in proportion to body size. They look, indeed, like a man's hands and form a strange contrast to the very small head and handsome feminine face of their owner. By their broad and muscular palm with short fingers they can be classified in the elementary group ; but the spatulate fingers present some striking peculiarities : the thumb is abnormally plump and closely resembles that of Mongolian imbeciles ; the index and middle fingers have a straight axis and are well proportioned, while the fourth and fifth fingers show a slight ankylosis. Their second phalanxes are waisted, and the tips are much thinner, comparatively, than those of the other fingers, giving them a 'retarded' appearance.

Even the untrained eye could discern in these hands an over-development of the second and third and an under-development of the fourth and fifth fingers. Such asymmetry in the hand of a working person is most likely to be due to manual activity, which chiefly employs the radial zone of the hand. The basal phalanxes are slightly enlarged.

Physical Qualities

Very dry ; normal colour ; stiff.

Crease-Lines

These are on the typical elementary pattern : broad well-designed principal transverse lines, without major defects, a less broad but defective long longitudinal line and accessory creases on the thenar eminences only.

Papillary Ridges

These show regressive arc-triangle patterns on the left thumb and third finger, and loops on both hypothenar eminences.

PERSONALITY DIAGNOSIS FROM HAND FEATURES

This is a person with degenerative traits and a low intelligence. She has, however, remarkable manual skill of a kind that one generally finds in men and not in women. These are the hands of a good mechanic, perhaps an electrician or a tool-maker. She is also gifted for sports and is on the whole a physically active person.

She is by nature cheerful, energetic and pushing, with a tendency to quick temper and emotional instability.

She represents an amorphous physical type which goes with a make-up which predisposes to the hebephrenic type of schizophrenia.

CLINICAL DIAGNOSIS

Dementia praecox with catatonic elements. She fell ill in 1936 and was then almost mute, very confused and showed all kinds of mannerisms. She had been trained for motor mechanics.

She has been cured by Electrical Shock Treatment and is soon to be released from hospital.

INTERPRETATION OF GESTURES

The expressive behaviour at work showed no striking peculiarity. It was that of an energetic person, with continuous underlying excitement which could be taken for a state of hypomania. That explains the high motor speed, the *élan* and rhythm of movement as well as her facial expression. The precision and spontaneity of movement showed that at this phase of her life the patient had full power over her motor activities and seemed to be well centralized. I have added this example of a cure in order to show the great difference of psycho-motor behaviour in severe cases of schizophrenia and after successful treatment.

Case XII. A young man of 24 years of age who was soleing shoes.

He smoked continually, kept entirely to himself, and did his work well. He worked with quick and efficient movements and evidently found satisfaction in his occupation. But he seemed to be easily distracted through some preoccupation, for he would interrupt his work to lapse into a state of day-dreaming, looking quite blank and sitting with folded hands. An extraordinary instability of facial expression was noticeable. While he worked he looked happy in a rather silly, puckish way, as if up to something that gave him great pleasure in anticipation ; but when he began to day-dream a wild and furious look would come into his eyes and he would make intense mouth and tongue gestures. There was an aggressive quality discernible in his movements and he pushed his way through the class-room without any regard for his companions. He walked in a swift, affected way, with one hand on his hip, almost taking dancing steps.

In his moments of day-dreaming I noticed jerky movements of the head and shoulders, while his folded hands were tightly pressed one against the other. He woke out of his lethargy as suddenly as he lapsed into it, with abrupt semicircular movements, shrugging his shoulders, as if to shake off some unpleasant idea or sensation, and then returning to his work.

He whistled while he worked and from time to time flipped his fingers. This gesture was repeated when he walked about.

HAND FEATURES

Measurements

Length of the Hands
Right, 17·0 cm. Left, 17·0 cm.
Length of the Medius Finger
Right, 8·0 cm. Left, 7·8 cm.
Width of the Hands
Right, 8·2 cm. Left, 8·0 cm.
Height of the Patient
5 ft. 2 in.

Hand Shape

These are the smallest male hands I have seen up to now. In spite of the small size of the patient's body his hands represent a case of acromicry. Apart from abnormality of length the fingers are disproportionately short in relation to the palm. The fifth finger is undersized and curved inwards. The thumb resembles that of a Mongolian imbecile and is at the same time abnormally inserted.

Generally in schizophrenics the nails are well developed, but in this patient they are of a rudimentary type.

Physical Qualities

Hyperflexible ; dry ; normal colour.

Crease-Lines

The crease-line system is on the typical elementary pattern. The main lines are broad and accessory lines lacking except for the thenar eminence, where there is a small number of creases. On the right palm there is a simian-like upper transverse line and a semicircular crease-line which encloses the third and fourth fingers.

Papillary Ridges

There is a whorl pattern on the left thenar eminence. Otherwise no abnormalities.

PERSONALITY DIAGNOSIS FROM HAND FEATURES

The patient is both physically and mentally defective. He is an endocrine case suffering from sexual and emotional infantilism. He is unstable and inclined to make bad blood. These traits, together with his defective intelligence, predispose him to criminal tendencies. The fact that his hands are so abnormally small places him among the amorphous subjects, who have, according to Kretschmer, a predisposition to schizophrenic psychosis.

CLINICAL DIAGNOSIS

Dementia praecox. Religious mania.

From the case papers : ' Patient is very destructive and impulsive in the ward but never attacks any one in the occupational therapy class. Alcoholism and mental illness in the family.'

INTERPRETATION OF GESTURES

The expressive behaviour revealed firstly, extreme emotional instability and impulsiveness; secondly a feeling of superiority and a contempt for others which showed in his face and in his ' self-confident ' gait. In his better moments the patient had a feeling of elation, expressed in his fast motor speed and accuracy and emphasis of movement. In his manner of walking he unconsciously stated to himself and others that he was a handsome, graceful and important person for whom every one else must make way. That this assurance had little solidity became evident in the brusque changes of attitudes and gestures.

He seemed to retain a certain self-control in moments of distress, from which he tried to extricate himself by shrugging his shoulders and by jerky movements of the head. Aggressiveness was expressed in his pushing arm movements while he was walking and in the contemptuous flipping of the fingers.

Case XIII. A young man of 25 years of age who cut material for book covers.

He was extremely slow at his work and often did the same thing over and over again. His movements were stereotyped and persevering and interrupted by long pauses of inertia. From time to time he looked at a fellow-worker with a fixed and empty expression, evidently without any perception of the exterior world but absorbed by an image or simply a void. While doing this his mouth twitched and his eyes remained fixed. In these pauses he always assumed the same posture, holding his hands on his thighs and his head raised, and so remained without moving for about a quarter of an hour. He came slowly back to life and gradually resumed his work or lighted a cigarette with clumsy ' staccato ' movements. All his gestures were interrupted by inhibitive impulses which gave them a zigzag pattern. The same abnormality appeared in his gait. He walked with spastic, dragging paces, as if his back were rigid, and with bent head. His advance was spiral, for he was incapable of walking straight, and he always held his arms in the same posture : the hands clasped, the elbows well away from the body. A typical catatonic gesture appeared in this patient. He lifted the right hand with the index finger raised, as if he were pointing out something to himself, for the movement was stereotyped and without any quality of persuasion.

HAND FEATURES

Measurements

Length of the Hands
Right, 20·0 cm. Left, 20·1 cm.
Length of the Medius Finger
Right, 10·2 cm. Left, 10·0 cm.
Width of the Hands
Right, 7·4 cm. Left, 7·3 cm.
Height of the Patient
5 ft. 6 in.

Hand Shape

These are long narrow hands, well proportioned to body size. Without knowing the details of finger measurements one would not discern any anomaly. But the digital formula is abnormal : the third and fourth fingers of equal length and the fifth finger too long. The finger-tips are spatulate and hyperflexible, bending backwards easily. The phalanxes are all waisted and very fragile. The thumb is small and thin and strangely immobile. The nails correspond to the long sensitive type of hand, being long and narrow with well-developed moons.

Physical Qualities

Palms stiff ; hands cold and red in colour.

Crease-Lines

These are few in number for this type of hand. The long longitudinal line is absent in the left and deficient in the right, where it consists of small fragments between the hypothenar eminence and the lower transverse line. The latter runs in a wrong direction in the left hand, ending very low on the hypothenar eminence. In the right hand the lower transverse line is abnormally short, terminating just below the medius finger. The few accessory lines are on the upper part of the thenar eminence and on the ' bord frappeur ' of the hand (see *The Human Hand*).

PERSONALITY DIAGNOSIS FROM HAND FEATURES

The anomalies of the digital formula and of the crease-lines are proper to a schizophrenic individual and to a catatonic in particular. Moreover, the restricted mobility of the thumb and the general composition as well as special qualities of the creases are frequently found in imbeciles.

The patient suffers from schizophrenia superimposed on mental deficiency.

CLINICAL DIAGNOSIS

Dementia praecox. Mental illness in the family.

INTERPRETATION OF GESTURES

In this patient the symptoms of cerebellar insufficiency were true to type : the catatonic postures, the ataxy of the hand-movements and of the gait.

Persevering and stereotyped gestures, abnormally slow motor

speed, and the annihilation of forward movements through movements of inhibition were pushed to an extreme, and all represented factors of a complete stagnation of inner dynamism and spontaneous activity. In fact one can describe the inner life of this young man as non-existent. Certain reflexes, such as the gesture of the index finger, might be indications of a lingering remembrance of his emotional past : he was probably trying to clarify a problem which had often haunted him and which had survived in this kinaesthetic form.

B. 5 CASES OF MANIC-DEPRESSIVE PSYCHOSIS

Case I. A woman of 30 but looking much younger.

She was sitting in the group of especially intelligent patients to which I have already referred, and was occupied in making a doll out of bits and pieces of felt, wire, and coloured silk. In spite of the fact that she showed remarkable skill in her work she was certainly not absorbed by it. She was easily side-tracked and very changeable in her expressions. She often interrupted her occupation in order to smoke, to talk and to walk round the other tables. For a certain time her face would be radiant with a calm and happy expression, as if she were absorbed by pleasant images, only to change quite suddenly into a countenance exhibiting extreme fear and gloom. When this happened she remained rigid in her chair with the hands pressed together and the thumbs hidden in the palm. This woman, who was as a rule an easy and sociable member of the class, would suddenly make the movements of withdrawal and suspicion characteristic of paranoiacs. But logical thought and initiative were never fundamentally inhibited. Seeing her like this I asked her if she were worried and received most reasonable replies, as, for example, that she was troubled about the length of her stay in the hospital and the chances of a cure. While she worked she had a perfect co-ordination of hand movements and their speed and accuracy would have made her an ideal factory worker.

HAND FEATURES
Measurements

Length of the Hands
Right, 20·0 cm. Left, 20·2 cm.
Width of the Hands
Right, 7·8 cm. Left, 7·6 cm.
Height of the Patient
5 ft. 6 in.

HAND SHAPE

These are long, bony hands, with long fingers and markedly long tips. The latter can easily be bent backwards. The hands are of a mixed type, the palm being muscular and the fingers fragile and tapered, as one finds them in the long sensistive type of hand. The nails are long and broad and furnished with big moons.

Physical Qualities

Cold ; dry ; normal colour. The palms very stiff.

Crease-Lines

Comparatively few, especially on the right palm. The principal crease-lines are all faulty, the long longitudinal being especially imperfect as well as too short in both hands. On the left palm there is a threefold semicircular line enclosing the third and fourth fingers.

PERSONALITY DIAGNOSIS FROM HAND FEATURES

The patient is a hyperthyroic subject with a strong inner dynamism, suffering from conflicting tendencies : on one hand she is able to take an interest in outdoor life and light sporting activities, on the other hand she is inclined to contemplation and introversion, interested in aesthetics and intellectual pursuits.

The diagnosis of mental illness could not be made from hand features. The hands suggest, if anything, a paraphrenic or schizo-phrenic psychosis. As in this case clinical diagnosis and hand inter-pretation are to a great extent at variance, I shall describe this case more fully.

CLINICAL DIAGNOSIS

Manic depressive psychosis with paranoiac features and megalomania.

From the case papers :

Patient comes from a good family and was of outstanding intelli-gence. She wrote newspaper articles as a schoolgirl and won a scholar-ship. She went to the university and studied literature. At the age of 24 (5 years ago) she became queer, developing megalomaniac ideas. Since then she has been mostly in a state of hypomania, alternating with periods of real mania and short intervals of depression. In the maniac state she is sleepless, aggressive and writes without a pause and without regard for the material. She wrote, for instance, on the walls of the ward as well as on the borders of trays and bits of paper. She posed for a certain time as a free lance detective who hunted big spies. While she is in the hypomaniac phase she behaves very amiably and is easily led. She was brought into the hospital because of her moral irresponsibility. She had a great number of men friends, was promiscuous and became pregnant. In spite of the fact that her emotional state seemed to be more balanced in the last two years, she cannot be released from hospital because of her lack of moral sense.

INTERPRETATION OF GESTURES

The most obvious deviation from the normal in the expressive conduct of this patient was to be found in the ambivalence and acuteness of her emotional expressions. It seemed that the co-ordination between the cortex and the subcortical regions of the brain had not suffered, except that the emotional centres were apparently under the influence of a constant hypertension. This state of affairs is often found in neurotics and it is a natural state in the emotional phase of the child (cf. Chapter III). Mental and expressive abnormalities were evidently less profound and definite in this patient than in the cases of schizophrenia previously described. Apart from the ambivalence of moods shown in facial expression this patient revealed the power of images over psycho-motor behaviour in individuals who are poorly adapted to reality. As with the child, the wall between the inner and outer world did not exist and the patient gave way to absorption in imaginary situations. Her hand gestures revealed anxiety and withdrawal from the world.

From the expressive conduct at the times of the observation it would seem impossible to diagnose any specific mental illness. One finds similar expressive traits in the beginning of schizophrenia, in paraphrenia or in certain forms of psychoneurosis.

One cannot foresee at this juncture of her illness in which way the patient will deteriorate later on, and I want to stress the fact, that a certain number of manic depressive patients are at a later stage recognized to suffer from schizophrenia and vice versa.

Apparently a rigid distinction between the two types of psychosis cannot be made at all.

Case II. A woman of 69 years of age occupied with knitting a duster.

Her face wore a childish expression of perfect contentment. She worked with slow motor speed and often interrupted her occupation to see if the table at which she was seated with six other women was untidy. She had, it seemed, a marked sense of order and would at once start to arrange scattered material. The teacher told me that she was an excellent worker in the ward. While she tidied up the table, the movements of her hands were uncertain and 'staccato' and reminded me of a flurried hen in front of a car. This sort of foolish agitation was the only peculiarity of her psycho-motor behaviour.

This old woman, who hardly ever talked and was always gay and alert to make herself useful, represented one of the happiest cases in the hospital, where she was conscious of no restriction and where she had found a perfect home.

HAND FEATURES

It is sufficient to mention that the hands are of an elementary type and very small (right, 17·0 cm. and left, 17·2 cm.) and that they are typical of a mental defective. The palm, which is muscular and broad, witnesses to the vitality and physical activity of its owner. The thumbs are particularly plump and large and the index fingers are abnormally short. The latter feature had been observed (C. Wolff and H. Rollin) in a certain number of hands of Mongolian imbeciles. The tips of all the fingers are abnormally short, measuring only 2 cm.

PERSONALITY DIAGNOSIS FROM HAND FEATURES

This is a feeble-minded woman of an extravert disposition. Psychosis could not be diagnosed from the hand.

CLINICAL DIAGNOSIS

Manic depressive psychosis and mental deficiency.

INTERPRETATION OF GESTURES

Anyone who has watched the expressions and gestures of high-grade imbeciles would recognize that this patient showed the typical psycho-motor reactions of mental defectives, many of whom are in a more or less permanent state of hypomania. As in the previous case the diagnosis of manic depressive psychosis could not be made from expressive behaviour, and both examples, but particularly the first, illustrate that the gestures which go with the lighter forms of psychosis correspond to emotional situations of the moment rather than to fundamental features of the illness.

Case III. A woman of 45, one of those who tried to hide in corners.

She was in a state of depression, did not reply when addressed, and remained standing, like certain schizophrenics which I have described, without the initiative to commence work. Her motor speed was so slow that it took her ten minutes instead of half a minute to walk from the door to her corner in the class. She remained standing for about an hour, then suddenly overcame her inhibition and sat down to her work on a duster. Her face had the haggard expression of melancholy. While at work her motor speed increased gradually until it was almost normal. She knitted well with a normal co-ordination of hand movements, but often interrupted her work to put the duster in her mouth.

HAND FEATURES

The hands represent the opposite type to those of the preceding patient. They are too long, measuring 20·5 cm. (right) and 20·7 cm. (left). In fact their length is rare in a woman. They are, moreover, narrow with long fingers exhibiting all the characteristic traits of the long sensitive type of hand.

They are abnormal for the following reasons :

1. An abnormal digital formula, with the third and fourth fingers equally long and a tiny index finger, the latter reaching only to the articulation between the upper and middle phalanxes of the medius finger.

2. A rigid thumb with a tiny terminal phalanx.

3. The presence of a simian line, a feature most uncommon in a hand of the long sensitive type.

4. The hands possess regressive patterns of the papillary ridges on both palms and the finger-tips of the index and medius finger of the left hand.

It is evident that these hands are composed of ' contradictory ' elements, commonly found in very degenerate subjects (see *The Human Hand*).

PERSONALITY DIAGNOSIS FROM HAND FEATURES

Degenerated subject of an amorphous physical type with a tendency to psychosis.

CLINICAL DIAGNOSIS

Manic depressive psychosis ; predominantly depressed. Paranoiac features.

INTERPRETATION OF GESTURES

This patient showed a classic picture of melancholy expressed in a mask-like face, slowness of motor speed, complete loss of initiative and voluntary action, perseverance of postures and poverty of gestures. As often with melancholics, she exhibited a regressive emotional pattern, revealed in her habit of putting the duster in the mouth as infants do with every object they can get hold of. Such regression goes with emotional and mental deterioration and can be found in mental defectives and schizophrenics as well.

Obviously the expressive behaviour of the patient does not allow for the diagnosis of a specific type of psychosis.

Case IV. A man of 54 years of age, continuing his ordinary profession of bookbinding in the occupational therapy class.

He worked in a small room by himself, where he had all the necessary tools. In the middle of the room was his work table and press, and his tools and materials were kept in perfect order on small shelves. I was only able to observe the patient on one occasion, for he was absent during my other visits. The teacher of the class informed me that he always disappeared when conscious of the approaching phase of depression. I caught him in a transition phase, when he was still working with great skill and energy. Apart from a marked tension of the mouth region, his face showed no sign of mental or emotional unbalance. He responded with agitated haste when asked a question and I noticed that he avoided the questioner's eye by looking down the whole time. His hand movements were rhythmic, graceful and rapid. He gesticulated a great deal when talking, emphasizing his words by emphatic movements which exhibited an aggressive element. One could discern in these gestures a nervous agitation which could easily develop into a frenzy. This man had a certain insight which forestalled the moments of crisis and enabled him to make the best possible preparations against catastrophy. This awareness of what was going to happen appeared in a feeling of responsibility, causing him to put everything in order before his departure. As a rule he did not remain in the ward during the periods of depression, but asked to be transferred to an agricultural job. This attitude seemed to me to be particularly interesting since none of the schizophrenic patients acted in the same way.

HAND FEATURES

Measurements

Length of the Hands
Right, 18·5 cm.   Left, 19·0 cm.
Width of the Hands
Right, 9·0 cm.   Left, 8·8 cm.
Height of the Patient
5 ft. 5 in.

HAND SHAPE

In spite of the relative smallness of these hands, they are muscular and broad with a conspicuously strong thenar eminence and thumb and broad short fingers with spatulate tips. The index finger is shorter than the ring finger. This is the fleshy motor type of hand. This classification is further justified by the composition and quantity of the crease-lines, which are deep and mostly horizontal. The accessory crease-lines are few in number.

PERSONALITY DIAGNOSIS FROM HAND FEATURES

The patient has a tendency to hypothyroidism (see *The Human Hand*), but has a strong physique and good vitality. He is an extravert type of man. His long and spatulate finger-tips reveal the artisan. The hypothyroic factor is likely to be responsible for an emotional instability in contrast to his physical stability. The combination of physical strength and emotional weakness might account for the marked impulsiveness. Tendency to manic-depressive psychosis.

CLINICAL DIAGNOSIS

Manic depressive psychosis.

INTERPRETATION OF GESTURES

The facial expression revealed nervous and emotional hypertension. He suffered from a fear of contact with others, a characteristic trait of anxiety. The gestures of the hands testified to an inner agitation with an undercurrent of aggressiveness. This kind of expressive conduct is typical of an extravert person, who remains still in touch with his surroundings in spite of his depression. A diagnosis of manic depressive psychosis was not possible from an observation of his gestures, which is a further proof that on the whole the state of mind rather than the psychosis is revealed by psycho-motor behaviour, except in those cases which go with severe dysfunction of the subcortical systems. It must be noted that my observation coincided with the beginning of a period of depression. If I had seen the patient either in a manic or really depressed state the result might have been different and the diagnosis of manic depressive psychosis might have been possible from psycho-motor qualities.

Case V. A girl of 20 years of age.

She was working on a hook rug with three other women. It was she who always took the initiative, chose the colours and was the quickest worker of the party. She threw the material about, from time to time put the hook in her mouth, and bent low over her work, which she carried out with emphatic and hypermetric movements, almost kicking the person next her. A lack of spatial measure was the outstanding feature of her motor behaviour. When I took the prints of her hands she let them fall on the paper with such a force that the prints were ruined, and I had great difficulty in checking her impatience and hyperactivity. All her psycho-motor responses were hypermetric, accelerated and emphatic and the teacher informed me that when she danced her movements were so exaggerated that she was practically on the floor. She was one of the most sociable members of the class. Though certainly very interfering, she liked to make herself useful and to take part in every kind of activity : cooking, housework, knitting, dancing, singing, &c. I observed her in a state of hypomania as well as one of depression. While in the former she sang all the time, made dancing steps while walking, laughed, joked, and addressed everybody as 'dear', with demonstrations of affection. Her face was animated, but even in these happy moments a painful tension was plainly visible in a twitching of the eyes and the mouth. When in a state of elation she took great pains with her dressing, decorating her hair with coloured ribbons and combs, and wearing bracelets and rings of a cheap quality. In periods of depression she used to put her head on the table and remain inert without speaking or replying when addressed. Her hypermetric and accelerated movements became hypometric and slow. She remained motionless for intervals of 20 or 30 minutes, but always resumed her work eventually, though slowly. Obviously she retained a certain amount of will-power and control during these negative phases.

HAND FEATURES
Measurements

Length of the Hands
Right, 18·2 cm.   Left, 18·6 cm.
Width of the Hands
Right, 8·2 cm.   Left, 7·8 cm.
Height of the Patient
5 ft. 1 in.

HAND SHAPE

These are fleshy motor hands with abnormally small thumbs and fifth fingers, as one finds in Mongolian imbeciles.

Physical Qualities
Warm ;   dry ;   of normal colour ;   hyperflexible.

Crease-Lines

The composition of the crease-lines is clear in spite of the fact that there are many accessory creases.   They are all well marked without any special defects.   Only the lower transverse line is too short, terminating in the middle of the palm just below the medius finger.

A certain number of the hand features are those which one finds in Mongolian imbeciles.   It is interesting to note that the face shows a resemblance to the Mongolian type.

PERSONALITY DIAGNOSIS FROM HAND FEATURES

The hands are those of a mental defective of the Mongolian group.   The patient shows the characteristics of the temperament generally attributed to Mongolian high-grade imbeciles : infantilism, ambivalence and shallowness of the emotions, sociability and strong dependence on the *milieu*.   She is quick-tempered but easy to deal with, and has a predominantly extravert personality.

CLINICAL DIAGNOSIS

Epilepsy with mental deficiency.   Emotional instability with marked hypomaniac and depressed phases.

She is quick tempered, unstable, kept jobs only for a few days.   Hypochondriac ideas.   Twitching face.   Speech : epileptic disarticulation.

INTERPRETATION OF GESTURES

I was particularly interested in reporting this case in full because
10

it enables me to show to what extent the different methods of diagnosis can compensate for one another. The interpretation of the hands shows clearly the mental deficiency and emotional instability, while the epileptic condition could not be diagnosed from hand traits, but from the psycho-motor behaviour.

Apart from her periods of depression, the gestures of this patient were hypermetric (typical of epileptics), emphatic, and of an accelerated motor speed. They were also highly ' decorative ', which is a characteristic feature of hypomania and they were arrhythmic. The lack of spatial measure and the resulting lack of motor-precision are symptoms of a lack of motor co-ordination which goes with the epileptic condition.

So far the gestures tallied with the make-up of a hypomaniac epileptic patient. But the facial tics introduced an element which is not usually found in this connexion : that of an obsessional complex. Epileptics are generally very intense people but not the real obsessionals. On the contrary, they are lacking in emotional memory and any fixation of images. That this patient was an exception from the rule was proved by her hypochondriac ideas, which also revealed, in spite of her predominantly extravert disposition, a slightly paranoiac element.

The swiftly changing expression of the face denoted the un-controlled emotional type. The speed and emphasis of gestures revealed a strong and intense inner dynamism and the kind of nervous agitation which was bound to end in periods of nervous and emotional exhaustion.

The richness of the many unnecessary decorative gestures, which one often finds in states of hypomania, might be explained as a combination of a heightened dynamism, which tends to find a safety-valve in movement, and narcissistic tendencies, which give to kinaesthetic impulses both an autistic and a pleasurable quality. The marked emphasis of gestures which were at the same time hypermetric revealed also aggressiveness and impatience.

The arrhythmy of movements betrayed an ' explosive ' make-up which soon accumulated emotional tension, requiring abrupt gestures to ease the congestion. In this context it is interesting to recall the Encephalograph of epileptics, which shows the cortical waves similar to fever waves. Epileptics are specially noted for impulsiveness and lack of control. These traits were certainly very marked in the subject under consideration. She was only able to live for the moment without foreseeing the consequence of her reactions and actions.   Such mental incoherence was, of course, in this case, much encouraged by the defective intelligence of the person.

C. 8 CASES OF PARAPHRENIA

Paraphrenics are particularly interesting for a study of gesture, since their conduct is to a large extent normal.   They have what is commonly called a ' kink '.   Their abnormality, often well concealed, is only apparent when their special complexes are touched upon.   They may be obsessed by religious, political or sexual ideas or by a combination of all three, but apart from these more localized anomalies they remain at times in reasonable touch with their surroundings, and for this reason their expressions and gestures are on the whole more adapted to exterior situations than those of other types of mental patients.

At the commencement of this chapter I described in a general way the expressive conduct of two paraphrenics, and I shall now investigate these two cases systematically without repeating the general description.

Case I.   A woman of 43 years of age.

She exhibited in moments of obsession all the expressions of fear and aggressiveness : the face tense with a fixed regard, the gestures of the hand emphatic and aggressive.   Her inner tension was further reflected in the predominance of extensor movements over flexor movements of the hand, and in the frequent opening and closing of the fists and demonstrative gestures of the index finger.   Even in her calmer moments she had a contemptuous expression, and this sentiment having become habitual was fixed in the physiognomy of her face.   Although, when carried away by her delusions, she was incapable of shaking hands in a frank and friendly way, she had often, when composed, given me her hand with every sign of contact : a warm and strong grasp.

HAND FEATURES

Measurements

Length of the Hands
Right, 17·2 cm.   Left, 17·3 cm.
Width of the Hands
Right, 8·0 cm.   Left, 7.8 cm.
Height of the Patient
5 ft. 1 in.

HAND SHAPE

The hands are small but muscular. The thenar eminences are specially strong, the hypothenar eminences flat and short. The right hand has the oval shape of the fleshy motor hand. The fingers are abnormally short, especially the fifth finger, which in both hands only reaches half-way up the second phalanx of the fourth finger. The thumbs, in spite of their smallness, are broad and strong, with bulbous terminal phalanxes. The basal phalanx of all the fingers is sausage shaped. The nails are of an elementary type, very short and broad and without moons.

Physical Qualities

Warm ; dry ; of normal colour ; stiff.

Crease-Lines

In the left hand the upper transverse line is simian-like and the long longitudinal line is lacking. The accessory crease-lines are few in number and only concentrated on the thenar eminences and below the fingers, whilst the hypothenar eminence is quite empty in both palms. All the creases are deep and without any particular defects.

Papillary Ridges

Primary arc-triangle patterns on the index finger of both hands.

PERSONALITY DIAGNOSIS FROM HAND FEATURES

Patient suffers from an endocrine deficiency probably of a hypothyroic type. She is physically strong and active, but emotionally weak, unstable, and uncontrolled. She is quick-tempered and impulsive and her capacity for adaptation is feeble or non-existent. Her endocrine make-up might have interfered with a normal sexual life, and it is likely that her unbalance has a root in sexual infantilism enhanced by temperamental defects. She has a tendency to anxiety neurosis and paranoia.

CLINICAL DIAGNOSIS

Paraphrenia. Religious mania.

From the case paper : ' Very deluded ; megalomaniac ideas. She was a housekeeper, but having developed ideas of persecution and other obsessions four years ago, she was certified.'

INTERPRETATION OF GESTURES

An expression of contempt was shown by the expression of the mouth, the lower lip being drawn down and the upper lip drawn up, showing the teeth. Her agitation and impatience were revealed in the opening and closing of the fists and the emphatic character of her gestures ; her aggressiveness by brusque and centrifugal movements. That the latter were the outcome of a paranoiac complex, which put her into a state of permanent inner defence, could be interpreted from the predominant extensor movements of her hands and the stiffness of certain postures. She was, for example, perpetually throwing her head back, a posture which exhibited a sense of superiority mixed with resentment. Her need of isolation was equally revealing of her self-esteem and her contempt for her surroundings (she was always seated with her back to the class).

Expressions and gestures such as these are exhibited under certain emotional conditions in any one of a strongly emotional make-up if the provocation is sufficient. The difference between a normal emotional reaction and an abnormal one consists in the fact that the former is a response to a real situation, the latter to a purely imaginary one ; though it is true that in normal people also imagination plays so large a part that the line of separation between the 'real' and the 'imaginary' is difficult to establish. Perhaps the line is drawn by the capacity for discrimination between the real and the unreal, a capacity always possessed in a greater or lesser degree by normal people, but entirely obliterated in cases of mental malady. The loss of a sense of reality is the decisive factor which separates the sane from the insane.

Case II. A man of 48 years of age who did odd jobs in the therapy class.

During these observations he rushed from one table to the other and only sat down to arrange bundles of newspapers or to write. He had certainly no wish to do manual work. He had a great sense of his own importance as a religious and social reformer who must spend his time in thought and propaganda by the spoken and written word. He was the only member of the class who did not insist on occupying a habitual place. His expressive conduct had something in common with that of the preceding case. The face was tense and had an expression of contempt, slightly softened, however, by an air of condescension towards those who could not share his knowledge of the truth. He made the same emphatic and menacing gestures of the hands as the previous patient, the fingers spread like a fan. This man was even more carried away by his obsessions than his female counterpart. He jumped up from the chair, took some steps forward and stamped with his foot, either in anger or with impatience that the other fellow (an imaginary person) or the listener did not see his point of view. He was very oratorical and frequently used his index finger to emphasize his political, humanitarian, and religious ideas. He did this in quite a different way to the preceding case, with spastic and abrupt movements and with a motor speed accelerated as if he was driven by an inner avalanche. He made sudden brusque gestures towards his forehead or temples when he tried to explain a difficult thought. An element of fanaticism and the urge to preach made for much more exaggerated expression than in his female counterpart, who showed her superiority rather by an attitude of withdrawal.

HAND FEATURES

It is sufficient to summarize the most characteristic hand features without going into detail. These are broad and short hands, with a simian line on the left palm and abnormal patterns of the papillary ridges (arc-triangle patterns) on thumb, index and medius finger of the right hand. With their few accessory crease-lines the hands belong to the group of elementary regressive hands (see *The Human Hand*). The fingers are spatulate, very mobile and longer than one generally finds in the elementary type of hand.

PERSONALITY DIAGNOSIS FROM HAND FEATURES

Neurotic subject lacking adaptability. He has an adventurous attitude towards life and is unreasonable in his ideas. Emotionally and mentally unbalanced. Prone to ideas of grandeur, likely to be forceful in his behaviour towards others.

CLINICAL DIAGNOSIS

Paraphrenia; megalomaniac ideas; strongly deluded. Has certain political and religious obsessions. Writes endless books and letters. Does not stop talking in the ward. Noisy at times; querulous and difficult.

INTERPRETATION OF GESTURES

The gestures were :

1. Emphatic
2. Abrupt and arrhythmic
3. Stereotyped
4. Predominantly centri- fugal
5. Of a fast motor speed

The psycho-motor behaviour of the patient was descriptive of an abnormal inner tension and agitation and of obsessional and fanatical ideas. The gestures were those of an oratorical dema- gogue. The combination of obsessional ideas and emotionalism produced a state of motor unrest and over-expressive behaviour. The obsessional character of the ideas was shown in the stereotyped repetition of the same gesture patterns. The aggressive element was revealed in the emphatic and expansive expressive movements in combination with the brusque and arrhythmic quality of the gestures. The frequent index gesture of the schoolmaster showed his feeling of mental superiority, and the autistic gesture of touching the forehead, corresponded to his difficulty in formulating a thought and to his despair of being properly understood.

Case III. A woman of 53 doing needlework.

She made incessant mouth and tongue movements. She looked round continually with an expression of fury as if some adversary were behind her. Her hands were skilful and the co-ordination of their movements was perfect. But the motor speed was unequal, changing continually : sometimes frantically accelerated, sometimes slowing or dying down altogether. This ambivalence seemed to be a mirror of the preoccupations of the patient. She was always seated in a stiff attitude, her head thrown back and on the alert for anything of a suspicious nature. She continually interrupted her work and wrung her hands or pressed them together. From time to time she pulled her hair or snatched some material from the table, throwing it away as if she wanted to attack somebody.

When talking calmly to her and asking her about her work she answered quite sensibly as if nothing were troubling her, but she continued to clasp her hands tightly on her stomach.

HAND FEATURES

The hands are small and broad, with short and strong thumbs of which the terminal phalanxes are spatulate. The basal phalanxes of all the fingers are sausage-shaped and the little finger is abnormally short. The hands are stiff. The crease-lines are extremely faulty and there are few accessory creases. They are elementary hands of a regressive type.

PERSONALITY DIAGNOSIS FROM HAND FEATURES

The patient is suffering from an endocrine insufficiency, probably of a hypopituitary type. She is an infantile personality with emotional instability and paranoiac tendencies. She has, however, quite good vitality and a strong inner dynamism.

CLINICAL DIAGNOSIS

Paraphrenia. Auditory persecutory delusions.

INTERPRETATION OF GESTURES

Facial Expression

The facial expression was the result of a purely imaginative process of an obsessional type. The mind was absorbed in auditory delusions which continually threatened the identity of the patient causing great distress and producing a mechanism of defence which was expressed in aggressiveness and fury. No explanation is necessary of the movements of the head and the eyes, which were continually turning round as if someone were just behind her. The patient was under the influence of chronic shock, released apparently by purely imaginative processes, but which produced all the reactions of real shock—rolling movements of the eyes, for example, which are the expression of panic. The mouth and tongue gestures might in this case also be attributed to a permanent feeling of catastrophe. As we have seen in the cases of schizophrenic patients, the mouth and tongue gestures are part of a syndrome of nervous dysfunction of a catatonic type. It is possible to assume that a dysfunction of this kind can be brought about through psychological causes. I must leave open, however, the question of whether this patient was not in fact a case of schizophrenia. There is still another psychological element in these mouth and tongue movements : an emotional regression to the most primitive phase of childhood. It is well known that neurotics whose direct expressions are cut off fall back upon infantile emotions and expressions. And this is especially the case with people suffering from anxiety.

HAND GESTURES

The arrhythmic and abrupt movements of the hands as well as the ambivalent motor speed seemed to depend on images alone and had no relation to exterior situations. The nervous agitation which was revealed in the accelerated speed seemed gradually to calm down, and with the acquiescence of the mind the tempo of movement changed to a slow one. But the moments of inner peace did not last. The same process of agitation, gradually fading out, was repeated over and over again. Nevertheless the manual work seemed to relieve the mind of the patient of a great deal of tension, for when she interrupted her work there was a visible change in her hand gestures, which became violently aggressive, destructive and fearful. The wringing, interlocking and pressing movements of the hands were typical of a state of acute anxiety.

It is hardly necessary to mention that a state of panic had completely broken up the identity of the patient.

Case IV. A woman of 57 years of age, who was engaged on such tasks as unpicking a garment or making slippers out of bits of old felt.

She was so concentrated on her work that she looked neither to right nor to left, and did not even notice the aeroplanes roaring overhead. In spite of her absorption she interrupted her work quite frequently and exhibited at these moments an extraordinary motor unrest. Her hands moved incessantly in graceful circular movements in the air and these gestures were accompanied by strident laughter. Sometimes she jumped from her chair and made movements in a semicircle as if she were the victim of an attack of St. Vitus's dance. Over-concentration and excitability were expressed in everything she did. When she was spoken to, twitchings of the mouth and eyes commenced at once and she went into fits of laughter. But she could maintain her poise and her sense of superiority when she addressed other people. When saying 'How do you do?' to me she put her hand on my head in a benevolent and condescending way and shook my hand with a pressure which caused me to wince. I often noticed her walking from one table to the other as if she were the supervisor of the class, taking the material and the tools in her hands without permission or excuse and upsetting all the work of her comrades. She would stand no criticism; the slightest admonition made her aggressive to the point of rage. Even without provocation she would murmur maledictions, making aggressive hand movements at an invisible adversary and throwing her scissors on the ground. She was always full of herself. Her decorative hand gestures were most fully displayed when walking through the class, when her swaggering walk was accompanied by the highly precious hand movements of an old-fashioned actress. While exterior phonetic impressions had no effect on her she paid special attention to everything which came into her line of vision. When an epileptic patient had a fit she ran towards her and at once took charge of the situation. Together with the nurse she supported the patient and observed her with fascinated absorption. She was so sure of herself that she gave orders, not only to the other patients but also to the staff. Her movements while running to help the patient were all hypermetric, emphatic and brusque. But her interest in the new situation was fleeting, and soon she returned without a word to her table. When walking at leisure her gait was very peculiar : she advanced with dancing steps, moving her hips as well as her shoulders. She used her hands and arms not only in the manner of the great actress but also to push aside those who interfered with her progress. Apart from these theatrical gestures she flipped her fingers and laughed loudly while walking about. Sometimes she burst into music-hall songs while crossing the classroom.

While cutting out material for slippers she constantly pointed the scissors at me or at the patients seated near her and then suddenly turned them towards her own face. She also made snipping movements or drew circles in the air with the scissors.

HAND FEATURES

The hand possesses a muscular but narrow palm and long fingers, with rheumatic nodes. The fingers are stiff and the thumb is especially immobile. The finger-tips are spatulate, furnished with long, narrow, and convex nails with large moons. In the right hand the long longitudinal line is missing and the lower transverse line is in an abnormal position : it joins the upper transverse line beneath the ring finger. Both the thenar and hypothenar eminences are covered with many accessory creases. The hands are of the bony motoric type with features of the elementary regressive hand.

PERSONALITY DIAGNOSIS FROM HAND FEATURES

The subject suffers from rheumatism, hyperthyroidism, and has probably been tuberculous. Her endocrine make-up may play a part in—

1. a strong nervous dynamism ;
2. a marked inner restlessness.

The patient has eccentric tendencies and has a marked aesthetic sense. She has manual skill of the kind which would make her a good dressmaker and even a good mechanic.

She belongs to the schizoid group of temperaments, representing the extravagant variety with instability of moods and lack of real emotions. She has no adaptation to her surroundings and suffers from depression and impulsiveness.

CLINICAL DIAGNOSIS

Persecution mania. Very deluded. ' Imagines that people are trying to kill her with laughing gas. Very noisy and destructive in the ward. Ill for ten years. Married with 5 children. Had been a dressmaker by profession.'

INTERPRETATION OF GESTURES

The gesture pattern of this patient had in my opinion a marked physiological background. She represented a case which fits into the Syndrome of Huntington's Chorea, as indicated by F. Walshe. A disease of the basal ganglia may have been responsible for both the athetotic character of her movements and the truly choreiform gestures.

Superimposed on this neurological background are the psychological manifestations of her mental disorder.

The Face

The hypermobility of facial expression showed both the lack of control over her inner sensations and an obsessional trend of thought and feeling. The explosive laughter might be explained through her special phobia, namely, that people were trying to kill her with laughing gas.

The Gait

The gait was particularly striking. It was essentially different when the patient was moving forward with a purpose from when she was walking at leisure. While she rushed to the aid of the epileptic woman her movements were clumsy and gross ; when she paid visits to other patients here and there her movements exhibited a mannered ' grace '. Then her walk seemed to have little or no relation to her age, social *milieu* and mentality. One may therefore assume that her gait was shaped by her imagination, by means of which she probably saw herself as a great actress. Carried away by such an idea of herself she produced these graceful but affected steps.

The Hands

Like the walk the hand gestures were affected. They did not correspond to the true nature of the patient but to her picture of herself. She moved her hands as if she were taking part in a pantomime. But the moment any one crossed her path the grand rôle was disturbed and her hand movements became gross and aggressive. Three fundamental traits of her mental disorder could be diagnosed from her typical hand gestures : megalomania, hysteria (theatrical poses) and impulsiveness. Both the gait and these hand gestures revealed an exaggerated feeling of self and a marked narcissism, whilst the symbolic gestures of pointing the scissors at her neighbours and towards herself showed aggressive tendencies not only towards others but also towards herself. They expressed the desire to attack a dangerous enemy as well as to injure herself. Her feeling of vindictiveness towards the world in general was expressed by the disorder she made of the work-tables of the other patients.

Case V. A woman whose expressive conduct was the opposite of the preceding case.

She occupied the next place to this agitated and aggressive patient, a circumstance which accentuated her own remoteness. She reacted in no way to what was happening round her, but was evidently frightened by the roar of aeroplanes overhead, which she followed with anxious eyes. She was very sensitive to noise, and approaching footsteps made her jump. She too was making slippers, with hand movements which were badly co-ordinated, very slow and abrupt. She often let her work drop and fell into a state of complete immobility. She spoke only when addressed. From time to time she made hair gestures with swift, abrupt and impulsive movements, as if she were afraid of contact. When asked questions about her work she replied like an ordinary person of inferior intelligence.

HAND FEATURES

The hands are long, narrow and flat. The fingers are tapered and so flexible as to appear boneless. The basal phalanxes are enlarged. The fifth finger is abnormally long. In the right hand there is a complete lack of accessory creases, which is contrary to the rule in this type of hand. The long longitudinal line is missing from both palms and the papillary ridges of all the finger-tips show regressive patterns. The hand belongs to the sensitive long type with elementary regressive features.

PERSONALITY DIAGNOSIS FROM HAND FEATURES

The patient has certain constitutional defects : an insufficiency of ossification, which is known as arachnodactyly. This anomaly always goes with an endocrine insufficiency probably of a pituitary type, and sometimes with mental deficiency. The vitality is feeble, the nervous dynamism is reduced, which produces a terrain for anxiety neurosis and introversion. It need hardly to be said that this woman belongs to Kretschmer's schizoid group of temperaments, and is of the dull and inhibited variety. Her identity is weak or non-existent, rendering her susceptible to obsessional ideas. It is possible that she is a case of schizophrenia.

CLINICAL DIAGNOSIS

Paraphrenia of a hypochondriac type. (It is well known that certain paraphrenics are borderline cases of schizophrenia. I suspect that the patient under investigation belongs to this group.)

INTERPRETATION OF GESTURES

It is not necessary to give a detailed interpretation of gestures in this case because they do not contribute any new element. Apparently the patient suffered from a state of depression and anxiety. The latter often goes with hypersensitivity towards noise. Her motor speed and bad co-ordination revealed both a marked inhibition and a defective intelligence. Her psycho-motor expressions were reduced to a minimum, testifying to a loss of initiative and a lack of inner dynamism, and the only movements she repeatedly made were autistic gestures towards her hair, a type of gesture often found in schizophrenia and in extreme anxiety.

Case VI. A young woman of 28 years of age who was a dressmaker by profession.

She did her work with a perfect co-ordination of hand movements. She made pretty dresses for dolls. The ease and facility with which she worked betrayed the skilled worker. The speed of her hand movements was, however, very unequal—for the most part accelerated, but changing abruptly to an abnormally slow tempo. This was accompanied by a change of facial expression. The face, as a rule tense and agitated, would suddenly change to an expression of profound fatigue. She continually talked and sang while working, but with a lack of coherence ; she would suddenly stop in the middle of a phrase or song.

The gestures of the hands had no special significance, but her gait was striking. She walked with tiny steps in a stiff manner, tiptoeing at high speed as if she were always in a great hurry. But there was grace in her manner of walking, a grace which went with an unconscious self-confidence.

I shook hands with her on several occasions and her grasp was prolonged and so strong as to cause pain.

HAND FEATURES

The hands are well proportioned to body size. The muscular palms, with strong, short and spatulate fingers, are typical of the fleshy motor type. The hands are stiff, dry, and warm. The nails are of the primary type, being abnormally short and without moons. The crease-lines as well as the papillary ridges show anomalies. The position of the lower transverse line, terminating very low on the hypothenar eminence, is abnormal in both hands. The papillary ridges are of a regressive pattern on the finger-tips of the index and medius fingers and there is a whorl on both hypothenar eminences.

PERSONALITY DIAGNOSIS FROM HAND FEATURES

A very vital person, physically active, possessing remarkable manual skill. She is, however, highly strung, agitated and impulsive. Her hands are virile, unlike her face and general appearance. She is a predominantly extravert type of person with emotional instability.

CLINICAL DIAGNOSIS

Confused psychosis. Disconnected talk. Very restless. Idiosyncratic about food. Defective in habits. Patient had recently been discharged but had to come back as she became agitated, violent, and depressed. Was found wandering about. She has two illegitimate children by different men. She made a home with each of them for several years.

INTERPRETATION OF GESTURES

The motor speed is comparable to a fever curve and reveals an abnormal agitation, impulsiveness and lack of mental cohesion. The only hand gesture of special significance was her handshake, which was characteristic of the anguished. Apart from the general tension expressed by too firm a grip, it contained an element of appeal. The facial expression was the mirror of an acute tension, quite different from that of the truly depressed person. The eyes were shining and the whole face reflected a rich inner life, even in moments of fatigue. It was the facial expression of a very emotional person lacking control over her feelings and images. Her gait contained a strong erotic element but was otherwise typical of anguished agitation and inner ' spasticity '.

Case VII. A woman of 54 years of age who had some expressive particularities in common with the preceding case.

She showed an instability of facial expression which was even more marked than in the previous patient. At one moment her face was radiant, as if she were filled with a sublime happiness, at the next it would change suddenly to an expression of insupportable grief. But as with children, no mood lasted for long nor did it seem to leave any trace.

Her working movements were unskilled and she was in the habit of pressing the third and fourth fingers on the needle as if she had cramp. When she was not working and while walking she made a recurrent gesture with the left hand, placing it on her cheek or her chest in a tense and almost cramped fashion. Her walk was the opposite of that of the preceding patient. She took long steps without lifting her feet from the ground as if held back by a stiffness of her back. These sliding paces are noted on several occasions in this chapter.

HAND FEATURES

It is sufficient to indicate that the hands are—
1. of the long sensitive type ;
2. have the index and medius finger of equal length ;
3. show an unusual poverty of accessory creases for their type ;
4. are cold, damp, stiff, and red in colour.

PERSONALITY DIAGNOSIS FROM HAND FEATURES

The patient belongs to Kretschmer's schizoid group of temperaments. Lacking contact with her surroundings she possesses little sense of reality and is apt to be easily disintegrated. Her emotions are shallow and distorted by abnormal inhibition. Her intelligence and vitality being feeble she cannot find compensation in physical activity. She is probably a borderline case between paraphrenic and schizophrenic psychosis.

CLINICAL DIAGNOSIS

Paraphrenic psychosis of long standing. Does not finish a sentence. Shallow emotions. Persecution ideas directed mainly against those she believes to be responsible for her detention at the hospital. She comes from a good family.

INTERPRETATION OF GESTURES

The instability of facial expression was produced more by fluctuating images than by emotions. Her abnormal inner tension and her depression were revealed in both hand movements and gait. The gait showed a profound inhibitive mechanism and resembled that of certain catatonic schizophrenics. The emphatic and cramped way in which she put her hand on her cheek or chest was an effort to revive the peripheric sensibility, designed to escape the feeling of anaesthesia which goes with a state of extreme fear and to reassure herself that she was still existing.

Case VIII. A woman of 46 years of age recently admitted to the hospital.

She was occupied in cutting out felt for making slippers and toys. She was concentrated on her work, which she executed with slow, cramped movements of the hands. Her face wore a tense and agitated expression with a look of anger and depression, the lips being drawn down. The patient was very communicative and interrupted her work from time to time to talk to other patients. Unlike other similar cases she was aware of her condition and asked me at every occasion if she were curable as she hated her depression. She became agitated and made emphatic and aggressive gestures with her hands when she described what she had suffered. This was especially so when she was complaining of a mistress who had illtreated her. She would implore the staff to rescue her and find her a good job. After these outbursts she would always become quite unreasonable and refuse to be helped, since it was useless as she then said. At the same time she let her hands fall as if her strength were exhausted and remained seated with bent head and a face pale as a sheet. At these moments the eye wore an expression of disorientation. Her gait was heavy but did not show any special anomaly apart from the extreme slowness of speed.

HAND FEATURES

The most outstanding feature of these hands is their width : 8·5 cm. in the right and 8·4 cm. in the left hand. The thumbs are misshapen, with a too short, enlarged, and immobile terminal phalanx. The fingers are short and tapered and their basal phalanxes sausage-shaped. The crease-lines are few in number ; the principal creases are deep and well drawn, but the papillary ridges show abnormal patterns. There are triangle-arc patterns on the index and medius fingers of the right hand and a whorl on the hypothenar eminence of both hands.

The hands are of the elementary regressive type.

PERSONALITY DIAGNOSIS FROM HAND FEATURES

Patient is a woman of remarkable physical strength and energy. She is gifted for the kind of work which demands physical force as well as a good intelligence. She could be equally useful in house, field and garden. She belongs to the athletic or amorphous type of Kretschmer, with a tendency to hypothyroidism. This latter condition might be partly responsible for an instability of moods. She is an impulsive and bad-tempered woman with paranoiac features. She has an adventurous outlook on life, no power of adaptation and is thoroughly self-destructive.

CLINICAL DIAGNOSIS

Nervous breakdown with paranoiac features.

INTERPRETATION OF GESTURES

A detailed interpretation of the gestures of this patient is super-fluous, since it is obvious that they were the result of emotional instability, depressive agitation and impulsiveness. She presented an expressive picture such as might be found among normal people in moments of crisis. In this case anxiety was mixed with an effort to maintain equilibrium and to be cured : through symbolic

11

movements of aggression as well as through her desire to communicate her preoccupations the patient tried to get rid of her unhealthy inner tension. The exaggeration of her gestures when she spoke about past miseries might be explained by the fact that she was a refugee who had suffered a great deal before she came to this country. For this reason I am inclined to think that she was only a case of nervous breakdown with acute depression and not a paraphrenic patient.

D. TWO CASES OF HYSTERIA

I treat these two cases in an abbreviated comparative way, combining the description and the interpretation of the gestures, while a short analysis of the features of the hand has also been made on a principle of comparison.

The two patients diagnosed as hysterical were inseparable friends. They occupied neighbouring places in the occupational therapy class as well as at meals. The expressive conduct of both was definitely different from that of all the other patients I have described. In this respect also they formed a unity of their own.

Case I was a young girl of 24 years of age recently admitted to the hospital. She was supposed to be making a sailor's scarf, but in reality was only pretending to work. Seated in front of her table, she gazed into space or talked to her friend. She was not interested in anyone else. Her face was blank and mask-like in expression but in quite a different way from that of the truly depressed, which is the result of real suffering. It was the mask of a narcissistic being without any real sensibility, who lived on autistic sentiments as the only stimulus of her existence. That she had a great opinion of herself was shown by the contemptuous expression of her mouth, which revealed her sense of superiority to those around her. One of her habitual postures was to throw her head back in a rigid position as if her neck were immobile. When addressed she moved her head towards the speaker very slowly as if it were hardly worth the trouble to listen. This posture and movement suggested haughtiness. And exactly the same posture, the same slow and stiff movement of the head could be seen in *Case II*, a girl of 28. She too was seated in front of her work and exhibited the same inertia as her friend, but her face was very changeable in colour and tension, demonstrating in a perfect way the relation between organic and expressive reactions. The instability which was reflected in her face was brought about by sudden changes of expressions of boredom, delight, and impulsiveness. But all these expressions had a different character to those of real emotions. In this patient inner tension appeared to be lacking, and it seemed that fleeting images affected the autonomic nervous system without touching the centre of emotional representation in the brain. For this reason she was only affected by organic and narcissistic sensations. The former were evidenced not only by the changeability of facial expressions but by autistic gestures of a hypochondriac type. She was in the habit of feeling her pulse and putting her hand on her heart as if to count her heartbeats. The latter were evidenced by the haughty and self-satisfied expression of her face and the condescending movements of her head. Fastidiousness and affectation were also visible in certain mannered hand gestures : when she took hold of an object she did it with a maddening slowness of movement, looking as infants do at her hand instead of the object. Another mannerism appeared in the hand gestures with which she arranged her hair, fastidiously and with obvious pleasure ; still another appeared in hiding gestures when she placed her hands on her temples, the fingers arranged fanwise.

The two patients showed the same motor characteristics in their gait : a display of muscular rigidity and self-consciousness. They walked with the same slowness with which they moved their hands, taking small steps, the whole body erect and rigid as if under the influence of a profound inhibition, the head thrown back.

The expressive conduct of these two examples of hysterical neurosis can be interpreted in the following way—

1. Emotional regression to the autistic phase of childhood.
2. Physical and mental narcissism.
3. Perversion of instincts through self-consciousness.

HAND FEATURES OF CASE I

The hands are of a mixed type : the palm belongs to the elementary regressive and the long and tapered fingers to the long sensitive type. This mixture is very rare and freakish. On the two palms one of the principal transverse lines is missing. The accessory creases are deep and concentrated on the hypothenar eminences. The general composition of the crease-lines is badly balanced.

PERSONALITY DIAGNOSIS FROM HAND FEATURES

In this case instead of giving an individual interpretation I prefer to quote the passage in my book *The Human Hand* (p. 49) on the mixture of the elementary regressive with the long sensitive hand type, since it contains all that can be said on the personality of the patient under consideration as far as hand diagnosis goes.

The mixture is a most negative one. All kinds of endocrine insufficiency and abnormality occur and the nervous health of a person with such a hand is extremely fragile. As the vitality is generally very low there is a natural tendency to frequent breakdowns. All the negative features of the schizoid temperament are exaggerated in this combination. The mentality is distorted, the eccentricity of the schizoid person being accentuated in the most negative way and an exaggerated suggestibility outweighing reasoned criticism and a realistic vision of the world.

CLINICAL DIAGNOSIS

Hysteria. Patient got worried about call up. Solitary and reserved. Had had breakdowns before.

HAND FEATURES OF CASE II

The hands are too long in proportion to the height of the patient, and belong to the long sensitive type. There is an anomaly in the digital formula, the index and medius fingers being of equal length. The crease-lines are irregular for the type of hand : on the right palm can be seen the simian line, showing a very interesting resemblance to the hand of Case I. The accessory creases are abundant and superficially drawn. In spite of the fact that the hands of Case II are on the whole more unified, the presence of the simian line adds also to these hands a trait which is typical of the elementary regressive hand. Thus there is a structural resemblance in the hands of the two patients. It must not be concluded from these two examples that the hands of all hysterical patients are on this pattern, but the described combination of structural elements reveals a tendency to destructive eccentricity typical of this rather ' problematic ' illness.

PERSONALITY DIAGNOSIS FROM HAND FEATURES

This schizoid personality combines the negative traits often exhibited by the different groups of this type of temperament : hyperaesthesia and eccentricity on the one hand and emotional dullness on the other. She is fastidious and has a certain amount of taste, and she is emotionally cold, obsessional and uncontrolled.

CLINICAL DIAGNOSIS

Hysteria, unstable, restless, full of mannerisms. Interfering. She is an illegitimate child whose mother is insane and an inmate of a mental hospital.

NOTE ON HYSTERIA

I append a note on hysteria because it is a malady which, perticularly in its lighter forms, is often found in men and women. The hysterical type is met with in all classes and in every profession. These people are rarely confined in mental hospitals, since hysteria is not a mental illness but a psychoneurosis. One of the difficulties of diagnosis lies in the differentiation between hysteria and anxiety neurosis, since symptoms of anguish are present in certain cases of the malady. But as I have been able to show in one of the two examples of this study, anguish may be entirely lacking. The most characteristic feature of hysteria is that of self-dramatization with the object of occupying the centre of the stage and becoming the focus of attention. The autistic attitude goes with a lack of real emotion and with an arrogant outlook. The latter explains the constant desire of hysterical people to interfere in the affairs of other people. Hypochondriacal symptoms are very frequent, but they are always used as a means to an end : namely to tyrannize. It is well known that many hysterical patients make themselves ill by scratching the skin, for example, until they produce a dermatitis, or they may simulate a fever by putting the thermometer in hot water. They consciously deceive their surroundings, which is not the case with victims of anxiety neurosis.

At the end of the first part of the clinical study I want to mention that the diagnoses from hand features were made independently of the clinical diagnosis and the notes from the case papers, both of which have been copied from the original texts.

The reader will find the necessary explanations of my diagnostic conclusions drawn from hand traits in my book *The Human Hand*.

II. GESTURES AT MEALS

I have already explained my reasons for investigating the expressive conduct of a certain number of mental patients at meals.

1. The action of eating releases emotional reactions which go far beyond the mere satisfaction of a primary instinct and in the case of the insane often shows a complete lack of self-control. Thus the subconscious urges which are at the base of mental and emotional aberrations appear in a transparent way.

2. As a rule the whole attention and interest is concentrated on the act of eating and the patients are quite undisturbed by a feeling of being watched.

THE MATERIAL OF STUDY

The material for this study consists of 39 patients, all of them women—

1. 8 schizophrenics.
2. 6 manic depressive patients.
3. 6 melancholics who had been treated with Electrical Shock Treatment.
4. 7 melancholics who had not been treated.
5. 2 cases of persecution mania.
7. 10 epileptics.

THE METHOD OF STUDY

I visited the dining-rooms of the different wards and observed each patient at least seven times. This gave me the opportunity to observe, for example, in one case of manic depressive psychosis the gestures in a state of hypomania and in the depressive phase. Most of the patients were known to me by the research work I had done on their hands. A certain number were members of the occupational therapy class and it was interesting to compare their expressive conduct at work and at meals.

This study was carried out on a different plan to the preceding one. I have not described every individual case separately, but have studied and reported the gestures from the point of view of the frequency with which they appeared in the same group, commencing with those which were common to all members of the group, then recording those which were to be found in a certain number and finally those which could only be observed in isolated cases.

The patients were seated at different tables in groups of 6, 8, or 10. At each visit I concentrated on one table at a time and registered the gestures of the patients on the spot. As a rule these groups were made up of sufferers from the same malady, a fact which facilitated my work. I gave special consideration in this study to epileptics, a preference which requires explanation.

NOTE ON EPILEPSY

Like hysteria, epilepsy is a condition which does not always necessitate admission to hospital. There are many epileptics, especially those who have fits only during the night, who are able to lead an ordinary life and to pursue an occupation. Their intelligence and aptitudes differ widely ; a certain number even have brilliant capacities, Napoleon Buonaparte and Dostoyevsky being historic examples. The epileptic type with mental deficiency, however, is much more frequent and represents a high percentage of the inmates of mental hospitals. The Encephalogram shows that there are also potential epileptics, who never have fits but who possess the same abnormal cortical waves as the true epileptics. The potential epileptics are not usually inmates of mental hospitals, but one can assume that they are always subject to nervous and emotional instability similar to that known as ' epileptic temperament '. I had no opportunity of studying the expressive behaviour of potential epileptics, but one can assume that it does not differ essentially from that of the true epileptic, who has a more or less normal intelligence and only occasional fits.

The potentially epileptic and the hysterical types can be found in every walk of life. It would be of great help to have means of diagnosing their make-up before their deficiencies bring them into conflict with society, as often happens with potential epileptics. Only recently the newspapers reported the case of a young man who had murdered his mother, driven by a sudden uncontrollable and apparently unconscious urge. The Encephalogram revealed his psychopathology : his cortical waves were on the pattern of epileptics.

It might reasonably be expected that the potential epileptic has a similar temperament to that of the true epileptic, which might reveal itself in his expressions and gestures. A certain number of neurologists deny the existence of an epileptic temperament. This negation is justified if one does not differentiate between epileptics with psychosis and those who have no mental malady, moreover, one can only take into account those who suffer from the ideopathic form of the illness.

The epileptic personality is distinguished by the following traits—

1. A subjectivism of ideas and judgement such as one finds in young adolescents.

2. Instability and superficiality of the emotions.

3. Impulsiveness and lack of control over actions.

4. Narcissism.

In Chapter III I mentioned that the phase which follows the emotional stage in the development of the child resembles the inner world of the epileptic. Certain expressions and gestures which I have described as 'Projective Gestures' are common, according to H. Wallon, to the child of about 5 or 6 years and to the epileptic.

A (1). GESTURES AT MEALS OF 8 SCHIZOPHRENICS

1. of a paranoiac reaction type (7);
2. of a hebephrenic reaction type (1).

The seven paranoiac schizophrenics were placed at the same table. Their social attitude was completely negative. No word was exchanged, no look cast on another patient only on the piece of bread of the next-door neighbour. It was interesting to see that four patients insisted on eating the bread which belonged to some one else.

The following expressive traits were common to the whole group :

1. Extraordinary motor unrest of the hands.
2. Arrhythmic and impulsive gestures.
3. Abnormally slow motor speed.
4. Habit of eating far away from the plate.

DESCRIPTION

HAND GESTURES

1. Four of the patients made frequent ' hair ' gestures in an abrupt way with movements of extension, as if frightened of the contact.

2. Two patients showed a similar catatonic mannerism as I have described in the preceding study. Each mouthful was accompanied by circular movements with the fork or spoon half-way between plate and mouth. One patient maintained this gesture of suspense for about 3 minutes.

3. In two others I observed an inhibitive anomaly of the same kind. They took up the fork and spoon in a normal way, but

were incapable of putting either directly into the mouth. They described a zigzag line. The speed of this one gesture was remarkably variable : normal to begin with, then becoming increasingly slow until the movement stopped altogether, to be followed by a sudden acceleration at the end. The patients gave the impression of making a painful effort to achieve the last phase of movement.

4. One of the patients, who ate nothing except some cake, was occupied in fingering the knife and fork with meticulous and precious gestures, holding the fifth finger well out. As in the preceding cases the motor speed of these gestures was abnormally slow.

5. One of the patients had a singular peculiarity : she got up every 3 or 4 minutes to turn round several times behind her chair and then sit down again. The motor unrest of her hands was even more marked than in the other cases. The hands were never still for a second ; she rubbed them together or on her body or crumbled bits of bread between her fingers.

THE FACE

Four out of seven patients showed symptoms of catatonic excitement. They made grimaces, laughed explosively and made mouth and tongue movements. The three remaining ones had an unmoved mask-like expression. It was interesting to note that those with the agitated facial expression were the patients who made hair gestures and whose gestures were particularly inhibited and stereotyped. But the patients with an apathetic facial expression also showed great motor unrest of the hands.

INTERPRETATION

Facial Expression

It is unnecessary to interpret the facial expression, as this differs in no way from what I have observed and tried to explain in the preceding study.

Hand Gestures

General Characteristics. The motor unrest of the hands was more accentuated during meals than while working, which is a proof that manual occupation reduces the abnormal nervous tension of schizophrenics. Such exaggerated motor unrest is probably due to subconscious impulses which continually interfere with the feeling of physical and mental identity. They may concern unbearable fears, for these are known to affect the sense of balance as well as the feeling of self. The gestures of the hand are designed, as Wallon and Osseretzky have shown, to maintain the nervous and spatial balance. The normal organism possesses a postural flexibility which continually adapts itself to interior and exterior situations through a self regulation controlled by the core of the personality—in other words—the ego. In an abnormal organism the ego is shifted from a central to an eccentric position and is more or less submerged in the subconscious. In cases where the self is dissolved in the id, the ego is annihilated. This, we may assume, is the case in schizophrenics. The patients still possessed the scheme of movements necessary for eating or working, but they were continually interrupted by subconscious compulsions which exacted other motor activities.

Arrhythmic and impulsive gestures have been interpreted in the previous study.

Eating far away from the plate indicates a lack of contact with the situation of eating caused by the same subconscious factors as I have just mentioned.

Special Characteristics. 1. Hair gestures have been interpreted earlier in this chapter as expressions of anxiety designed to combat a nervous anaesthesia in order to retain a feeling of identity.

2. Writhing movements, which are typical of schizophrenics, have also been dealt with in the first part of this study ; but I want to put forward here a psychological explanation of these kinaesthetic arabesques which I have not mentioned before. They may be understood as an outcome of superstitious urges similar to the stereotyped habits of certain children and of native tribes. They show a complete lack of self-confidence which implies the idea that the person cannot succeed in any action however ordinary without the aid of a power greater than himself. These gestures represent a sort of kinaesthetic prayer designed to conciliate the Gods. 'The Gods' are the creation of a subconscious fear.

3. The stereotyped habit of displacing knives and forks on the table is not confined to schizophrenics and other mental patients ; but with them such obsessional traits take an exaggerated form. This habit is in line with another frequent in schizophrenics : the obsession for arranging papers in a meticulous fashion and then disarranging them in order to tidy them up again, a process which may go on for hours. The sense of order in this perverted form represents a refuge and is the exteriorization of a need for stability,

as if the mind found reassurance in a symbolic action with a fixed pattern.

4. In the mannerism of the patient who gets up from her chair to make circular movements, one is faced with a very individual obsession which may unconsciously reproduce the memory of a child's game. It is possible that an agreeable feeling is attached to this practice, for it exercises a calming influence on the nervous system. The mannerism is also one of the stereotyped superstitious expressions which, as with all these gestures, serves to reduce the inner tension produced by subconscious obsessions.

(2). GESTURES AT MEALS OF ONE SCHIZOPHRENIC OF THE HEBEPHRENIC REACTION TYPE

This singular case can be treated in a summary fashion. It represents the opposite of all the expressions and gestures of the seven preceding cases.

DESCRIPTION

1. Instead of a motor unrest with a predominance of inhibitive movements, this patient employed only the strictly necessary movements to get the food into her mouth.

2. Her gestures were emphatic to the point of violence.

3. She ate with her head close to the plate, and

4. with an accelerated motor speed.

5. All her movements showed lack of inhibitive traits.

HAND GESTURES

She had no table manners at all and devoured her food like an animal or a savage. She used both hands as knife and fork and ate with a greed which I have never seen even in starving people.

THE FACE

The expression of the face, as is often the case in mental defectives, was one of radiant happiness, but there was an underlying tension and agitation which was discharged from time to time in fits of laughter.

INTERPRETATION

The general reader will probably fail to understand how it is possible that the same malady produces opposite expressive symptoms and I must stress the following points—

1. The patient under investigation had been treated with insulin. Before the treatment she was mute.

2. The hebephrenic form of schizophrenia differs from the paranoiac form in the survival of primary instincts and often goes with a state of hypomania. As a rule the hebephrenic reaction type ends in a state of catatony, which involves the complete inhibition of voluntary activity. Thus, even in the same type of the illness, one finds at different stages different symptoms.

Hand Gestures

The hand gestures resembled those of certain mental defectives and the patient was in fact a case of schizophrenia superimposed on mental deficiency. It was, moreover, interesting to note that she suffered from hypothyroidism, a condition which often goes with an inferior intelligence. It is evident that the eating gestures of this patient represented a regression towards the most primary form of life.

The patient had no mechanism of inhibition, nor was there any indication of the existence of an emotional life. All her expressions came from a survival of primary instincts which came to the surface through lack of self-control. These instincts were only satisfied by the most direct movements possible, as was indicated by her approach close to her food and by the speed and urgency of her gestures.

Facial Expressions

It was only in the facial expression that an element of nervous tension and catatonic suspense could be discerned : the tightness of the mouth region was often distorted by fits of explosive laughter.

B. 6 CASES OF MANIC DEPRESSIVE PSYCHOSIS

I was able to observe three patients in a state of hypomania and three in a depressive phase. One of the patients changed while I was making this study from the first into the last state.

(a) Hypomaniac Phase

DESCRIPTION

In the hypomaniac phase there were the following common traits—

THE FACE

The patients wore an expression of happy reverie with a radiant look and a smile of contentment. They were not entirely absorbed by their imagination but took a certain amount of interest in their surroundings. They were the only patients among those under investigation who looked at me attentively and smiled, without, however, asking any questions or realizing that I was studying them.

GENERAL CHARACTERISTICS OF HAND GESTURES

1. Slow motor speed.
2. Many unnecessary movements.
3. Expansive gestures.
4. Rhythmical gestures.
5. Affected or ' precious ' gestures.
6. Autistic gestures.

SPECIAL CHARACTERISTICS OF HAND GESTURES

Whilst the expression of the face was essentially the same, the gestures of the hands showed a certain individual variety.

Two patients ate far away from the plate and with very slow chewing movements. Their hand gestures whilst eating indicated a pleasure in suspense : they were long and circular, the hand describing a graceful curve in the air. The fifth finger was raised at the same time and the regard was fixed with visible satisfaction on the hand and not on the food. They were, in fact, not interested in what they were eating. From time to time they sat with their elbows on the table, placing one or both hands on the temples, still with the fifth finger raised. These two patients also indulged in hair gestures, but of quite a different kind to those of schizophrenics : slow and decorative movements, conveying the pleasure of contact.

The third patient was more agitated than the other two, and while expressing herself in monologue held the left hand tightly closed with the thumb extended.

INTERPRETATION

General Characteristics

Unnecessary movements are the result of subcortical activity either of an emotional or purely reflex type. They appear in those cases where the dynamism is accelerated, as in hypomaniacs, or impoverished as in schizophrenics. In the former case they go with a slight psycho-motor inhibition, in the latter with a profound motor inhibition. One might expect that an accelerated dynamism would go with accelerated motor speed, but I have observed that this is not the case with maniac patients. For this reason slow motor speed alone is not a sufficient indication of an inner disposition. It is necessary to consider the ensemble of expressive traits to arrive at a proper estimate.

Apart from slow motor speed and many unnecessary movements, gestures of expansion could also be observed which were at the same time rounded and rhythmical. They were the expressive movements which accompany emotions evoked by joy and self-love and are the signs of narcissism.

Special Characteristics

The raised fifth finger is a pretentious and self-conscious gesture, and the decorative hair gestures (which are autistic gestures) belong to the same category. In these two expressive traits can be seen a resemblance to the gestures of the two hysterical patients. The 'thumbs up' gesture of the third patient indicates, as I have explained in *The Human Hand*, a heightened feeling of self and an aggressive spirit.

(b) Depressed Phase

DESCRIPTION

GENERAL CHARACTERISTICS

Face

Tension, general disturbance and disgust.

Hands

1. Slow motor speed.
2. Few unnecessary movements.
3. Gestures of withdrawal, e.g., hiding gestures.
4. Arrhythmic gestures.
5. Autistic gestures.
6. Perseverance of postures and gestures.

SPECIAL CHARACTERISTICS

Face

The expression of the face varied between a mask-like calm and hypermobility, according to the nature of the depression, which took either the form of agitation or melancholy. The region of the mouth was the most expressive in the depressed phase.

In all three patients the mouth was tight and had a bitter expression, but I did not observe any twitchings either of the mouth or the eyes.

One of the three patients was so affected by noise that she bit her lips ; even the most usual sounds, such as those made by the knife and fork on the plate, produced this reaction. She also indulged in monologues and the expression of the face changed in accordance with the images evoked, which appeared to be either painful or aggressive.

The two others were much calmer. One of them never moved throughout the meal, but remained with her eyes closed making no attempt to eat.

It was particularly interesting to study one patient who had been in a hypomaniac state the week before. Her face was hypermobile with a continually changing expression. She gazed alternately at the ceiling, the distance or her own body. Her lips also moved incessantly as if in a monologue without words.

1. HANDS

Autistic gestures : Two patients made hiding gestures, one by placing her left hand on her profile, the other (the one who ate nothing) by covering her mouth with her hand.

2. IMPULSIVE GESTURES

The third patient, whose depression took the agitated form, and who indulged in monologues, moved her hands in an emphatic and aggressive fashion. She put her plate on the table with an impulsive movement and helped herself to the bread and cake of her neighbours in a brusque way. She was in the habit of holding her hands closed with the thumb hidden in the palm.

3. ARRHYTHMY AND PERSEVERANCE OF GESTURES

These were specially noticable in the patient who was in the transition stage, between the hypomaniac and the depressed phase. She alone made many unnecessary movements so characteristic of the hypomaniac phase, but her gestures had lost the *élan*, precision and rhythm of the preceding phase. The pattern of gestures was still the same but deprived of the dynamic force which had animated them before. Thus all the movements had become listless, slower and lacking in conviction. They showed two new qualities : a purely mechanical execution of movements and a more marked element of inhibition. The latter was further expressed in a recurrent posture : that of crossing the arms and holding them tightly clasped to the chest.

INTERPRETATION

General Characteristics

Depression is a state of interior contraction which affects the two nervous systems, the autonomic and the central. The vaso-motor symptoms are all those of inhibition, as shown for example in the paleness of the face and the haggard expression. The motor symptoms are those of motor inhibition which leads to a more or less marked incapacity to transform the nervous tension into expressive action. The former increases in proportion to the reduction of the latter. This disproportion between tension and discharge constitutes the basis of the suffering endured by the depressed.

In such a condition of emotional congestion without any refuge in expressive movements, reflex activity alone survives and often becomes excessive, as is shown in the abnormal intolerance of noise which results in protective movements.

In the agitated form of depression, where the aggressive instinct persists, the nervous dynamism is stronger and penetrates the barrier of motor inhibition, but with unsatisfactory results : on the background of psycho-nervous rigidity the discharge in move-ments is limited to impulsive, awkward and arrhythmic gestures.

The six general characteristics of the gestures in the depressed phase can be explained logically by the preceding consideration.

Special Characteristics :

Of all the special traits mentioned only two require to be explained, since the interpretation of the others would only be repetition.

Face

The bitter trait : The bitter expression of the mouth is common to all the depressed, and is one of the most obvious characteristics.

Bitterness is a mixture of gloom and disappointment. In the tabulation reproduced in Chapter III of the emotions of the child according to K. Bridges, gloom is denoted as the most primary emotion, gradually developing into rage and disgust. And like all the emotions experienced in infancy, gloom and disgust are expressed in the region of the mouth.

The bitter mouth of the depressed reveals, in the first place, emotional poverty. Then it testifies to a sense of disappointment which, as in the case of elder children and adults, is essentially a disappointment in oneself.

This sense of failure in depressed adults is psycho-biological and cannot be cured by insight. It is the incapacity to gain self-mastery that they resent and which gives them the feeling that they are victimized.

Hands

It only remains now to interpret the gesture of hiding the thumb in the closed fist. I showed, by a series of examples in my book *The Human Hand*, that the thumb represents the ego and willpower ; the gesture ' thumbs up ' corresponds to the desire to act and fight, or in other words to live and realize the personality. The gesture ' thumbs down ' reveals the opposite tendencies : resignation and self-abnegation.

C. (1). GESTURES AT MEALS OF SIX MELANCHOLICS WHO HAD BEEN GIVEN ELECTRICAL SHOCK TREATMENT

Five out of six patients had responded to the treatment. Their social attitude was almost normal except that they remained silent throughout the meal. They ate tidily and one of them excelled in her sense of order and the desire to make herself useful. She helped to clear the table and fold the tablecloth. This patient was the outstanding success of the cure. Before the treatment she had been mute, faulty in habits and impulsive.

GENERAL CHARACTERISTICS OF GESTURES

Face

The five patients who had been successfully treated had a calm but still slightly depressed facial expression. All the patients ate very near the plate.

Hands

The gestures of all the patients were characterized by—
1. Very slow motor speed.
2. Lack of emphasis.
3. Few unnecessary movements.

12

Face

Among the improved cases, one still suffered from slight twitchings of the mouth, a second was in the habit of smelling the food before eating it. The only patient who had not profited by the treatment showed signs of extreme tension, the head bowed, the eyes shut. She did not touch her food.

Hands

Apart from this last patient who kept her hands locked together on her chest, three others made no involuntary gestures. The remaining two made stereotyped gestures either by repeatedly cleaning their knife, fork, and spoon, or by tapping movements with the spoon on the plate.

INTERPRETATION

An interpretation of the general characteristics is superfluous since the preceding text has made their meaning familiar to the reader, but I will give a brief interpretation of the special characteristics. The habit of smelling food is the sign of an obsessional fear of being poisoned, an idea which is common to melancholics. A similar fear was demonstrated by the constant cleaning of the cutlery. Tapping movements like those which one of the patients performed on the plate are characteristic of people suffering from anxiety with or without depression.

(2) GESTURES AT MEALS OF SEVEN MELANCHOLICS WHO HAD NOT BEEN GIVEN ELECTRICAL SHOCK TREATMENT

SOCIAL ATTITUDE

In contrast to the preceding cases the social attitude of these patients was completely negative, neither word nor glance being exchanged. Two patients with agitated melancholia were isolated and had to be spoon-fed.

GENERAL CHARACTERISTICS

Face

The five apathetic melancholics had haggard faces and mask-like expressions. The two agitated melancholics exhibited on the contrary hypermobility of the face and general motor unrest more acute and more pronounced than all other mental patients. The face was distorted by intolerable suffering and all the expressive regions, forehead, eyes and mouth, shared in this distressing exhibition. Wailing and screaming kept the mouth region in continual distortion; the eyes rolled in every direction, and the forehead was furrowed by the suffering caused equally by the tremendous inner agitation as by the self-induced mutilizations. The patients habitually tore their hair, scratched their faces, especially the forehead, and plucked their eyebrows.

Hands

In all seven cases the gestures were : purely autistic.

In the five apathetic melancholics the characteristics of the gestures were :

1. Very few unnecessary movements.
2. Of an abnormally slow motor speed.
3. Stereotyped gestures.

SPECIAL CHARACTERISTICS OF FIVE CASES OF APATHETIC MELANCHOLIA

Facial expression and hand gestures revealed the highest degree of motor inhibition, which was also reflected in the tense postures, the legs crossed, the body bent stiffly towards the table. During seven observations the attitudes never varied and gave proof of an extraordinary perseverance. One of the patients forgot to put the morsel into her mouth and kept it in the air for several minutes as certain schizophrenics did.

The four other apathetic melancholics made occasional hiding gestures by putting the left hand on the side of the face or on the mouth in a stereotyped and persevering manner.

SPECIAL CHARACTERISTICS OF TWO CASES OF AGITATED MELANCHOLIA

The two agitated cases revealed the greatest possible motor unrest of the hands. They pressed them together or interlocked them and tore their fingers to the point of dislocating the joints. They also gnawed their fingers.

INTERPRETATION

An interpretation of the expressive traits of these cases is un-necessary, since those of the apathetic melancholics differed from psycho-motor reactions of the depressed who suffered from manic depressive psychosis only by the absence of impulsive gestures and a complete lack of nervous dynamism. The amount of psychomotor inhibition in the apathetic cases was also carried to a higher degree.

The gestures of the agitated melancholics differed in no way from those which were characteristic of certain forms of anguish, except that they also were carried to an extreme pitch.

(3) GESTURES OF TWO PATIENTS WITH DELUSIONAL INSANITY (PERSECUTION MANIA)

Owing to the fact that I have to report on only two cases of this type of mental malady I shall describe their gestures separately.

Case I never changed her posture during all seven observations. She sat with her back turned to the rest of the company in a tense posture with her legs and arms crossed, her hands held tight to the chest with the thumbs hidden in the palm. She never ate anything, but sat with her mouth hidden in her coat, which she always wore at meals. The reader will remember a description of the behaviour of paranoiacs in the professional therapy class. The same hostile attitude towards others was manifested by the manner of choosing a place at table. In the case of this patient the depression was most strongly marked and not only induced her to withdraw from every one but also to hide her face and to remain immobile. The way she sat and the posture of the hands with the thumbs turned inwards were, as I have already mentioned, typical of depression.

Case II was seated in a similar fashion at table and in the same hostile isolation, but her expressive conduct was quite different from that of the other patient. She sat with her elbows firmly on the table, legs apart. The face had a tense and furious expression with frowning forehead and piercing eyes. From time to time she made nodding movements of the head, which was thrown back.

The hands were never still and made small mechanical gestures like those of a puppet. She only interrupted these kinaesthetic obsessions to wipe her mouth. These stereotyped movements were repeated during seven different observations. She used the left hand for gestures but supported it with the right. She only ate dessert or cake, of which she nibbled small morsels without looking either at the table or the food. She smelt the cake in a suspicious manner.

INTERPRETATION

That both these women were obsessional is evident. Their persecution mania was not only shown in their approach to food but also in their attitude towards the other patients. The mixture of anguish and aggressiveness typical of many paraphrenics was revealed in facial expression, postures and gestures in Case II. The stereotyped hand gestures of the latter indicated an obsessional conflict probably below the level of consciousness which, as with many schizophrenics and imbeciles, was repeated over and over again.

(4) GESTURES AT MEALS OF TEN EPILEPTICS

Amongst the ten epileptic women there were only two of normal intelligence. The others were either mentally defective or psychotic or both. All the patients suffered from the ideopathic type of epilepsy.

In spite of the fundamental differences of the mentality and the level of intelligence, there were certain expressive traits common to the whole group and which for this very reason can be considered as most typical of the epileptic.

GENERAL CHARACTERISTICS

Face

The expression of the face alone would never, according to my experience, betray the epileptic, but I observed, in all the patients under investigation, a singular expressiveness of the eyes. They were more animated than any other part of the face. This special expression may be described as one of anxious expectation and the rolling movement of the eyes, characteristic of a failing sense of equilibrium, occurred more or less frequently in all these patients independent of an epileptic fit.

Hands

Much more notable than the facial expression was the pattern of the hand gestures, the most frequent and characteristic of which were—

1. The bending backwards of the hand with the fingers wide apart like a fan. This is a movement of extreme extension. I propose to call this gesture the 'stretching hand gesture'.

2. The lack of spatial orientation was most obvious in the clumsiness of hand movements. These were either hyper- or hypometric.

3. I noted autistic gestures of different kinds in all the patients under investigation, as well as

4. A very marked motor unrest of the hands.

The last traits are to be found in other mental maladies and are therefore less valuable from a diagnostic point of view.

SPECIAL CHARACTERISTICS

The individual traits of expressive conduct in epileptics depend on two factors :

1. The intellectual level.

2. The presence or absence of a psychosis.

The ten epileptics included six with mental deficiency, two with psychosis, two without mental deficiency or psychosis.

The six mental defectives showed all the expressions of anxiety in their face and above all in their postures and gestures, the most frequent of which consisted of :

1. holding the right hand firmly with the left in the intervals of eating ;

2. stroking gestures of one hand over the other or over other parts of the body ;

3. hiding gestures, putting the hand over mouth or profile.

In *the two psychotics* the expressions and gestures were the same as those of the schizophrenics I have described. Stretching gestures of the hand occurred in all epileptics.

The two patients of normal intelligence were the only ones with a normal social attitude. They helped the nurses to lay and clear the table. They were considered with the other patients. They took a pride in their appearance. They were not only neatly dressed but wore ear-rings, coloured combs, &c. Their hands were spotlessly clean. They ate in the grand manner. Their upright posture would have enchanted many mothers trying to instil good table manners into their children. The eating movements were slow, slightly hypermetric and mannered. Both held the fifth finger raised. Between whiles anxiety gestures were observable in the pressure of one hand on the other, &c. In both, the facile change of colour and tension of the face revealed strong emotionalism, also a display of uncertain mood : serious sad expressions suddenly changing into smiling and contented ones, recalling the expressiveness of the child. But even in moments of apparent contentment symptoms of a fundamental anguish were revealed in rolling eye movements.

INTERPRETATION

In epilepsy we are concerned with a psycho-biological condition in which the organic factor is more tangible than in most cases of mental malady. The epileptic fit in itself is proof of an anomaly of the brain which attacks consciousness and the sense of balance. And in the expressions and gestures which are limited to those suffering from this malady it is easy to discern the defects which exist in certain cerebral functions. These are the stretching gestures of the hands and the hypermetric movements which announce the failing sense of balance in the epileptic subject. The expression of anguish in the face and the corresponding gestures of the hands are more a secondary psychological consequence of the epileptic condition. I have already stressed the fact that in all cases where the sense of equilibrium is feeble, a chronic state of anxiety and anguish is established.

The expressive conduct of the two patients of normal intelligence is particularly interesting, for it throws light on the epileptic temperament manifested also in potential epileptics.

The facial expression of both patients was similar and reflected the ambivalence and superficiality of the emotions, differing from the infantile pattern only in the permanent tension produced by subconscious anxiety.

The gestures of the hand revealed self-consciousness and a decorative sense as well as a certain impulsiveness. The last automatically produced hypermetric movements as an anticipatory unconscious measure of defence against latent catastrophe—the fit.

It is true that the traits of temperament which I have enumerated here as seen in the expressions and gestures of these two examples do not account for all the typical qualities of the epileptic make-up, but they show its essential structure.

I conclude the chapter on the pathology of gesture with those two cases because they were nearest to the normal and stood a good chance of returning to normal existence.

CHAPTER VI

RESULTS AND CONCLUSIONS

IN this study of gesture I have confined myself to certain aspects only of a vast subject. My object has been to investigate the laws of those psycho-dynamics which are the basis of emotional gestures and of the expression of identity.

Through a genetic theory and a clinical study I found sufficient evidence that correlations exist—

1. Between emotional make-up and gesture.
2. Between the degree of integration and gesture.

A scientific study of gesture requires as premise the consistency of psycho-motor responses. This has been proved to exist by Allport and Vernon, among others, in their *Studies in Expressive Movements*.

The investigations of both authors were concerned with normal people. In my own study, based on pathological material, I have been able to show that consistency of psycho-motor response increases with the severity of a mental malady. The more advanced the disintegration of the personality the more stereotyped and restricted do the gestures become. This result has a great deal of scientific and practical interest, since it is applicable not only to the psychology of the insane but also to psychology in general.

I commence this chapter with some of the most striking results and conclusions so that the reader may the more easily understand the detailed ones which follow.

In the psychotic patients a regression of emotions into childhood patterns can be observed along with a high degree of disintegration. The disagreeable emotions such as gloom, fear, disgust and rage prevail over the agreeable ones and, as in children, appear in a direct and uninhibited form.

The power of the imagination as an incentive to emotional upheaval as well as emotional expression is one of the most striking facts arrived at through the clinical observations. This influence grows in proportion to the disintegration of the personality and the consequent failure to adapt to reality. The more the power of adaptation is restricted the more subcortical functions prevail and take the place of voluntary activity.

The clinical studies further demonstrate that subcortical expressions are not rigidly limited to one type of mental malady. Similar expressive traits can be found in different mental illnesses and, in a lesser degree, in normal people. The fact that, on the whole, no strict correlation can be found between a certain type of psychosis and a certain type of gesture is proof in itself that the latter is more determined by the psychological than the neurological element of mental abnormality.

An exception, as I have pointed out, is presented by the epileptic condition, in which abnormal brain functions, rather than psychological factors, dominate the scene of psycho-motor behaviour.

These are the most obvious conclusions to be drawn from the clinical observations. I shall now discuss the outcome of each and in the same order as the studies were made.

I. GENERAL DEDUCTIONS FROM THE SOCIAL ATTITUDE OF THE PATIENTS IN THE FEMALE AND MALE OCCUPATIONAL THERAPY CLASSES

The general observations throw some light on the social attitudes of mental patients. The women are more gregarious than the men and exhibit more emotional intercourse, both in its positive and its negative form. They are more inclined to form themselves into groups and cliques and their lack of self-sufficiency seems to be more marked than that of the male patients. They are superior in creating a lively and homely atmosphere and in deriving some emotional gratification out of group life and group work. They are also, as one might expect, more easily disturbed by each other than the men. Their comradeship resembles that of children with its emotional display and ambivalence. The men, even those suffering from complete disintegration, as in the case of schizophrenia, retain a more natural aloofness from each other, which points to a stronger individuality. Individuality must be understood here as the capacity to live and behave as a separate entity. Though the inclination to form groups is more marked in the women, the opposite tendency, that of complete isolation, appears in them also in a more extreme form than in the men. This is not, as would appear, a contradiction. Melancholics, paranoiacs and some schizophrenics hide in corners or choose seats where they are unobserved by their fellow-patients. This behaviour is only the reverse side of that previously described :

the clustering together. It shows a greater need to demonstrate aloofness than the men seem to require, and this corresponds, I think, to a weakness of their individuality which produces an unconscious desire to exhibit an independence that is really non-existent.

Who are the most social and who are the most antisocial types among the patients *apart from sex difference* ?

I have already answered the question who are the most anti-social types : certain paranoiacs, melancholics, and deteriorated schizophrenics. It has been interesting to observe that the most social patients could not be easily classified in accordance with the type of their illness. Certain paraphrenics, who had been diagnosed as suffering from confusional psychosis, or depressed psychosis, as well as patients with a milder form of schizophrenia, mixed just as well as some epileptics and patients with manic depressive psychosis in the hypomaniac phase. If the typology of Kretschmer into schizoid and cycloid groups of temperament is correct one would expect epileptics and hypomaniacs to be far better mixers than schizophrenics, who, according to Kretschmer ought to be entirely devoid of any capacity for contact. I wonder therefore if the typology suggested by Kretschmer has a solid foundation. The material of this study is not extensive enough to answer the question positively one way or the other ; but questionable it certainly is.

A strong group feeling does not seem to depend on psycho-biological types but rather on a state of reduced identity. Un-certainty of self seems to provide a stronger link with others than a well centralized ego. Either a fully established or an entirely abolished identity acts as a bar to group attachment. The extravert type of Jung and the cycloid of Kretschmer in their purest forms represent the most independent human entities, those who can most easily do without any reassurance and reinforcement from others. They look for companionship rather to expand their ego than to merge it into a group personality. Perhaps this explains why such introvert or schizoid people as the Germans can be so completely absorbed into a national group while the much more extravert Frenchmen remain individualists and discourage group units. Whatever may be the answer to the puzzle of human typology the inclination to form groups does not depend on the type of man but on his state of inner stability. That is why, in some lighter cases of paraphrenia and even schizophrenia, where centralization is weak without being completely broken up, one finds group feeling very much alive.

While the social attitude of sufferers from severe paranoia is actively hostile, that of melancholics is marked by negativism and indetermination. In a lesser degree a similar behaviour is noticeable in normal people suffering from depression. Again it is the state of mind rather than the type of personality which dictates social or asocial behaviour.

Another trait characteristic of the social attitude of the patients is the conservatism of habit. They regroup themselves each day in the same way. This stereotyped behaviour indicates a lack of spontaniety and sense of adventure and can be found in many people outside the mental hospital, who feel the need of a solid background to counteract a feeling of inner instability. At the same time indolent and inert people also prefer fixed habits, for in both the capacity for adaptation is reduced.

II. DETAILED DEDUCTIONS

The method of study consisted in comparing the gestures with the clinical diagnosis and in a great number of cases with a diagnosis from hand features. This approach makes it possible to establish correlations between :

    I. Types of gesture and types of mental illness.

    II. Types of gesture and hand-types.

    III. Types of gesture and types of personality, the latter being assessed by means of a psychology of the hand (see C. Wolff, *The Human Hand*).

I have tabulated the most frequent gestures I observed, and Tables I and II show the psycho-motor reactions of the patients at work and at meals respectively.

Table I consists of 33 items, starting with the most habitual type of gesture in schizophrenics and continuing in the order of their frequency. Table II contains 37 items arranged in the same order as in Table I. The reader can thus see that the frequency of certain gestures changes considerably in the same mental malady at work and at meals. I have not included the two cases of hysteria in Table I and the two of paranoia in Table II as their number was too small for useful comparison.

For a depth study of personality the number of subjects is necessarily limited ; but there are sufficient to arrive at valuable conclusions because they are mental patients and mental maladies produce similar psycho-motor symptoms.

In the Introduction to this book I have expressed my doubts as to the value of the statistical method in individual depth psychology. I give the tables in this chapter only in order to show the complexity of results in as simple and concentrated a form as possible so that the characteristic expressive traits can be read at a glance. I must stress the fact that no tables can ever replace individual description, since subtle differentiations cannot be shown in them : and it is just those subtleties that count in a subject as delicate and difficult as the interpretation of gestures.

The reader will find Table I and II together with Tables III and IV at the end of the book.

A. DISCUSSION OF TABLE I (GESTURES AT WORK)

The first six items of Table I represent symptoms of extreme psycho-motor inhibition.   They are most marked in schizophrenics, least so in manic-depressive patients.   In the latter, arrhythmic and stereotyped gestures occur also in the hypomaniac phase, a fact which proves that even under the influence of an euphoric animation the mechanism of inhibition persists up to a point.   Autistic gestures (see Table II) are also found in a lesser degree in hypomaniac patients, which in my opinion is a proof of their characteristic narcissism.   In schizophrenics and paraphrenics the same type of gestures has a different meaning, namely the maintenance of identity.   In the first case the autistic gestures refer to an infantile exhibitionism which goes with self-satisfaction ; in the latter cases they refer to a complex of uncertainty of self which goes with anxiety.   The term ' autistic ' covers therefore an expressive complexity which requires a detailed classification to make it valid for a psychological interpretation.   For example, ' autistic gestures of an exhibitionistic type ' or of an ' anxiety type ' must be differentiated, for they are due to different psychological causes.

Arrhythmic gestures are less frequent in normal people than in abnormal, but they are certainly not limited to mental patients.   In the latter they are present in opposite psycho-dynamic conditions : those, for example, of hypomania and depression.   They go equally with spatial exaggeration of movement as with spatial reduction of movement.   Rhythm of movement, on the contrary, is due to a perfect balance or co-ordination between impulse and expression. It is evident that arrhythmic gestures are the natural consequence of a lack of mental balance. In distress and rage, but also in exuberant joy, the co-ordination between nervous tension and expressive actions is imperfect. But why are arrhythmic gestures a symptom of inhibition if they accompany the states of elation and even euphory ? I have already mentioned in Chapter III that agreeable emotions when pushed beyond a certain point develop into disagreeable emotions. From this one can understand that every inner condition lacking balance contains an element of inhibition, which is expressed by abrupt changes of movement. In schizophrenic and melancholic patients the forward impulse is at its lowest and abrupt movements occur all the time. In hypomaniacs, on the contrary, the forward impulse is strong but may also be hindered by an underlying inhibition. Arrhythmy of gesture does not serve as a diagnostic indication for a single state of mind or a particular mental illness. It only indicates a mental and emotional want of balance.

Complete inhibition of forward impulses is distinctly more marked in schizophrenics than in other patients and has a similar significance to that of perseverance. Both complete inhibition and perseverance are evidently characteristic of schizophrenia or, in a lesser degree, of a schizoid make-up and thus have a more definite psycho-diagnostic value.

Perseverance of gestures is an expressive trait which has been much studied in psychological laboratories as an indication of a schizoid make-up. As Table I demonstrates, the percentage (92 per cent) of persevering gestures is highest in schizophrenia and occurs only in one case of manic-depressive psychosis in the depressed phase.

Stereotyped gestures reveal obsessional traits which, because of their nature, always release inhibitive mechanisms. It is interesting to note that their frequency is almost equal in the three types of mental malady. For this reason their value for differential diagnosis is negative. As I mentioned in Chapter III, stereotyped gestures are specially connected with the sense of balance, and it is these which develop in the first place the kinaesthetic consciousness. This form of consciousness precedes the mental phase in the development of the child, and it is evident that in mental disorders a regression to this more primary phase of mental expression takes the place of an adequate expression of thought.

Obsessions prevent the proper functioning of voluntary impulse and objective consciousness.

As stereotyped gestures always go with an obsessional make-up they reveal a limited spontaneity and subjectivism, but, as in the case of autistic gestures, they may express both agreeable and disagreeable emotions.

In the hypomaniac person they are similar to the enjoyable kinaesthetic arabesques of children, while in paranoiacs and schizophrenics they are only designed to re-establish a certain self-assurance and are coloured with anguish.

Quantity of unnecessary movements is neither characteristic of the nature of a mental malady nor significant of the type of temperament ; schizophrenics, for example, make as many unnecessary movements as hypomaniac patients. Unnecessary movements are only the symptom of an inner agitation which can take many different forms of expression. Combined with extreme inhibition (as in schizophrenia), unnecessary movements are entirely reflexes of an extensor type ; combined with strong forward impulses, they take on an emotional and pleasurable quality, as can be seen in the many decorative gestures of hypomaniac patients. To arrive at a true interpretation of their meaning it is always necessary to specify their character as being either inhibitive or expansive.

Hair gestures. I shall now, before coming to slow motor speed, discuss hair gestures, since they, too, have a significance similar to that of many ' unnecessary movements '. They are autistic gestures of a special type. One comes across them outside the mental hospital and more often in women than in men. They always contain a strong element of self-consciousness. They are very frequent in schizophrenics, for whom, as I have explained, they appear to be an outlet for nervous tension and at the same time a source of self-assurance. In these cases they are anxiety movements characteristic of a feeble or shattered identity. But they are also very frequent in hypomaniac patients (see Table II), in whom they have quite another significance, since they are carried out in quite another way.

Hypomaniacs touch their hair and arrange it, with obvious pleasure, whilst schizophrenics seem to fear contact with it. The gestures of the former are made slowly, with the hands relaxed, and are movements of flexion ; those of the latter are, as a rule, made quickly and are movements of extension. To find a psychodiagnostic value in hair gestures it is necessary to observe at the same time the motor speed and the quality of the movement (extensor or flexor).

Motor speed is naturally an indispensable quality of gesture and a *slow motor speed* seems to be specially characteristic of schizophrenics and, as we shall see later, melancholics. But this quality of movement is nevertheless not limited to a specially inhibited dynamism since it is to be found in hypomaniac patients as well (see Table II). Considered apart from other psycho-motor traits, slow motor speed is not an indication of a state of mind. Its diagnostic value changes if it is combined with decorative or anxiety movements, with centripetal or centrifugal gestures, with or without emphasis of gesture, &c. But slow motor speed is certainly most frequent in those mental states that go with marked inhibition.

Here I must interrupt the sequence of my discussion of Table I to discuss the different types of motor speed together.

Fast motor speed (Item 20) is most marked in manic-depressive patients, but oddly enough in the cases of hypomania (see Table II) slow motor speed is more frequent. Owing to the fact that it occurs also in 3 out of 13 schizophrenics this quality of gesture has no special significance which can be used for differential diagnosis. It depends neither on a strong nor a weak dynamism, but rather on conflict between forward impulse and inhibition, and is therefore most marked in the agitated, whether depressed or not. It represents an energetic attempt to overcome the obstacle of inhibition. As far as could be seen from this clinical study motor speed is not correlated with the type of temperament as Enke, among others, maintained.

Ambivalent motor speed (Item 30) must be understood as an abrupt change from a fast tempo to a slow one and vice versa. As Table I illustrates, this trait is absent in schizophrenics and is found in the majority of paraphrenic patients. It is they who exhibit in the most marked degree instability of mood and impulsiveness. From this one must conclude that ambivalent motor speed goes with a lack of cohesion of emotion as well as of images. A trend of thought or of feeling is easily interrupted and replaced by another, often the opposite, and this lack of pattern produces a state of psycho-dynamic confusion. It must be remembered that paraphrenic patients are people with kinks who, apart from localized delusions, behave like normal people. This make-up explains the irregularities and bizarre quality of all their expressions and in particular their motor speed. In ordinary life a lesser degree of irregular tempo can be seen in persons with emotionalism and paranoiac tendencies.

Non-emphatic gestures are lacking in verve. They are slight and without conviction. This characteristic is most common in schizophrenics and, as is seen in Table I, does not occur in manic-depressive patients. Non-emphatic gestures are not limited to any mental malady but most frequently go with a state of depression. They are the outcome of an impoverished dynamism which is unable to produce sufficient nervous tension. For this reason they are to be found in all cases where the nervous vitality is exhausted.

Mask-like Expression. I have explained the term in the previous chapter. This expression, or rather lack of expression, was more frequent in schizophrenics at work than at meals. But the trait is most frequent in apathetic melancholics (see Table II).

Sniffing, smelling, and giggling are particularly noticeable in catatonic schizophrenics. These movements are known as an expression of catatonic excitement. They have a diagnostic value for mental malady, especially for schizophrenia. However, the fact that they are met with in cases of paraphrenia and in some cases of melancholia shows that this peculiarity is not limited to one mental condition only. But when found in other maladies or in persons who are not inmates of a mental hospital it is always proof of a schizoid element.

Writhing Movements. These gestures of the hands are definitely limited to mental malady. I have never observed them in neurotics or normal people but almost exclusively in schizophrenics and in only one case of paraphrenia. Writhing movements can therefore be considered as frequently associated with schizophrenia.

Impulsive gestures are much less frequent in schizophrenics at work than at meals (compare Tables I and II). But they are not limited to one mental malady and, as everyone knows, are quite common outside the mental hospital. They are a marked characteristic of epileptics and paraphrenics and originate from a ' spastic ' state of mind which is produced by a mixture of anguish and aggression. Taken alone they have no value for differential diagnosis, but when they appear habitually with emotionalism they are indicative of nervous and emotional instability combined with aggressiveness.

General motor unrest is a common trait of psycho-motor behaviour and is neither limited to a mental malady nor to a single type of neurosis. It is the result of a nervous agitation which cannot find a satisfactory outlet.

It occurs in 5 out of 8 paraphrenic patients at work and in all epileptic patients at meals. It is particularly evident in the agitated melancholics, who cannot remain still for a moment (see Table II).

Hypermobility of the face forms part of general motor unrest and is to be found in lesser percentage in patients at work than at meals.

It is evident that hypermobility of facial expression is also not limited to mental malady, but is a sign of emotional and nervous instability. It is most often noticeable either in those suffering from anxiety and impulsiveness such as paraphrenics or in manic-depressive patients in the transition phase.

Quiet and contented expression of face is to be found in certain hebephrenic and imbecile psychotics. In paraphrenics this type of facial expression is rare since most of them suffer from ideas of persecution.

Facial tics were comparatively rare in the mental maladies which I investigated, but occurred most often in cases of schizophrenia. They occur in cases of cerebellar insufficiency but are by no means restricted to mental illness ; they are often to be found in nervous people, children, and adults. According to Dr. Earl they are linked with an obsessional complex. Obsessional fixation and the anguish which results can affect cerebellar functions particularly in neurasthenic people. These often lack calcium, which encourages a spastic type of nervous reaction.

Wringing, pressing, and interlocking of the hands occur most often in depressed people and are found in 3 out of 5 manic-depressive patients. It must be remembered that one of the cases investigated was in a depressed phase and two others in a transition phase. This psycho-motor feature (see Table II) is characteristic of the agitated form of depression and always expresses profound anguish. These gestures are well known outside the mental hospital in people who are in the throes of expectation or haunted by fear. They are also to be found in schizophrenia and paraphrenia, which shows that they are not limited to a specific malady.

Centrifugal gestures are directed towards the surroundings and differ essentially from centripetal and autistic gestures. Centrifugal gestures occur often in paraphrenic patients, according to Table I, and in hypomaniac patients according to Table II. They seldom occur in schizophrenics, who, as I have shown, excel in autistic gestures. Centrifugal gestures are often expansive, in which case

13

they indicate a strong and living dynamism. Such a condition is realized in the highest degree in hypomaniac patients, in the lowest degree in apathetic melancholics. But centrifugal gestures can also be without emphasis, in which case they appear to be purely mechanical or reflex movements.

Hiding gestures are a special form of autistic gesture and reveal fear of contact with others. They are well known in ordinary life in very shy people and in mental patients they are most often found in the depressed. It is interesting to note that their frequency in melancholic patients who have received Electrical Shock Treatment exceeds that of those who have not been cured. The gesture goes with a certain self-consciousness as well as with a certain consciousness of surroundings. In profound depression the latter ceases altogether.

Mouth and tongue gestures are typical of schizophrenia and are part of the syndrome of catatonic excitement. They are also to be found, but in a very low percentage, in paraphrenics and melancholics and these cases must be considered as fundamentally schizoid. I had occasion to observe these gestures outside the mental hospital in two cases of hysteria.

Emphatic gestures are most definitely marked in paraphrenia, where one also finds the highest percentage of impulsive movements. The person who employs them wishes to convince either himself or others or both. Emphasis has always a more or less unconscious element of persuasion. The ego is in the ascendant in people with emphatic gestures, whether they are mental patients or not : an ego which is in fact feeble but pretends to be strong.

Aggressive expressions of the face rarely occurred in schizophrenic patients but was to be seen in the majority of the paraphrenic and in 50 per cent of the manic-depressive patients.

It is interesting to note that none of the melancholics had an aggressive look and that amongst the manic-depressive patients observed at meals, none of the hypomaniacs exhibited this expressive quality. A permanent aggressiveness goes with a strongly emotional make-up, combined with an obsessional complex.

Rolling eyes seem to be connected with a failing sense of balance. The symptom always reveals a state of acute anxiety or panic.

Index gestures should be divided into two categories. I noticed them in two schizophrenics and described their manner of raising the index finger as ' passive ' and not demonstrative. In such a case it is more correct to speak of a posture rather than a gesture as it persists for some length of time. The same posture can be seen in small children who are still uncertain of their balance. This posture is connected with a deficient sense of equilibrium so marked in schizophrenics. The demonstrative gesture of the index finger was observed in two religious maniacs who behaved like ' orators '.

Expansive gestures are centrifugal gestures of a special type. They are characteristic of elation and the desire to convince others. That is why they are most often found in hypomaniacs whose dynamism is increased or in religious and other maniacs (paraphrenics) who are possessed by the desire to impose their ideas on others. Certainly expansive gestures are not confined to mental patients. They are habitual with orators, demagogues or people who want to convince others. They also often express exuberant joy and other pleasurable emotions of an egoistic type.

Pulling hair and plucking eyebrows do not occur in schizophrenic and hypomaniac patients. These gestures are most frequent in agitated melancholics, (see Table II) in manic-depressive patients in the depressed phase, and in paranoiacs.

Opening and closing of the fists has been observed in one case of paranoia and is due to an aimless excitement, and represents a regression to early childhood similar to that of hiding the thumb in the palm.

Hyper- or hypometric gestures are due to lack of motor balance and to a lack of instinctive judgement of proportion, which affects not only the insane but also normal people. It is characteristic of states of anguish and rage, both of which impair the sense of equilibrium.

Thumb-in-palm posture was only observed in one manic-depressive patient, but this posture is well known in normal people in a state of abnormal fatigue or depression. It is a regressive infantile posture expressing the desire for repose and protection.

B. DISCUSSION OF TABLE II (GESTURES AT MEALS)

The material of Table II has a wider range than that of Table I and includes melancholics (treated and non-treated) as well as ten epileptics.

Taking the first seven psycho-motor items together—(1) autistic gestures, (2) persevering gestures, (3) stereotyped gestures, (4) reflex movements only, (5) arrhythmic gestures, (6) forward impulses entirely inhibited, (7) slow motor speed—one can see that all these traits of extreme inhibition are present in 100 per cent of schizo-phrenics and 100 per cent of apathetic melancholics who have not been given Electrical Shock Treatment. The manic-depres-sive patients who were in the depressed phase exhibit, as one would expect, the same psycho-motor characteristics apart from ' entire inhibition of forward movements'. The group of epileptics show the same characteristics in an overwhelming majority. This demon-strates two things :

1. That the same expressive reactions are much more pronounced when tested at meals than when tested at work.

2. That no single psycho-motor trait of inhibition is character-istic of one mental malady, since certain underlying psycho-dynamic conditions are similar in different mental diseases.

The six treated melancholics, five of whom benefited from the treatment, showed that these seven traits of profound motor inhibi-tion disappeared to a great extent. Amongst the three hypomaniac patients one finds the complete absence of the same traits except for Items 1, 3 and 7. The last, slow motor speed, is particularly marked. From this observation one can conclude that, in the hypomaniac phase, an underlying obsessional pattern persists independent of changes of dynamism, mood, and vitality.

With regard to the ten epileptics with marked inhibitive traits I must repeat that a large percentage among them were schizophrenics.

Many unnecessary movements (Item 8) is found in 100 per cent of schizophrenic, hypomaniac, and epileptic patients, in the two cases of agitated melancholia, and in none of the apathetic melan-cholics. This trait is also, on the whole, more marked at meals than at work. Two fundamentally different conditions, schizo-phrenia and hypomania, exhibit the same psycho-motor quality, which proves that this quality is not connected either with an increased or a decreased dynamism. In schizophrenia many un-necessary movements are the result of increased reflex activity which involves the spine, in hypomania they are the result of an emotional animation which involves the interbrain, especially the hypothalamus region. They are movements of defence in the former and movements of expansion in the latter condition.

The same explanation can be applied to *hair gestures* (Item 9). These occur in the same category of patients as item 8, but according to Table II are comparatively more frequent in hypomaniacs than in schizophrenics. Moreover, they are to be found in the two agitated melancholics not treated, in whom they can be interpreted in the same way as in schizophrenic patients, namely as expression of profound anguish and as an attempt to maintain a feeling of identity.

Mask-like expression is typical of melancholia or profound depression. It does not, naturally, occur in the two cases of agitated melancholia, and it is interesting to note that all those patients who had been successfully treated with Electrical Shock Treatment had lost this typical trait of melancholia. As a mask-like expression also occurred in the depressed phase of manic-depressive psychosis and in schizophrenia, it has only a limited value for diagnostic purposes.

Sniffing, smelling, and giggling, especially the first and the last, are, on the contrary, typical of schizophrenic psychosis. Smelling might be considered separately, for this regressive psycho-motor habit occurs in other mental illnesses, especially in melancholia and paraphrenia. In the material of this study it only occurred in one of the apathetic melancholics who had not reacted to the Electrical Shock Treatment.

Writhing movements, characteristic of schizophrenics, were much more marked in those patients tested at meals than those tested at work. This might be explained through the calming influence of manual occupation, which reduces the profound nervous tension and inhibition of schizophrenics.

Impulsive gestures appeared in 100 per cent of schizophrenics at meals in comparison with about 30 per cent at work. The difference in frequency is probably due to the same reason as the differences in the previous category, namely the soothing effect of the work in the occupational therapy class. Impulsive gestures appeared in 100 per cent of the epileptics. Impulsive gestures, as I have already explained, are produced by an agitation which conflicts with strong inhibitions. There are different types of impulsive gestures, due to different mental and expressive mechanisms. Impulsiveness can be produced by images, which arouse aggressive emotions ; this is the case in paraphrenics and in certain epileptics. Impulsive gestures which express such a state of mind are the result of a mixture of mental and emotional activity. The same holds good for normal people who react in an impulsive fashion ; in their case impulsive reactions and expressions are likely to be aroused by a real interference from the outside world. In deteriorated schizophrenics, impulsive reactions are on a purely reflex level and seem to have no connexion with any mental or even emotional process. The food on the neighbour's plate is more attractive to them than their own food, which makes them snatch the piece of bread which does not belong to them. This is a regressive impulsive reaction on the level of a child of 2 years old, and seems to be revived on a subconscious level without any mental repercussion.

General motor unrest results from increased reflex activity leading to automatism. Automatism is particularly pronounced in those mental and emotional states which go with the disintegration of personality.

Hypermobility of facial expression was found in 100 per cent of hypomaniac and epileptic patients and in four out of seven schizophrenics. In the last it occurred more often at meals than at work, another proof of the calming effect of occupation.

Quiet facial expression occurred only in four melancholic patients who had been successfully treated. No schizophrenic patient had a quiet face at meals, while some of them, and one manic-depressive patient, looked contented and peaceful at work.

Facial tics were only observed in one melancholic and one epileptic patient.

Wringing, pressing, and interlocking of the hands were entirely absent in schizophrenics at meals, but they occurred at work. At meals they were most frequent in agitated melancholics and epileptics.

Fast motor speed only occurred in the two agitated melancholics and in those two epileptic patients who were not psychotic.

Centrifugal gestures are the opposite of autistic gestures and occurred in all hypomaniac patients.

Hiding gestures go with depression and anxiety. They are movements of self-protection, either against other people or against painful sensory impressions such as loud noises.

In the first case they are more on an emotional, in the last case more on a purely reflex level. It may be noted that they occurred in all melancholics who had been successfully treated and in none of the cases of extreme agony, represented by the two agitated melancholics. Hiding gestures are not only movements of self-protection but also of self-consciousness. The latter vanishes when the mind is in the throes of unbearable despair.

Mouth and tongue gestures, typical of schizophrenia, were also more frequent at meals than at work.

Emphatic gestures belong properly to epileptic patients (100 per cent) but they appeared also in two cases of agitated melancholia. It is interesting to note that the hypomaniac patients showed no emphasis in their movements, which were, on the contrary, rather light and floating. In Table I the manic depressives were noted for their emphatic gestures. It must be remembered that only one of the five patients observed at work was in a geniune state of hypomania, the three others in an ambivalent state, and one completely depressed. It is evident that the transition stage produces a painful agitation, a conflict between elation and depression together with an attitude of resistance to the enfeeblement of the ego and the consequent urgent necessity for self-assertion. Epileptics are by nature 'childish', who try to make a good effect and to show off. This tendency may account, in the two patients who were otherwise normal, for emphatic gestures. In the other epileptic cases (psychotic and imbecile) this explanation does not hold good. With them the same trait can be interpreted as the result of continual suspense and nervous tension, together with a lack of spatial measure which has a biological basis but produces the same results as psychological causes. Naturally biological and mental factors cannot be rigidly divided, for they are inseparably linked, but either the former or the latter have the predominant influence on psycho-motor behaviour.

Aggressive facial expression and rolling eyes. None of the schizophrenic patients showed an aggressive expression at meals, while they behaved much more impulsively then than at work. This might be explained through the fact that their impulsiveness is devoid of any real emotion and mental association.

The 'rolling eyes' are typical of epileptics in 100 per cent of whom they appear. They refer to a state of continual underlying panic, which can be explained as a permanent subconscious expectancy of an epileptic fit.

Expansive gestures occur in all hypomaniacs and in those two epileptic patients who were neither imbecile nor schizophrenic. Expansive gestures are the outcome of an enriched dynamism and, contrary to centrifugal gestures, with which they are closely allied, they have a certain emphasis and vigour.

Items 29–31 do not need special mention. They occurred rarely in the patients investigated and their meaning is obvious.

Hyper- and hypometric gestures are characteristic of epileptics and hypomaniacs in whom there is a lack of spatial judgement. A nurse informed me that one of the latter was in the habit of writing on the walls of the ward in immense letters when she was excited. This exaggeration of movement goes with abnormal emotionalism.

Thumb-up and thumb-in-palm gesture occurred in isolated cases, the first gesture in a hypomaniac, the last in a depressed patient.

The fifth finger raised was observed in one schizophrenic, two hypomaniacs and two epileptics. This gesture is a pretentious mannerism of an exhibitionist type.

Affected or precious gestures were used by all hypomaniac patients who, in this respect, resemble the two hysterical women that I have described in the clinical study. This type of gesture has its origin in a marked narcissism.

Stretching gestures of the hand are limited entirely to epileptics and are therefore the most outstanding feature of the psycho-motor behaviour of this illness. Their origin has already been explained.

CONCLUSIONS

It is evident that an isolated trait of psycho-motor behaviour has no diagnostic value and even a certain number of traits of the same type are insufficient for diagnosis. But, as we shall see, there are different expressive motor patterns which reflect the psycho-dynamic state in mental illness and health.

C. FIVE FUNDAMENTAL PSYCHO-MOTOR PATTERNS DERIVED FROM THE CLINICAL OBSERVATIONS

PSYCHO-MOTOR PATTERN. I : EXTREME INHIBITION

(a) Reflex movements of an extensor type predominant.
(b) Movements of withdrawal predominant.
(c) Forward movements more or less entirely inhibited.
(d) Stereotyped movements.
(e) Arrhythmical movements.
(f) Perseverance of movements.
(g) Autistic gestures of an anxiety type (especially hair gestures).
(h) General motor unrest of a reflex type.
(k) Slow motor speed.
(l) Many unnecessary movements. (This pattern is most indicative of schizophrenia.)

PSYCHO-MOTOR PATTERN. II : DEPRESSION

(a) Slow motor speed.
(b) Few unnecessary movements.

(c) Traits of extreme inhibition according to degree and nature of depression.
(d) Hiding gestures.
(e) Non-emphatic and fugacious movements.
(f) Hesitating gestures.
(g) Mask-like expression of the face.
(h) Thumb-in-palm gesture.
(k) Perseverance of tight postures.

PSYCHO-MOTOR PATTERN. III : ELATION

(a) Many unnecessary movements.
(b) Fast motor speed.
(c) Expansive gestures.
(d) Autistic gestures of an exhibitionist type.
(e) Rhythmical movements.
(f) Spontaneous gestures and postures.
(g) Emphatic and self-assertive gestures.
(h) Slightly affected or mannered gestures.
(k) Thumbs-up gesture.
(l) Radiant facial expression.

PSYCHO-MOTOR PATTERN. IV : ANXIETY (CHRONIC)

(a) Autistic gestures of the anxiety type—hiding gestures and hair gestures in particular.
(b) Perseverance of gestures.
(c) Increased reflex movements.
(d) Many unnecessary movements.
(e) Pressing, wringing, interlocking of hands.
(f) Ambivalent motor speed.
(g) Hypermobility of facial expression.
(h) Centrifugal gestures mixed with autistic gestures.
(k) Rolling eyes and staring.
(l) Forward impulses more or less inhibited in proportion to the degree of anxiety.
(m) Closing and opening of the fists.
(n) Plucking eyebrows, pulling hair, scratching face, &c.
(o) Aimless fidgeting movements of the fingers.
(p) Supporting one hand with the other.
(q) Holding on to some object—handkerchief, &c.

PSYCHO-MOTOR PATTERN. V : SPASTIC EMOTIONAL REACTION TYPE

(PATHOLOGICAL EXAMPLE : EPILEPSY)

(*a*) Many unnecessary movements.
(*b*) Stereotyped movements.
(*c*) Reflex movements increased.
(*d*) Perseverance of movements.
(*e*) Impulsive gestures.
(*f*) Emphatic gestures.
(*g*) Expansive gestures.
(*h*) Hyper- and hypometric gestures.
(*k*) Stretching hand gestures (only in epileptics).
(*l*) Opening and closing of fists.
(*m*) Autistic gestures of both types.
(*n*) Ambivalent motor speed.
(*o*) Hypermobility of facial expression.
(*p*) Facial tics (seldom).

(1) *Diagnostic Value of Psycho-Motor Patterns for Mental Illness*

The grouping of single expressive traits in five fundamental psycho-motor patterns permits a classification which has a relative value for the diagnosis of certain mental illnesses. It is obvious that to a great extent the patterns contain the same elements, but it is their combination which counts, as in chemistry, where the same elements differently blended form different chemical substances. It must also be stressed that different psycho-motor patterns can combine one with another in proportion to the character of the malady and the individual predispositions of the patient.

There is one other difficulty in the diagnosis of mental maladies from gesture which needs elucidation. The reader will understand that the patterns described are largely common to normal people besides mental patients, but with this difference, that in the insane these psycho-motor responses are mostly based on imaginary situations. That is the crucial point. The same reactions produced by exterior causes are characteristic of emotional patterns in general and represent a valuable aid in personality diagnosis. Only in schizophrenics and epilectics can postural and motor behaviour directly indicate the malady. In the latter, stretching gestures of the hand, together with marked hypermetric movements as well as other expressive traits, are characteristic of the malady. I must here mention that the staccato voice so often found in epilepsy is also contributive to diagnosis. There are circumstances in which means of assessing this illness, other than the epileptic fit itself, would be invaluable, for there are many epileptics who may be free from fits for a long period. And certain traits classified under the spastic emotional reaction type can reveal an epileptic or quasi-epileptic disposition. In Courts of Justice the understanding of such a disposition is of the first importance. Certainly diagnosis according to gesture alone would not be absolutely convincing, but it could guide the physician and psychologist in the right direction. The last word in the diagnosis of real or potential epilepsy remains with the Encephalograph of Berger and Adrian of which I have already spoken.

It now remains to indicate the line to be followed for the diagnosis of other mental maladies which I have treated in the Clinical Study.

Paraphrenia. Paraphrenics are emotional and unstable obsessionals. In them, the illness only concerns a part of their being and at certain times they have the closest resemblance to ordinary people. The difference between the unstable and obsessional type of personality and the paraphrenic consists in the unrestricted power of the obsession in the latter over the imaginative and expressive processes. It is hardly necessary to say that in the case of paraphrenia this power is omnipotent and destroys the judgement of what is real and what is imaginary. Identity becomes reduced or abolished by an overpowering obsession. Expressive traits described in pattern 5 are characteristic of paraphrenia when they appear, so to speak, out of the blue in an entirely irrational way and solely due to the reality of an imaginary situation.

Manic-depressive Psychosis. As the term indicates, two opposing elements form the underlying structure of this malady. Taken alone, the traits, described respectively under the psycho-motor patterns of Depression and Elation, would be deceptive. The former is characteristic of melancholy, the latter of a state of exuberant joy, which is perfectly normal. In manic-depressive psychosis the elements of obsession are united to those of depression and euphory, and one finds in these patients gestures characteristic

(*a*) of depression or elation ;
(*b*) persevering and stereotyped gestures.

The two tables make this point clear. In manic-depressive psychosis the behaviour has always a stilted quality. In the phase of depression the patients seem to be somewhat more alive than genuine melancholics, while in a state of hypomania they behave in a more affected, self-conscious and strained way than people without psychosis under the influence of elation. This behaviour is produced and maintained by images alone, the loss of contact with the surroundings being more or less complete. But, as the Clinical Study has shown, it is not always possible to make a differential diagnosis between the depressed phase of Manic-depressive Psychosis and Melancholia.

Melancholia can take an apathetic or agitated form. The former may be recognized from the psycho-motor pattern of Depression (II) together with that of extreme inhibition. In the latter the psycho-motor pattern of depression is replaced by that of anxiety. The extreme inhibition which is characteristic also of the agitated form of melancholia goes with movements of self-destruction.

One can conclude therefore that a correlation between types of gesture and types of mental illness exists, but a diagnosis of the malady from gesture alone is difficult, particularly in cases of paraphrenia and manic-depressive psychosis.

(2) *Diagnostic Value of Psycho-Motor Patterns for Personality Study Gesture Types and Hand Types*

To study the correlation between types of gesture and hand types another tabulation was necessary.

According to E. Kretschmer, the hands of schizophrenics differ from those of manic-depressive patients, and in the former, Friedmann and C. Wolff have recognized that there are different types of hands in the different types of the illness.

In the Tables III and IV I have compared the psycho-motor patterns observed in 49 patients with their types of hands. As a rule, hands comprise a mixture of types, and a note is necessary on the classification I apply. Detailed information can be found in my book *The Human Hand*; here I can provide only a short explanation.

The hand serves two functions—touch and prehension: and according to whether the former or the latter predominates I differentiate I, Sensitive hands; II, Motor hands. The sensitive hands I subdivide into small sensitive and long sensitive; the motor hands into elementary, fleshy motor, and bony motor. The elementary hand often exhibits regressive traits, shown either in the presence of the simian line, a too short thumb or papillary ridges of the type found in monkeys, &c. I draw a distinction between the elementary simple and the elementary regressive hand. The latter is often found in degenerates, especially mental defectives, but also in neurotic people, often of high intelligence.

The six types of hands, then, are as follows :

    I.   Elementary simple.
    II. Elementary regressive.
    III. Bony motor.
    IV. Fleshy motor.
    V. Small sensitive.
    VI. Long sensitive.

I must repeat that as a rule one finds a mixture of two or even three of these types.

I have dealt at length in *The Human Hand* with the form and other features of the hand corresponding to the constitutional and personality types. Here it must suffice to indicate that the first four types belong mostly to active personalities, the two last to passive personalities. The elementary simple and fleshy motoric hands are to be found in the pyknic type : the elementary regressive in an amorphous person : the bony motoric in the leptosome type : the sensitive small and the sensitive long in the asthenic type. The sensitive small hand is broad and muscular, when it indicates an element of activity which is lacking in the narrow variation of the same type.

Kretschmer has correlated constitutional types with types of temperament and I followed this classification in the above-mentioned book. But I am no longer convinced that this classification is entirely satisfactory, and in the correlation between gesture-type and personality-type, treated later in this chapter, I use only the physical types described by Kretschmer, whilst employing another method of describing personality types.

D. DISCUSSION OF TABLES III AND IV

In Table III I have had to omit all detailed indications which, as can be seen in the clinical study, were significant for the presence of a psychosis. I also omit those peculiarities of crease-lines and papillary ridges which are indicative of more individual personality traits. They have been discussed in the preceding chapter.

I have supplemented Table III, which bears entirely on the

observations of the clinical study (Chap. V), by Table IV, which registers the psycho-motor patterns of 25 patients—13 paraphrenics and 12 schizophrenics in correlation with the types of their hands. I have chosen these cases at random from hand prints collected at St. Bernard's Hospital. Attached to each of these prints was a detailed description of the hand features, along with notes on the expressive behaviour of the patient during the process of making the prints. These notes were considerably enlarged by the personal information supplied by the nurses and by notes in the case papers.

(1) *Correlations between Hand-types and Psycho-motor Patterns*

The results obtained from the two tables lead to the following conclusions :

Psycho-motor Patterns I and I + II represent a mechanism of extreme inhibition characteristic of the lowest level of inner life, which is expressed in reflex activity only. This behaviour pattern shows lack of emotion and the absence of contact with others, and witnesses to the complete disintegration of the personality.

The 17 patients possessing these traits have hands of—

Long sensitive type, 13.

Small sensitive type, narrow variety, 4.

These types of hands are the most passive among the six types which I have indicated. They are the hands of devitalized people with the least possible power of adaptation. It is obvious that the owners of such hands have a tendency to become the victims of complete disintegration. By their lack of dynamism they easily react with negativism. These are the hands which prefer to make extensor movements and their shape and flat muscles can be explained by this psycho-motor habit.

As Goldstein pointed out, the predominance of extensor movements goes with disintegration and impoverishment of mental life, while the predominance of flexor movements goes with its enrichment. This consideration may throw some light on the link which exists between the form and expressive functions of the hand. In all the cases falling within this category inhibition and disintegration can be considered as constitutional traits.

Psycho-motor Patterns I + V. The combination of these patterns was found in 7 out of 49 cases. It is characteristic of a mechanism of extreme inhibition together with impulsive reactions, which means that a residue of emotional life is maintained. These patients are more human than those of the preceding category, since they react more emotionally to their obsessions, thus indicating that a certain dynamism is still alive in them. It is interesting to note that six of the patients had the same type of hand and only one, a congenital mental defective, had the Mongoloid type of hand. The six hands were of the small sensitive type of the broad variety.

The small but broad sensitive hand contains, in spite of its passive nature, an element of activity. It is a hand which goes also with a tendency to disintegration but with a good potential of self-defence and with a stronger ego than the two hand forms previously mentioned.

The small but broad sensitive hand with which the psycho-motor patterns I + V seem most often to be combined is the hand of antagonistic reactions, with a tendency to profound emotional and mental disturbances. This hand type seems to be characteristic of schizophrenics of a paranoiac reaction type.

In normal people the same type of hand shows a predisposition to nervous and emotional conflicts, as can be seen in easily dislocated personalities who fall ill from anxiety neurosis, especially of an obsessional type.

Psycho-motor Pattern V was found in 8 cases—4 with fleshy motor, 2 with bony motor, and 2 with elementary hands, all representing the active type of hand which goes with a strong physical and nervous dynamism. The fleshy motor and elementary simple hands are of the same pattern, the only differences being the greater simplicity of the composition of the crease-lines in the latter and an element of muscular rigidity with restricted mobility. From this one may conclude that 6 out of 8 cases had similar hands. All these patients were cases of paraphrenia, characterized by emotional instability of a spastic reaction type and obsessional complexes.

The psycho-motor pattern V is characterized by an element of impulsiveness and lack of a sense of proportion. This lack on the mental plane is shown by rigidity of judgement and subjectivism. But even in the form of mental malady the predominance of this psycho-motor pattern reveals a strong ego and a lively nervous dynamism.

There are two pairs of bony motor hands in the same category, and one may conclude that the obsessional element predominates over impulsiveness in this type. They are, as a rule, the hands of more intellectual people. Their mental dynamism, which is stronger than their emotional dynamism, may be responsible for a marked predominance of the imaginative processes over the emotional processes.

Psycho-motor Patterns V + III were present in 8 cases, 4 of which possessed elementary regressive, 2 small but broad sensitive, and 2 bony motor hands, one of the latter showing regressive traits. The latter and one elementary regressive hand belonged to mental defectives with manic-depressive psychosis.

This mixture of psycho-motor patterns is characteristic of a maniac and impulsive personality with ideas of grandeur.

Two pairs of elementary regressive hands were those of hebephrenic schizophrenics, and the two pairs of small sensitive hands belonged to hypomaniac paraphrenics. The owners of the four regressive pairs of hands were certainly most deteriorated and degenerated subjects.

The small sensitive hands belonged to less deteriorated personalities : two patients of an infantile make-up, one imagining herself to be the Queen of France, the other a princess, both continually distributing favours. The same type of hand, especially with an endocrine factor, is to be found in a certain number of paranoiac schizophrenics. It is possible that the two opposite mental conditions—hypomania + megalomania and depressive impulsiveness + micromania—are the two opposites of the same type of malady. The fact that most of the individuals with psycho-motor patterns V and III (two of them being mental defectives) had very abnormal and degenerated hands, shows perhaps that hereditary deficiency encourages this type of psycho-motor behaviour. It is highly probable that a large number of hypomaniac impulsive personalities exists outside mental hospitals.

Psycho-motor Patterns I + III observed in 4 cases is to be found in what one can call the 'stilted' hypomaniac person, in whom the element of inhibition is betrayed by pretentious and precious gestures, perseverance of movements, &c. He is emotionally different from the preceding type of man but mentally the same. Combined with this make-up one finds the small but broad sensitive type of hand (2 cases) and the bony motoric hand. The emphasis is in these cases on the imaginative side, and as I have already mentioned, the small sensitive hand-type probably indicates an infantile personality with highly developed imagination and a temperament betraying either shallow emotions or impulsive emotional reactions. But this point will be treated later on in this chapter.

Psycho-motor Patterns IV + V. I have only to mention three other cases, representing a mixture of psycho-motor patterns IV and V— typical cases of anxiety reactions. The hands of these three cases were in the main of the same type : 2 fleshy motor and 1 elementary, and all three had symptoms of hypothyroidism. I might have classed these cases along with those exhibiting the traits of psycho-motor pattern V, for their anxiety is only superimposed on an underlying impulsive emotional reaction-type. These cases possess the same type of hands as most of those belonging to pattern V.

To sum up : There exists a correlation between certain psycho-motor patterns and certain types of hands.

Psycho-motor behaviour of extreme inhibition accompanied by loss of voluntary activity and emotional drive is linked with narrow flat hands either long or small.

The more inhibition is counteracted by strong dynamic impulse the more one finds the broad and muscular type of hand. The elementary and fleshy motor hands are therefore representative of all psycho-motor patterns which go with a strong emotional reaction and the capacity of self-assertion. In the pathological material of these investigations they are most often hands of paraphrenics with profound but impulsive emotional responses. Midway between the hands of the most and the least inhibited types are the small but broad, sensitive, and the bony-motor hands. The former I have always found connected with a certain infantilism and difficulty in adaptation. This type of hand is mostly found in dislocated imaginative people whose emotional dynamism is weaker than their mental dynamism. Such people are more easily disintegrated than the owners of fully developed broad and muscular hands and on the whole possess less nervous resistance. This type of hand is of course much more frequent in women than men. The bony motor hand is found in tall leptosome people (men and women) who are rather wiry but much less centralized than the owners of fleshy motor hands, and therefore exhibit a greater tendency to obsessional traits and extravagances.

Since a correlation exists between psycho-motor patterns and hand types I am convinced that the former are linked with personality types. I have produced evidence in support of the correlation between hand-traits and personality in my previous writings as well as further proof in the Clinical Study in this book, where personality diagnosis from hand features is compared with clinical

14

notes, both showing a considerable agreement. It is a fact that the same types of hand are found in the sane and the insane. The difference is to be found in those special hand features which accumulate with the severity of the mental aberration. But the underlying personality remains fundamentally the same outside or inside the mental hospital. Certainly a deteriorated schizophrenic has lost his personality, since his malady has absorbed it. Before the outbreak of this malady he presented the same emotional instinctive and intellectual qualities as other people, apart from the fact that his reactions had probably always been more irrational. For this reason one can find a personality type in the patient as well as in the sane individual. The same holds good for fundamental psycho-motor patterns. They appear in everybody, the difference between their normal or abnormal expressions being one of degree and of the power of the imagination over the sense of reality.

(2) *Correlations between Personality Types and Psycho-motor Patterns*

Psycho-motor Patterns I and I + II and Corresponding Personality Type. The hand most frequently found in the profoundly inhibited is the sensitive hand, long or small, but always narrow. This type of hand belongs to the kind of man who is asthenic and devitalized. The small narrow variation is characteristic of the asthenic infantile. Both have little dynamism, are physically lazy and easily depressed. Their ego is feeble and their will power non-existent. With such poor equipment they become on the smallest provocation the victims of disintegration.

The asthenic type is emotionally feeble and takes refuge in the imagination and introversion.

The infantile variety of the asthenic is more vivacious but lacks concentration, and is always dependent on his surroundings. This dependence may be responsible for reactions of anxiety and obsessional traits. The latter are characteristic of the owners of both the long and the narrow small sensitive hands. They are often very gifted mentally and receptive to aesthetic impressions. But they rarely possess creative talent. It need hardly be said that in spite of their dependence on surroundings their capacity for adaptation is limited and they have great difficulty in accepting responsibility. They are happiest when living under the wing of a strong personality which protects and supports them.

Psycho-motor Patterns I + V and Corresponding Personality Type.

These psycho-motor patterns are most often linked with the small sensitive hand of the broad variety. This type of hand belongs to a mercurial type of personality, physically asthenic but possessing a certain amount of nervous and mental energy. Excitability is one of the most marked traits of this type. With little concentration or depth of emotional sentiment the owner of the small and broad sensitive hand is volatile and undertakes too much. His appetite is greater than his powers of assimilation. Anxiety as an expression of insecurity and a poorly stabilized ego provides a field for conflicts and constitutional difficulties. He is versatile and has the infant's gift of mimicry and is often a good actor on the stage and in life. But he has a tendency to nervous breakdowns, anxiety neurosis, and an irrational attitude in general. He relies by his vivacity on a certain amount of self-assertion, which, however, most often takes an aggressive and impulsive form and rarely develops stability and centralization of personality. The temperament of this type is marked by a want of proportion and balance. An extravert urge throws him into the company of others, but the fundamental emotional force being feeble he fails to develop depth or any responsibility and reliability in human relationships and either becomes the victim of other people or breaks away from them.

This is the superficial and unstable type.

A temperament of this kind encourages the development of imagination and intuition at the expense of reasonableness and logical judgement.

[1] *Psycho-motor Pattern II + III and Corresponding Personality Type.* These, according to Kretschmer, are characteristic of the cycloid personality, which has periods either of predominant elation or of predominant depression, and this type of Kretschmer is identical with the extravert type of Jung. In my experience the pure extravert type rarely exists in reality. The cycloid most often shows traits of psycho-motor pattern V and possesses elements of impulsiveness and obsession in the depressed phase as well as in the elated phase. The type nearest to that of Kretschmer is the one whose predominant patterns are I + V or V only.

Psycho-motor Pattern V and Corresponding Personality Type. This most often goes with elementary and fleshy motor hands, both being large and long with strongly developed muscles and strong

[1] This personality type is purely theoretical and does not refer to the Clinical Study.

and short fingers. Kretschmer considered this type of hand as being characteristic of the pyknic type. The man with such a hand is of medium size with broad shoulders and an almost athletic physique, but without the muscular hypertrophy of the real athlete.

He has a tendency to get fat when middle-aged.

This description suggests the jovial fatherly man with physical strength and remarkable emotional dynamism, controlled as a rule by a natural discipline. But, as Kretschmer pointed out, once roused this type can become emotionally excited to the point of aggressiveness. He is more inclined to be angry than anxious, since his ego is strong and he is emphatic and self-assertive. In all that concerns the physique and personality traits I have described, I am in agreement with Kretschmer's classification, but I differ from him when it comes to the fundamental psycho-motor patterns of this type. The word cycloid is in itself proof of emotional instability. Thus the cycloid is far from being balanced and equally far from being centralized and free from obsessions. It is true that he has much more self-defence and inner security than other human types, but he is also more volcanic. The volcano may remain quiescent for long periods but it is liable to sudden violent eruptions. Pathologically the pyknic type of man represents a caricature of the cycloid make-up, which, in my opinion, is more closely allied to the paraphrenic than to the manic-depressive individual. In paraphrenics no distinct line is drawn between the elated or the depressed type, but they have also cycles in the form either of more elated or aggressive or more depressed and submissive phases. Compared to the manic-depressive personality the paraphrenic is more unified and consistent.

Psycho-motor Pattern V + III and Corresponding Personality Type. The type of hand which is the most frequent in combination with psycho-motor patterns V + III is first the elementary regressive (50 per cent), then the small but broad sensitive and the bony-motor types of hand (each 25 per cent). I have already mentioned that this psycho-motor pattern is the expression of an impulsive hypomaniac personality which seems to be less definitely allied to a special constitutional type than the patterns previously described. The elementary regressive hand belongs to the 'amorphous' type of Kretschmer, with a rather freakish physique. Often the chest and arms are overdeveloped—hypermasculine, so to speak—while hips and legs show feminine traits. The face is often badly proportioned, with a very low forehead and a very big chin. And the ears are frequently abnormal. This type is also mentally freakish and comprises all sorts of unbalanced people as well as moral defectives. Emotional extravagance, found in the neurotic variant of this type of man, includes adventurers of every kind. Explorers, great soldiers, as well as eminent artists, belong to this category. Apart from a strong dynamism they often possess a blind courage. They are very egocentric and their lack of adaptation makes them natural rebels. Their impulsiveness renders them destructive not only for others but for themselves.

The two owners of the small and broad sensitive hand, both women, had less emotional and physical force, and in their case a state of hypomania was produced and maintained primarily by a vivid imagination. The two bony motor hands seemed to me to be uncharacteristic of these psycho-motor patterns, since one of them possessed regressive traits which placed the owner among the amorphous type with leptosome physique.

Psycho-motor Patterns I + III and Corresponding Personality Types. This psycho-motor pattern does not occur often in other than psycho-paths, whom I have called stilted hypomaniacs. The hands of the four cases classified under this pattern are of the bony motor and small but broad sensitive type. In both types, as I have already mentioned, the power of the imagination is greater than that of the emotions. And both types of hands show a tendency to marked inhibitions.

The bony motor hand, which is typical of the leptosome type of man, occurs relatively seldom in the pathological material at my disposal. The characteristics of this type were studied from different material and treated at length in *The Human Hand,* but a few words on this subject must be added here. Leptosome people are tall and slender but have well-developed muscles. They possess physical and nervous energy and are generally very graceful in their movements. Their temperament is marked by hypersensitivity and inhibition, which makes them shy away from human contacts, and their introversion is responsible for their notorious love of beauty and the arts. But their strong nervous dynamism tempts them to take part in human affairs. They are people with a divided mind, excitable and enthusiastic as well as easily bored and inclined to give in. There is no emotional warmth about them and they are therefore often prone to extravagance and sensationalism. Their emotional coldness and a lack of natural instinct contributes possibly to their feeling of insecurity and restlessness.

According to the correlations which exist between certain psycho-motor patterns and certain hand types, Five Personality Types have been established by a method of comparison between hand features and psycho-motor patterns.

These are :

1. The asthenic inhibited type :
   (*a*) predominantly depressed ;
   (*b*) predominantly obsessional.

2. The infantile type with emotional instability.

3. The pyknic type with predominantly impulsive emotional reactions.

4. The amorphous type with emotional and mental instability :
   (*a*) impulsive and megalomaniac ;
   (*b*) mentally inferior or mentally defective.

5. The leptosome type with intellectual capacity and inhibited emotions.

It must be stressed that a classification of man according to his emotional expressions does not mean that he is fixed in a certain pattern but only that this particular one is the most marked. In every living being there exists a whole scale of psycho-dynamic qualities, but only the most characteristic ones find easy and frequent expression.

Gestures correspond not only to the type of personality but also to the emotional make-up, since the two are intrinsically linked.

(3) *Psycho-motor Patterns reveal the Degree of Integration or Disintegration*

Psycho-motor patterns indicate also the degree of integration of the individual.

The more extensor and reflex movements appear in the expressive language of a person the greater is his disintegration. These movements are particularly those of the hand. They are unconscious gestures of defence against a situation which endangers identity. As a rule, in ordinary life gestures of disintegration are to be found as a reply to exterior situations, but imaginary situations can also release them, a fact which I have illustrated in the examples in the Clinical Study.

If an individual responds to a situation (real or imaginary) with an exaggerated motor unrest of the hands and face one may conclude that he is preoccupied with inner conflicts. He is deprived of

presence of mind and suffers from a lack of adaptation to circumstances. Disintegration may come from the emotional or imaginative life, or both. The latter is most often responsible since repressed
emotions have a disintegrating influence on the imagination by
giving it an exaggerated preference for certain fixed images. The
persistence of these images and their obsessional character is betrayed
by inhibited as well as stereotyped gestures.

Apart from the general motor unrest and the quantity of reflex
movements, disintegration is revealed by autistic gestures, often of a
regressive type, such as nail-biting, thumb-in-mouth and thumb-
in-palm gestures. Other autistic movements, such as hair gestures
or an aimless fiddling with tie or clothes, reveal insecurity and
anxiety, not only about the appearance but also about the self,
and indicate disintegration.

Such a state of mind was well illustrated by one of my private
patients who was in the habit of turning up the lapels of his coat
in a sort of hiding gesture betraying fear. The same man had a
nervous cough which showed an inhibition to speak frankly.
Another rearranged his trousers and made brushing movements on
his shoes without any real reason for doing so. He used to dream
that he was reprimanded in the army for not having cleaned his
shoes properly. His autistic gestures as well as his dreams revealed
a feeling of insecurity about his identity. He did not feel clean.
The dream had no reference to a real situation, for he had never
been in the army. Another patient used to carry a button in his
pocket which he moved between his fingers when he had to talk
to strangers, especially superiors or officials. He explained that this
habit gave him some self-assurance which he seemed to lose through
anxiety when any situation arose in which he felt inferior. A
woman patient suffering from claustrophobia calmed her mind by
pulling her handkerchief tight over her thumb or holding one
hand firmly in the other. These last examples are less characteristic
of obsessional conflicts than of anxiety neurosis, which has just the
same disintegrating effect. Another woman with the same com-
plaint used to drum with her fingers, a habit which betrayed both
impatience and anxiety. One could give endless examples of the
kind. All these gestures represent a safety valve for nervous and
mental tension and are therefore means of self-protection in an
ill-adapted organism. To be able to diagnose the well and the
badly integrated person is of course extremely valuable, not only
for tracing maladjustment but also for practical purposes such as

placing the right man in the right job. We have overcome the prejudice that badly integrated people are completely useless. They are only useless if their work is antipathetic. If they are given a profession which saves them from nervous catastrophe they may even do better than well-balanced people, through having more vision, or through especially conscientious execution of their duty, or through an extraordinary drive and heroism. As with all diagnostic schemes, which demand not only knowledge but great experience, infinite care is needed in applying them. Half-knowledge and dilettantism are the most dangerous enemies in everyday life. It must therefore be left only to the psychiatrist and trained psychologist to make use of gesture interpretation, otherwise it is liable to misuse and will do more harm than good. If ever test-methods of personality are to be introduced on a large scale, every institution—hospitals as well as factories, government departments, big businesses and schools—should have trained psychologists as advisers.

As I have tried to show, psycho-motor patterns, expressing both personality-types and the degree of integration, are linked with certain hand types and it would contribute greatly to the diagnostic value of the first to take the latter into consideration. Compensating methods must be used in order to get an all-round view of personality and to give more real substance to psychological judgement and classification.

III. PREFERENCE FOR THE LEFT HAND IN EXPRESSIVE MOVEMENTS

I have left to the end of the book this fascinating problem of expression.

It is undoubtedly a fact that it is the left hand which is predominantly used in subconscious gestures (see Clinical Study). I observed this also in patients whose hand-prints I took. I remember one especially impressive case, a melancholic woman who used to dig her left fingers into the skin just over her right shoulder and cause deep scratches. Both hands were very stiff, but the fingers of the left remained so tightly closed that it was impossible to take a hand-print.

The psychological significance of right and left hands has been described in *The Human Hand*, where I have shown that in a great majority of normal as well as abnormal people accessory crease-lines are more numerous in the left than in the right palm. This can be explained by a preference for using the left hand in subtle movements, such as subconscious gestures. As the left hand (in right-handers) is under the control of the right hemisphere of the brain, one may conclude that the latter has a closer link with emotional than voluntary impulses, or as Werner Wolff suggests (*The Experimental Study of Forms of Expression*) : 'The right cerebral hemisphere governs the collective functions of the unconscious mind.'

Werner Wolff observed that the two sides of a face show entirely different physiognomies. In one of his experimental studies showing profile photographs the subjects recognized the portrait of the left profile as being their own but rarely that of the right, while the opposite occurred in recognizing side views of other people. Werner Wolff concludes from this that the left profile embodies the wish-image of an individual—how he sees himself—and the right represents his conventional face—as others see him. The right side of the face roughly agrees with the impression given by a full-face photograph where all traces of the peculiarities of the left side alone are lost.

The right and left problem attracted attention long ago. As far as I know, the first to write about it was a German Jewish physician, Dr. Robert Fliess, at the end of the last century. Fliess maintained that the whole left side of the body, but especially the face, expressed characteristics of the opposite sex. In women and men whose left side was more developed than the right he saw either a masculine or feminine streak. He held that bisexual tendencies exist in every human being but that in a certain number either the hetero- or the homosexual side is more developed than the rest. The homosexual part does not necessarily extend into the sexual sphere but may exist in a sublimated form. Asymmetry of the face is particularly marked in creative people ; and Fliess mentions Goethe, Beethoven and Bismarck as examples. It is also well known that a great number of famous artists as well as homosexuals are also left-handed, which may contribute to the truth of Fliess's theory. More recently Wilhelm Ludwig investigated the same question in his book *Das Rechts-Links Problem im Tierreich und beim Menschen* (in English : *The Right-Left Problem in the Animal World and in Human Beings*). Ludwig points out that in man and animal one always finds two opposite or R.L. (right left) agents, and though one of them may be entirely responsible for the appear-

ance, the other still exists though it remains latent. He also noted
that in homosexuals the left gonads are often more developed than
the right and in heterosexuals the other way about. Such a development is determined by the genes and is therefore inherited.

Ludwig mentions that the left has always been associated with
evil—the devil fiddles with the left hand ; in the Roman Augurs
the birds of ill omen flew to the left ; and so on.

But how far does the homosexual significance, if it exists,
account for the preference for the left hand in subconscious movements ? Homosexual tendencies must be understood as including
those qualities which are the opposite of the person's own sex.
It may well be that the tension which produces emotional reactions
is determined by a continual conflict between opposite innate
tendencies, the male and the female, and that it is our repressed or
less developed half that rules our subconscious impulses. It would
mean that in ' masculine ' men and ' feminine ' women the irrational side and its expressions come from his or her opposite sex
tendencies. We may further conclude that in all ill-balanced people
these tendencies are accentuated and that it is their homosexual
component which deepens and widens their emotions but also
leads to neurotic responses and disintegration. It must be remembered that the subconscious expressive movements of which I speak
here are quite different from gesticulation, in which either both
hands or preferably the right is used as, for example, in the case
of the ' schoolmaster ' emphasizing his point by raising the index
finger of the right hand. Those gestures with which I am concerned in this context are not connected with thought. The more
a person's gestures are of a reflex type, the greater the use of the
left hand. It seems therefore possible that subconscious conflicts
of a more or less hidden homosexual side in all of us predispose
both to emotionalism and disintegration, and this may also explain
why homosexual tendencies are so often found in psychotics,
particularly schizophrenics.

In this country an emotional man is considered to be ' feminine ' ;
or at least the Englishman's shyness about the expression of emotion
and the humiliation he feels when he lets himself go, indicate a
refusal to appear effeminate.

The French are less self-conscious in this respect, and one of
their greatest novelists, André Gide, in *L'Immoraliste*, illustrates in
the following phrases both his strong emotionalism and the rôle
which the left hand plays in expressing it.

Je m'épouvantais de ce calme et brusquement m'envahit de nouveau comme pour protester, s'affirmer, se désoler dans le silence le sentiment tragique de ma vie, si violent, douloureux presque et si impetueux que j'en aurai crié si j'avais pu crier comme les bêtes.

Je pris ma main, je me souviens, ma main gauche dans ma main droite, je voulus la porter à ma tête et la fis. Pourquoi ? Pour m'affirmer que je vivais et trouver cela admirable.

(Quoted from an article ' André Gide ' by Peter Quennel, *Horizon*, June, 1942.)

COMMENTARY ON THE ILLUSTRATIONS

I. GESTURES OF CHILDREN

Photo 1 shows a child of six months in a situation of suspense which is revealed more by the gesture of the hand than by facial expression. The hand looks like a ' foreign body ' not yet properly connected with the brain.

Photos 2, 3, 4, and 5 show the predominant influence of the developing sense of balance on hand gestures in two children of eighteen months of age. The face of the little girl in photo 2 shows signs of insecurity and anxiety, for she is walking on unsafe ground. Her right hand is held in a tense ' stretching ' gesture, such as can be seen in epileptics and ballet dancers performing acrobatic steps. The same child is more self-possessed in photo 3, where she stands on even ground. Her left hand, however, with the index finger raised, still reveals uncertain sense of balance.

The same gesture is observable in the little boy in photo 4.

Photo 5 is an example of the charming clumsiness of gesture in a child of eighteen months. The whole body takes part in the attempt to point out an object which has caught his interest. Note the twisted gesture of his hand with the index finger pointed.

Photos 6, 6a, and 6b show gestures of surprise in a boy of thirteen months and a girl of two years. The latter holds her hands open but closer together than the little boy does his. This shows the improvement of psycho-motor co-ordination with age. Compare the same type of hand gesture in the child in photo 1.

Photo 7 shows the global expressiveness of a child of eighteen months. The whole body takes part in her ' giving ' gesture.

Photos 8 and 9 show two boys of three and a half years, the first in a passive situation of surprise, the second in an active situation of running towards an object. Note the intelligent understanding of the situation revealed in the facial expression of both, and the marked control and co-ordination of hand movements and gait in the boy in photo 9. The ' surprised ' boy makes, naturally, a more clumsy hand movement ; but note the difference of this gesture to similar gestures shown in previous photos. Control of the situation is revealed in his facial expression and also in the pointing gesture of the index finger.

Photo 10 shows a boy of seven years, with a forced smile and clasped hands, both characteristic of a state of anxiety.

Photo 11 shows a boy of nine with a sensitive, calm face that does not disclose any preoccupation or feeling of discomfort. But the thumb-in-palm posture reveals fear of the outside world and a desire to go back to an earlier period of childhood. This is an introverted child.

Photo 12. This girl of eight is of the opposite type to the child in the previous picture. She has a happy facial expression and her inner ease and relaxation are also revealed by the gesture of her hands, which are put lightly together with the thumbs up.

Photo 13. Note the strained facial expression of this girl and the tense gesture of extension of her right hand ; she feels very uneasy. The boy, on the contrary, is master of the situation.

Photo 14 shows the perfect inner relaxation of two boys, especially the one with the closed eyes. The inner relaxation is mirrored in muscular relaxation : the hands are slightly flexed in a posture of ease.

II. HOW TWO GROUPS OF IMPORTANT PEOPLE FACE THE CAMERA

Group A

Photo 15. General Devers is the most extravert personality of this group. He is absolutely at ease. Note his happy facial expression and the relaxed, slightly flexed posture of his hands.

Mr. Eden is right outside of the situation : he keeps his eyes shut and holds his hands behind him.

Mr. Winant has a friendly smile but holds his hands in a tight gesture of unease. He is apparently very shy, and certainly an introvert.

Lord Mountbatten is a ' reserved ' extravert, holding himself back (note the hand gesture), but enjoying the situation with a certain superiority.

The late Sir Kingsley Wood puts up with the situation in a friendly way, but not without self-defence (see his hand gesture).

Lady Joseph is an extravert personality, much enjoying the situation, but she is not as relaxed as General Devers.

Group B

Photo 16. Note the physical and postural resemblance of Captain Flanagan (U.S.A.) and Lord Mountbatten.

Mr. Winant is more relaxed in this photo but shows in the ' gauche ' gesture of his hands an adolescent type of shyness.

The extraverts of this group are Mr. Churchill, who sits in a posture of perfect ease, and the First Sea Lord, Mr. A. V. Alexander. Admiral Stark feels tense and uneasy to the point of suffering (note his facial expression and strained hand gesture).

III. GENERAL EISENHOWER AND AIR-MARSHAL TEDDER IN AN AUDIENCE

Photo 17. General Eisenhower leans forward. He has an absorbed facial expression and his hands are folded with the thumbs up. He is a strong extravert personality.

Air-Marshal Tedder leans backward, with a calm and reserved facial expression. His hands, which have a boyish look, clasp the pipe very lightly, a gesture which shows a 'receptive' and contemplative person. He is an imaginative introvert.

IV. GENERAL EISENHOWER AND AIR-MARSHAL TEDDER WALKING

Photo 18. General Eisenhower shows again a typical hand gesture (fists with thumbs up) of the extravert personality.

Photo 19. Air-Marshal Tedder feels self-conscious and shy. His hands perform an uncertain and retiring gesture, revealing his sensitive and introvert make-up.

V. THE DEGREE OF INTEGRATION SHOWN IN HAND GESTURES

Photo 20. The hand of General Eisenhower rests in a perfect gesture of relaxation and certainty on the map, showing the complete unity of thought and motor function, which is the sign of a well-centralized and integrated personality. His face shows an expression of happy contentment and self-confidence.

Photo 21. The slightly flexed hands of Mr. Miles also reveal a state of inner relaxation and poise. Like General Eisenhower he is a predominantly extravert personality but of a more contemplative type. The relaxed gesture of his hands has a passive and receptive quality, characteristic of a contemplative and imaginative person. He is well integrated, but has not the same strength of personality as General Eisenhower.

VI. DISINTEGRATION OF PERSONALITY SHOWN IN HAND GESTURES

Photo 22. General Ritter von Thoma, after his capture by British officers, has a facial expression of despair and bewilderment. While he is able to control his face, his hand gestures have lost control and co-ordination. He clumsily grasps his despatch case at a corner with his right hand, while the left hand is held in a fist, showing abnormal inner tension. His negative emotion prevents purposeful voluntary activity. The integration of personality is disturbed.

Photo 23. The Belgian Fascist leader Degrelle while making a speech holds his hands like claws, with the thumbs extended. This gesture reveals the determination to hold on and to subdue. The extended thumbs also reveal a state of profound unease and the cramped tension of a strong and negative emotion : hatred and the will to conquer.

Photo 24. Darlan does not face either General Eisenhower or General Clark while talking, but he is able to control his facial expression, which appears to be calm. His hands, however, which are clasped, with the left thumb hidden in the palm, reveal inner strain, insecurity and embarrassment. This is a gesture of self-protection and reserve, tinged with fear. It is the gesture of a disintegrated personality with a bad conscience.

Photo 25. Hitler's face is that of a maniac. His hand gesture conveys anxious appeal. The fingers are held apart in a movement of extension, characteristic of a negative emotion, a mixture of anxiety and aggression. Note the relative smallness of his hands.

VII. HAND AND FACE

Photo 26. Mr. Aldridge (author of *Signed with their Honour*) has a bony-motor type of hand with long, sensitive, tapered fingers. He is both an active and an imaginative person, with a high degree of intuitive comprehension. On Jung's typology of personality, he is an introvert. The hand is held in a posture of medium extension, revealing an undercurrent of unease.

Photo 27. Lieutenant Luducilla Pavlichenko has a fleshy motor hand with tapered fingers. She is an extravert personality, a physically and mentally strong woman of a high degree of integration. Her face reflects ease and naturalness. She holds her hand in a gesture of medium flexion, characteristic of inner relaxation and perfect contact with surroundings.

VIII. ESMOND KNIGHT'S HANDS SPEAK

Photo 28. Esmond Knight's hands are endowed with an unusual quality of expression. They communicate his thoughts to Madame Rosay. Having almost lost his sight, he has developed the highly sensitive and imaginative expression of the hands characteristic of blind people.

Note also the hand gesture of Madame Rosay. The hands are lightly clasped with the thumbs up, showing her poise and self-confidence.

IX. HAIR GESTURES

In both examples hair gestures are made in a state of fatigue as a means of reviving the perepheric sensibility.

Photo 29. The man, who holds his head with his hands and touches his hair, is apparently listening to a lecture. He is strained and tired and wants to make sure by this gesture that his brain still works all right.

Photo 30. Wendell Willkie is seen here waiting for the results of the Republican Presidential Nomination. His hair gesture reveals fatigue (as does the posture of his whole body) and an element of anxiety, which is inevitable in a situation of expectancy.

X. GENERAL MONTGOMERY IN CONVERSATION WITH GENERAL EISENHOWER

Photo 31. General Montgomery shapes his thought with a gesture of his hand. His eyes are half closed. These are traits of an imaginative and creative mind.

General Eisenhower makes a corresponding 'listening' gesture, which shows the capacity of receptive understanding in an extravert and very active personality.

XI. GESTURES OF SPEAKERS

Photo 32. Lord Strabolgi uses the 'teacher's' gesture with the index finger pointed. He is concerned with what he has to say and he rubs it in.

Photo 33. In Mr. Morrison hand gesture and facial expression tally. He feels and lives what he says. Note his broad, fleshy-motor hands with a marked zone of the imagination. He is both an active and an imaginative personality.

Photo 34. Mr. Shinwell has his thumb extended and pointed while speaking. He knows how to put his personality across.

Photo 35. This speaker wants to bring his point home by a 'fighting' gesture. The gesture is, however, stronger than the emotion behind it, for the face remains comparatively unmoved. The gesture is used for effect.

Photo 36. The Belgian Ambassador is seen here in private conversation vividly emphasizing his words by a hand gesture characteristic of his Latin temperament.

Photo 37. An habitual, jovial gesture of Mr. Churchill, full of cheerful self-possession and inner warmth.

Photo 38. Michael Redgrave in the play *Uncle Harry*. Note the expressiveness of his hand-gesture: the index and medius fingers are tightly pressed against the table and the whole hand is held in a posture of extreme tension. While the expression of the face rather conceals what is going on in his mind, the hand reveals his inner state : *a state of desperate determination and anxious expectancy.*

Photo 39. Michael Redgrave as 'Uncle Harry' when he has just been told by Lucy (the woman for whom he has murdered his sister) that all is finished between them. [Continued on page 207.]

PLATES

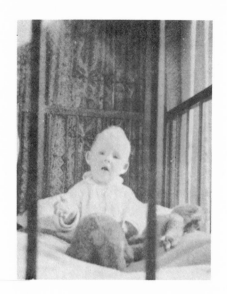

1

2

5

6

4

3

6a

6b

7

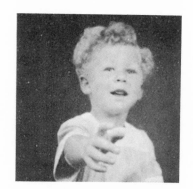

8

9

12

10

11

13

14

Photo by] ['*Daily Sketch*'

15

16

Photo by]   17   [' Daily Sketch '

Photo]

['Daily Sketch'

18

Photo by]

[Associated Press

19

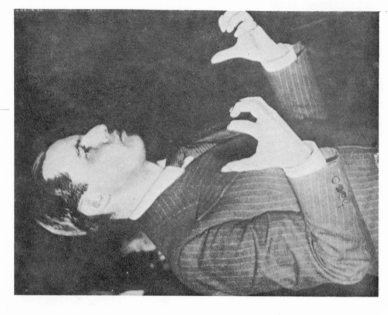

23

22

24

25

Courtesy of] [Michael Joseph Ltd.

26

Photo by] [Planet News Agency

27

Photo by]

[Pictorial Press

Photo by]   [' *Picture Post*'

Photo by]   [*Associated Press*

Photo by]

31

[Planet News Agency

32

33

36

hoto by]　　　　　　　　　　　　　　['*Picture Post*'　*Photo by*]　　　　　　　　　　　　　['*Picture Post*'

34　　　　　　　　　　　　　　　　　35

Photo by]　　　　　　　　　　　　　　　　　　　'*Daily Sketch*'

Photo by]   ['Picture Post

39

Photo by]   [John Vickers

38

Photo by]   [John Vickers

41

42

43

44

The face is torn by cynically despairing laughter. The right hand supports his thigh, the left hangs down like a faded flower, showing that *all life has gone out of ' Uncle Harry '*.

Photo 40. The actress Rachel Kempson as Lucy in *Uncle Harry*. Note her radiant face and the posture of her hands with thumbs up. This posture reveals that she is master of the situation and that she has freed herself from a frustrating bondage.

Note. It is interesting to note that the hand gestures of both artists were subconsciously performed. They were produced by the ' images ' in their minds, which dictated their psycho-motor behaviour.

Photo 41. The British Attorney-General presents the British case for the prosecution of the Nazi war leaders. Sir Hartley Shawcross's gesture is indicative of the utmost concentration. He is holding his whole case in his hands. He is a man who grasps essentials and holds them with iron determination. The fact that he looks at his own hands —not at the audience—shows that he is concerned solely with what he has to say and not with the effect of his words. His is the summing-up gesture of a clear, determined, imaginative and perfectly detached mind.

Photos 42–44. The pictures of Herman Goering show all the characteristics of emotionalism, untruthfulness and theatricality ; indeed, they are the gestures of a third-rate actor. Note especially the hand-on-heart gesture so typical of the cheapest form of demonstrative behaviour, revealing both hypocrisy and lack of culture.

A GLOSSARY OF TECHNICAL TERMS

Acromegaly.—A disease in which the extremities—the face, hands and feet—are too big. Such abnormal proportions, especially of the hands and feet, occur in dysfunction of the pituitary gland resulting in an over stimulation of the growth of the bones of the limbs and face.

Acromicry.—The opposite condition to that of acromegaly. Reduced activity of the pituitary gland results in reduced stimuli of growth. The term acromicry is, however, only used in regard to the hands and feet, which are abnormally small in proportion to body size.

Adrenals.—There are two adrenal glands, situated just above the kidneys. They belong to the endocrine gland system and play a very important part in the regulation of the blood pressure in autonomic nervous and sexual functions. For example, a hyperfunction of the adrenal glands leads to virilism in women and to feminism in men.

Agoraphobia.—Fear of open spaces.

Amorphous.—Shapeless. An amorphous type of man (according to E. Kretschmer) is a man with a physique composed of different types of structure and which lacks unity.

Ankylosis.—Stiffening of an articulation leading to complete rigidity of the joint. It occurs most frequently with the joints of the fingers, especially the fifth finger, and is a condition which may be hereditary as well as congenital.

Anxiety Neurosis.—A state of mind in which irrational fears govern both feeling and behaviour. A constant underlying current of anxiety, sometimes amounting to panic, leads to abnormal inner tension and introversion. The symptoms of anxiety neurosis may take very different forms according to the cause and type of the anxiety and to the temperament of the patient. Claustrophobia is a frequent symptom of anxiety neurosis.

Arachnodactidy.—A term applied to fingers in which ossification is incomplete. They are abnormally thin and flexible and so fragile as to resemble a spider's legs.

Asthenic.—Weak. The term is generally used of physical qualities.

Athetosis.—An abnormal condition of the nervous system, going with muscular hypertone and irregular jerky movements, especially of the hands. The postures of the hands and limbs are also peculiar and reflect the abnormal tension. Sometimes, but not as a rule, the movements of the face and tongue are distorted. The condition of athetosis occurs in brain diseases but also without any cerebral lesion, apparently brought about through purely psychological causes.

Auditory Delusions.—The purely imaginative perception of voices. Auditory delusions, which are absolutely real to the sufferers, are very frequent in mental patients, especially in schizophrenics and paraphrenics.

Aura.—A state of acute hypersensitivity preceding an epileptic fit. Such a state of aura has been admirably described by the Russian novelist Dostoevsky (himself an epileptic) in his novel *The Idiot*.

Autism.—An exaggerated form of egocentricity ; a type of existence which feeds on organic stimuli only, and which is therefore devoid of any contact with other individuals or the community.

Autistic.—Directed towards the body or arising from bodily stimuli.

Automatism.—A reaction type on the lowest level of inner life. It is expressed by reflex activity only and is therefore devoid of voluntary and conscious activity.

Autonomic Nervous System.—The nervous system which innervates the inner organs and the blood vessels. It is essentially different from the central nervous system. It maintains the organic functions and transmits organic sensations to the brain. It has a predominating rôle in the origin and expression of the emotions.

Basal Ganglia.—Part of the 'ancient' brain, called by some authors the interbrain. They are situated beneath the cortex and consist of the thalamus and the corpus striatum.

Catatonic.—An abnormal postural quality. Catatonic postures are the result of a dissociation of mental and postural activity. In normal people the two work in harmony ; in abnormal people, such as schizophrenics, they lead an isolated existence. Catatonic postures are seen in the perseverance in the same attitude for a prolonged period, and seem quite independent of any normal feelings of comfort. For example, a catatonic schizophrenic can keep his arms stretched out or twisted for hours without attempting to relax the 'uncomfortable' posture.

Cerebro-spinal.—The cerebro-spinal nerves form the central nervous system. They consist of two types of nerves, sensory and motor. The former connect the periphery of the body (skin and exteroceptive senses) with the brain, the latter link the brain with the muscular apparatus. Both types of nerves are closely linked with each other through their neighbouring position in spine and brain as well as through their interdependent functions.

Choreiform.—Choreiform movements are those of an illness called St. Vitus's Dance. There are different forms of chorea, linked either with rheumatism (rheumatic chorea) or with mental disorder (Huntington's chorea). The choreiform movements are involuntary, jerky and inco-ordinate, and (if the illness is severe) affect the whole body with continual spasms. The movements are incoercible and occur, according to Walshe, on the background of diminished muscular tone.

Claustrophobia.—The fear of being 'shut in'. It is a frequent symptom of anxiety neurosis. People who are unable to go into a basement room or to travel by tube without suffering agony are victims of claustrophobia. The fear is, of course, irrational and must be worked out from the psychoanalytical angle.

Corpus Striatum.—A part of the 'ancient' brain or interbrain and one of the basal ganglia. It is most important for the regulation of muscular tonus and co-ordination of movements.

Cortex.—The most developed part of the brain. It is the seat of all voluntary activity and of every capacity which is typically human : thought, judgement, and action.

Cortical.—Cortical functions are those which depend on the various nervous qualities of the cortex.

Delusional Insanity.—Any form of mental illness which goes with delusions.

Dementia Praecox.—The early name of schizophrenic psychosis, used before the different forms which this illness may take were discovered. The name is still used for a special schizophrenic reaction type, mostly found in young

15*

patients who show catatonic symptoms together with a rapid deterioration of intelligence.

Dermatitis.—An inflammation of the skin.

Digital Formula.—The term was coined by Professor Wood Jones to signify the sequence of the fingers in regard to their length. Normally the medius finger is the longest, then follows either the fourth or the index finger ; after that the thumb and the fifth or ' little '. In human beings in whom the second finger exceeds the fourth in length have, according to Wood Jones, a typically ' human ' digital formula, while one speaks of a ' simian ' digital formula when the fourth finger is longer than the index. The digital formula 3 : 4 : 2 : 1 : 5 occurs in most monkeys and apes. An abnormal digital formula—one, for example, in which the index, medius and fourth fingers are of equal length—occurs in a high percentage of mentally abnormal people.

Electrical Shock Treatment.—A new type of treatment with an electric current (galvanic) used in cases of schizophrenia and melancholia. The electrodes are fixed on both temples of the head and through an electrical shock the activity of the brain seems to be revived.

Encephalogram.—The registration of cortical waves. The Encephalogram was discovered at the end of the last century by the Austrian Professor Hans Berger, but has been elaborated and completed by Professor Adrian of Cambridge. Adrian has shown that the cortical waves of real and potential epileptics differ from those of normal people. In a recent lecture at the Royal Institution he pointed out that other abnormal conditions than those of epilepsy produce abnormal types of cortical waves and that perhaps one day it will be possible to detect criminal tendencies as well as any other ' extravagances ' of the mind by means of the Encephalogram.

Endocrine Glands.—Glands producing ' inner ' secretions, called hormones, which are poured into the blood stream. The knowledge of endocrine function is of fairly recent date, but their vital importance for the general state of health and for most organic functions is now an established medical fact. The endocrine glands govern not only the physical dynamo, but the emotional dynamo too. They influence the type of temperament and play a great part in the origin of emotion and in emotional expression.

Exteroceptive Senses.—The senses which connect the body with the outside world : the eyes, the ears, the sense of touch, the sense of smell and the sense of taste.

Extrapyramidal system.—' The old motor system ' conveys involuntary movements. It constitutes the entire motor system of the lowlier forms of animal life.

Ganglion.—A conglomeration of nervous fibres or a nerve centre which leads to a highly concentrated nervous activity. Both types of nervous systems, the central and the autonomic, possess numerous ganglia, which have special functional tasks to perform apart from their general heightened nervous activity.

Gestalt Psychology.—A school of psychology which originated in Germany. Its founder was Professor Wertheimer of Berlin. Gestalt means ' form ' or ' shape ' in the sense of an organised unit, and, according to Gestalt psychologists, underlies for example all perceptive and adaptive functions of man.

Global.—In the psychological sense this means the whole or undifferentiated. A global reaction is one in which the whole body takes part and where single traits of expression can scarcely be differentiated. Children have more global emotional reactions and expressions than adults.

Gonads.—The sex glands.

Hebephrenic.—(*See* Schizophrenia.)

Hyperaesthesia.—A morbid form of sensibility in which impressions of the outside world are registered in an exaggerated and most painful manner. Hyperaesthesia is found in certain types of neurosis.

Hypomania.—A state of elation and heightened vitality generally taking a pathological form. It goes with flights of fancy, lack of common sense and moral sense, and with ideas of grandeur. It resembles a state of mania without its extreme manifestations. The maniac is violent, aggressive, tremendously tense, while the hypomaniac is happy, extremely self-contented and without malice towards others. A state of hypomania is found in patients of manic-depressive psychosis and in many mental defectives as well as in a certain number of other types of mental patients. Up to a point hypomania can be considered as a ' normal ' state of mind, for in some cases a certain amount of insight and common sense are maintained.

Hypothalamus.—Part of the interbrain. It gets its name from its position just below the thalamus. It is much smaller but even more important than the latter because of its functional significance. It is linked with the cortex of the brain as well as with ganglia of the autonomic nervous system and the pituitary gland. It plays a foremost part in emotional as well as in sexual function.

Inner Dynamism.—The potential and active force of nervous energy. It differs individually. Inner dynamism is the source of any form of human activity, physical, emotional and mental. Inner dynamism always depends on an appropriate amount of nervous tension, which is necessary to maintain physical, emotional and mental life.

Integration.—The capacity to co-ordinate conscious and subconscious energies into a perfect whole. In an integrated person physical, emotional and mental reactions are in harmony with each other.

Kinaesthetic Sense.—The feeling of one's own movements. The kinaesthetic sense is linked with a special type of consciousness and imagination which is strongly developed in children of from 4 to 6 years of age. There is a certain type of adults in whom kinaesthetic consciousness and imagination are more marked than in others : the ' dancer ' type, with a highly developed motor-imagination. Kinaesthetic or motor imagination can develop in a special type of aesthetic perception which is not restricted to one's own body. One finds kinaesthetic perception of objects in certain abstract paintings, such as those of Paul Klee, Kandinsky and many modern surrealists ; these artists do not represent the shape of things but the subjective feeling of the inner rhythm of them.

The kinaesthetic sense is strongly linked with the feeling of identity.

Leptosome.—A physical make-up. The term is used by E. Kretschmer in the description of his physical types. Leptosome means a physical make-up which is slender, graceful, but muscular and strong. The ' bony ' sportsman is of a leptosome physique.

Manic Depressive Psychosis.—A mental illness, called in French ' Folie circulaire , which goes with states of mania alternating with those of depression.

Between the two the patient goes through hypomaniac phases. Delusions and ideas of grandeur, and often also ideas of persecution, are features of this mental illness.

Medulla.—The nervous substance of the spine. The medulla oblongata is part of the hind brain and the direct continuation of the medulla of the spine.

Megalomaniac.—Suffering from ideas of grandeur.

Mental Representation.—The imprint of perceptive or organic processes in the brain. The organ of mental representation is the cortex (q.v.).

Mongolian imbecility.—A form of imbecility which goes with a special appearance recalling features of the Mongolian race.

Neuro-Humor.—A liquid produced by the sympathetic and parasympathetic nerves at the points at which they contact the muscles.

Neurology.—The knowledge of the anatomy and functions of the nervous system.

Neuron.—A nerve cell.

Paraperception.—I have used the term in this book in a special sense, namely, as a form of registration of outside impressions without consciousness of them. Generally, paraperception means a registration of phenomena which cannot be perceived through the senses ; in this sense telepathy is a form of paraperception.

Paraphrenia.—Can be translated as a state of mind in which the patient is always beside the point. It is a mental illness or psychosis in which the mind has lost the capacity of proper co-ordination between the real and the unreal. Paraphrenic patients suffer from delusions, which are, however, more localized than in sufferers from manic-depressive psychosis or schizophrenia.

Paralysis agitans, or Parkinson's Disease.—Described by Parkinson himself as consisting of ' involuntary tremulous motion, with lessened muscular power, in parts not in action, and even when supported ; with a propensity to bend the trunk forwards, and to pass from walking to a running pace ; the senses and intellect being uninjured. (*See* Walshe, F. M. R., *Diseases of the Nervous System*, p. 186.]

Parasympathetic nerves.—One of the two parts of the automatic nervous system, the other being the sympathetic.

Pathology.—The science of dysfunction and disease.

Pituitary Gland.—An endocrine gland situated in the brain in a small cavity of the skull called the sella turcica. The pituitary gland is considered in modern endocrinology as the most important of the endocrine glands. It has a decisive influence on the development of the bones, on blood pressure, metabolism and sexual function.

Proprioceptive Senses.—Those senses which register impressions of bodily feelings and organic sensations.

Psycho-dynamics.—Those qualities of the mind which are in continual fluctuation and development. The psychodynamic conception of personality has been especially developed by the Gestalt psychologists. It is a conception which attempts a depth-knowledge of the mind in contrast to the static conception of personality. The latter is based on physical measurements, from which it derives mental and temperamental qualities of a constitutional or permanent type.

Psychosis.—Mental illness.

Pyramidal Pathway, or Pyramidal Tract.—Nerve system probably arising from pyramidal cells in the cortex. It conveys voluntary motor impulses from the brain to the muscles. The pyramidal fibres decussate at the lower end of the medulla oblongata.

Pyknic.—A physical make-up. It is used by Kretschmer in the description of his physical types. The pyknic type of man is short and broad, rather heavily built, with strong muscles and round forms. He has a broad face with a small nose. He tends to get fat in middle age. He is slow in his reactions, both physically and mentally.

Regressive.—The term means a going back to an earlier stage of existence. Regressive qualities are those which belong to childhood or those which belong to an earlier phase of evolution.

Schizoid.—A type of temperament which, in a much milder form, is on the pattern of the schizophrenic personality. It is distinguished by a weak identity, a lack of spontaneous response and emotional warmth. The schizoid personality is always introvert.

Schizophrenia.—' Split personality ', the most severe type of psychosis. It can take different forms, but always goes with loss of identity. One distinguishes the hebephrenic, the catatonic, and the paranoiac reaction types in schizophrenia. The hebephrenic type is associated with sexual preoccupations and obsessions ; the catatonic—frequently a later stage of the hebephrenic —type goes with complete dissociation of mental and postural reaction leading to dementia on one hand and abnormal, stereotyped and persevering postures on the other. The paranoiac type of schizophrenia is associated, as the name indicates, with ideas of persecution, as well as with impulsiveness and depression.

Sclerosis.—The process of calcification which leads to hardening of the tissues ; artero-sclerois, for example, is hardening of the arteries. Sclerotic processes can occur in any type of tissue, not only in the blood vessels.

Sensory pathway.—A relay of neurones which pass from the periphery of the body to the brain, where they occupy a special area in the cortex. This area is responsible for consciousness of sensory stimuli.

Splanchnical Nerves.—The nerves of the autonomic nervous system which innervate the intestinal tract.

Static Sense.—The sense of balance.

Sympathetic Nerves.—A part of the autonomic nervous system which, on the whole, works antagonistically to the parasympathetic nerves of the autonomic nervous system.

Syndrome.—The unit of symptoms which are significant for a disease.

Thalamus.—More exactly, the optical thalamus, is one of the basal ganglia of the interbrain.

Thyroid Gland.—The endocrine gland which ' embraces ' the larynx. Its overdevelopment leads to Grave's disease. The thyroid gland is especially important for the fat metabolism of the body. The underfunctioning of the gland, called hypothyroidism, leads to abnormal fatness, often accompanied by low intelligence. The opposite condition, hyperthyroidism, goes with a slim physique, nervous restlessness, sleeplessness, &c., and often with a high intelligence.

Vasomotor-symptoms.—Symptoms, such as easy blushing or sweating, caused by a hypersensitive autonomic nervous system.

Writhing movements.—Slow, profoundly spastic, bizarre movements which occur in the condition of athetosis. They are due to an abnormal muscular tone leading to stereotyped and convulsive psycho-motor behaviour.

BIBLIOGRAPHY

ALLPORT, G. W. *Personality*, a Psychological Interpretation. Constable, London, 1938. Chapters III and IV.

—— and VERNON, PH. *Studies in Expressive Movements.* Macmillan, New York, 1933. Pp. 1–182.

—— and VERNON, PH. *A Scale for Measuring the Dominant Interests in Personality.* New York, 1940.

ARNHEIM, R. *Experimentelle psychologische Untersuchungen zum Ausdrucksproblem.* Psycholog. Forschungen, 1928. Vol. II, pp. 1–132.

BEHANAN, KOVOOR, T. *Yoga*, a Scientific Evaluation. Secker and Warburg, London, 1937.

BELL, CH. *The Anatomy and Philosophy of Expression.* George Bell & Son, London, 1890.

BILLS, A. G. 'The Influence of Muscular Tension on the Efficiency of Mental Work.' *Amer. J. Psychol.* 1927. Vol. 38, pp. 227–51.

BOGEN, H. and LIPMANN, O. 'Gang und Charakter', *Ergebnisse eines Preisausschreibens, Beihefte zur Zeitschrift fuer angewandte Psychologie.* Leipzig, 1931. Vol. 58.

BOHERTAG, O. 'Bemerkungen zum Verifikationsproblem. *Beihefte zur Zeitschrift fuer angewandte Psychologie.* 1934. Vol. 46.

BRIDGES, K. T. 'Le Développement des Emotions chez le Jeune Enfant.' *Journ. de Psychologie.* Paris, 1936. Vol. XXXIII.

BRUNSWICK, E. *Wahrnehmung und Gegenstandswelt*, Deuticke, Leipzig und Wien. 1934.

BULWER, J. Article by Norman, H. J., *Proc. Royal Soc. Med.*, London, 1943. Vol. XXXVI.

BRAUN, F. 'Untersuchungen ueber das persoenliche Tempo.' *Arch. f.d. ges. Psychol.* 1927. Vol. 60, pp. 317–60.

CANTRIL, H., RAND, H. A. and ALPORT, G. W. *The Determination of Personal Interests by Psychological and Graphological Methods* (Psychol. Lab. Harvard Univers.) Character and Personality. 1933–4.

CHAMBERS, E. G. 'Statistics in Psychology and the Limitations of the Test Method.' *Brit. Journ. Psychol.* 1943. Vol. XXXIII.

COLLINS, M. and DREVER, J. *Experimental Psychology*, sixth edition. Methuen, London, 1941. Pp. 275–300.

COOMARASWANG, A. and JUGGIRALA, G. K. *The Mirror of Gesture.* Cambridge, 1917.

CRITCHLEY, M. *The Language of Gesture.* Arnold, London, 1939.

DARWIN, CH. *The Expression of the Emotions in Man and Animals.* London, 1934. The Thinkers Library, pp. 4–23.

DUFFY, E. 'Tensions and Emotional Factors in Reaction.' *Genet. Psychol. Monog.* 1930. Vol. 7.

—— 'The Measurement of Muscular Tension as a Technique for the Study of Emotional Tendencies.' *Amer. Journ. Psychol.* 1932. Vol. 44, pp. 146–62.

DUNLAP, K. *Elements of Psychology.* London, 1936. Pp. 324–45.

EISENBERG, PH. 'Expressive Movements related to Feelings of Dominance.' *Arch. of Psychol.* New York, 1937. No. 211.

—— 'A Further Study in Expressive Movements' (Psychol. Lab. Columbia Univers.). *Character and Personality*, 1937. Vol. V., No. 4.

ENKE, W. 'Die Psychomotorik der Konstitutionstypen.' *Zeitschrift fuer angewandte Psychol.* Leipzig, 1930. Bd. 36, pp. 238–87.

FÉRÉ, quoted by VASCHIDE, N. in *Essai sur la Psychologie de la Main.* Paris, Rivière, 1909. P. 478.

FLACH, A. 'Psychologie der Ausdrucksbewegung.' *Arch. f.d. ges. Psychol.* 1928. Vol. 65, pp. 435–534.

FLIESS, R. 'Periodenlehre,' quoted by Ludwig W. in *Das Rechts-Links Problem im Tierreich und beim Menschen.* Berlin, 1932. P. 427.

FRIEDEMANN, A. 'Handbau und Psychosis.' *Arch. f. Neurol. u. Psychiat.* 1928.

GALTON, F. *Inquiries into Human Faculty and its Development.* Macmillan, London, 1883.

GESELL, A. *The First Five Years of Life.* Methuen, London, 1942. Pp. 1–107.

GIDE, A. *L'Immoraliste*, quoted in an article by Quennel, P. *Horizon.* London, June 1942.

GOLLA, F. L. and ANTINOWITSCH, S. 'The Relation of Muscle Tonus and the Patellar Reflexes to Mental Work.' *Journ. Ment. Sci.* 1929. Vol. 75, pp. 234–41.

GURWITCH, A. 'Le Fonctionnement de l'Organisme' d'apres K. Goldstein. *Journ. de Psychol.* Paris, 1939, Janvier-Mars.

HANSEN, K. 'Ueber humorale Nervenwirkung und Ausdruckssymptom', in *Die Wissenschaft am Scheidewege von Leben und Geist.* Festschrift zu L. Klages, 60, Geburtstag, Barth, Leipzig, 1932.

HARVEY, O. L. 'The Measurement of Handwriting considered as a Form of Expressive Movement.' *Charact. and Person.* 1933-4. Vol. 2, pp. 310–21.

HEAD, H. 'Head's Concept of the Scheme and its Application in Contemporary British Psychology,' by Oldfield R. O. and Zangwill O. L. *Brit. Journ. Psychol.* 1942. Vols. XXXII and XXXIII.

HERZ, E. 'Physiognomik and Mimik,' *Fortschr. d. Neur. u. Psychiat.* Grenzgebiete. Vol. II, Bd. 12.

HUEBEL, W. 'Ueber psychische Geschwindigkeit und ihre gegenseitigen Beziehungen,' *Zschr. f. angew. Psychol.* 1930. Vol. 35, pp. 447–96.

HUXLEY, A. *The Art of Seeing.* Chatto and Windus, London, 1943.

ISAACS, S. *The Behaviour of Young Children.* London, 1937.

JACOBSEN, W. 'Charaktertypische Ausdrucksbewegungen.' *Zschr. f. Paedag. Psychol.* 1936-7. Pp. 307–17.

JAMES, W. *Précis de Psychologie*, Eighth Edition. Rivière, Paris, 1929. Chap. 24.

KLAGES, L. *Ausdruckswissenschaft und Gestaltungskraft*, 5 Auflage. Barth, Leipzig, 1936.

—— *Handschrift und Charakter.* 13 Auflage. Barth, Leipzig, 1932.

KOEHLER, W. 'Les Forces Motrices du Comportement.' *J. de Psychol.* Paris, 1930. Vol. 27, pp. 367–90.

—— *Gestaltpsychology.* New York, 1929.

—— *Dynamics in Psychology.* Faber & Faber, London, 1942.

KOFFKA, K. *Principles of Gestalt Psychology.* Kegan Paul, Trubner, &c. London, 1940.

KRETSCHMER, E.   *Koerperbau und Charakter.* Berlin, 1931.
——— 'The Experimental Method treated as an Instrument of Psychological Investigation.' *Character and Personality.* 1933. Vol. I, No. 3.
KROUT, M.   *Autistic Gestures.* An experimental Study in Symbolic Movement, Psychol. Monographs, Psychol. Review Comp. Princeton, New York, 1935. No. 208.
——— 'The Social and Sociological Significance of Gestures,' *Journ. Gen. Psychol.* 1935. Vol. 47.
LAYARD, J.   *Stone Men of Malekula.* Chatto & Windus, London, 1942. Pp. 310–59.
LEIBNITZ, E.   *Opera omnia,* Part 2. Geneva, 1768. Vol. VI, p. 207.
LEWITAN, C.   'Untersuchungen ueber das allgemeine psychomotorische Tempo.' *Zschr. f. Psychol.* 1927. Vol. 10, pp. 321–76.
LHERMITE, J.   *L'Image de Notre Corps.* Paris. Editions de Nouvelle Revue Critique, 1939.
LUDWIG, W.   *Das Rechts-Links Problem im Tierreich und beim Menschen.* Berlin, 1932. Pp. 423–9.
LURIA, quoted by KROUT M. in *Autistic Gestures.*
MOUNTFORD, E. G.   'An Experimental Study of some German Type-Theories.' (Kings College, London.) *Character and Personality,* 1939–40.
MUENSTERBERG, quoted by VASCHIDE N. in *Essai sur la Psychologie de la Main.* Rivière, Paris, 1909. P. 478.
OMWAKE, K. T., DEXTER, E. S. and LEWIS, L. N.   'The Inter-Relations of Certain Physiological Measurements and Aspects of Personality.' *Character and Personality.* 1934–5. Vol. 3.
OSSERETZKY, N.   'Psychomotorik.' *Beihefte z. Zschr. f. angew. Psychol.* Barth, Leipzig, 1931. No. 57.
PAVLOV, J. P.   *Lectures on Condition Reflexes.* Third Edition. Lawrence and Wishart, London, 1941. Vols. I and II.
PIDERIT, TH.   *La Mimique et la Physiognomie* traduit par A. Girot, Alcan, Paris. 1888.
PINDER, W.   *Zur Physiognomik des Manirismus.* Zschr. z. 60. Gebrtst. L. Klages, &c.
POPHAL, R.   *Die Doppeldeutigkeit lebendiger Bewegungen im Lichte ihrer zwiefachen Entstehungsmoeglichkeit.* Zschr. z. 60. Geburtstag v. L. Klages. Barth, Leipzig, 1932.
REYMENT, M. L. and KOHN, H. A.   'An Objective Investigation of Suggestibility.' *Character and Personality.* 1940.
RIBOT.   *Problèmes de Psychologie Affective.* Alcan, Paris, 1909.
ROHRSCHACH, H.   'Le Diagnostic Individual chez l'Enfant au Moyen du Test de Rohrschach,' par M. Loosli-Usteri, Hermann et Cie Paris, 1938. *Actualités Scientif. et Industr.* No. 639.
ROSENTHAL, J. S.   'Typology in the Light of the Theory of Conditioned Reflexes' (Lab. of Leningrad Inst. f. Exper. Med.). *Character and Personality.* 1940.
SAMUELS, M. R.   'Judgement of Faces.' *Character and Personality.* 1939–40.
SEELIG, E.   'Die Registrierung unwillkuerlicher Ausdrucksbewegungen als forensisch psychodiagnostische Methode.' *Zschr. f. ang. Psychol.* 1927. Vol. 28, pp. 45–84.

SHELDON, W. H. *The Varieties of Human Physique.* Harper, New York, 1940.
—— and CHILD, J. L. 'The Correlation between Components of Physique and Scores on Certain Psychological Tests.' (Harv. Univ.) *Character and Personality.* 1939–40.
SHIRER, N. *Last Train from Berlin.* London, 1940.
SITTL, K. *Die Gebaerdensprache der Griechen und Roemer.* Treubner, Leipzig, 1890.
SPAERMAN, CH. 'German Science of Character.' *Character and Personality.* 1931. Vol. VI, No. 1.
STRATTON, G. M. *Developing Mental Power.* Boston, 1922.
TILNEY, F. and RILEY, H. A. *The Form and Functions of the Central Nervous System.* Lewis Co., London, 1938. Pp. 506–657.
UEXKUELL, I. V. *Der Gedachte Raum.* Zschr. z. 60. Geburtstag L. Klages. Leipzig, 1932.
VANCE, I. G. *A Mirror of Personality.* London, 1927.
VALENTINE, C. W. *The Psychology of Early Childhood.* Methuen, London, 1943.
VASCHIDE, N. *Essai sur la Psychologie de la Main.* Rivière, Paris, 1909. Pp. 399–414 and 475–88.
VERNON, PH. E. *The Measurements of Abilities.* University of London Press, 1940.
WALLON, H. 'Comment se développe chez l'Enfant la Notion du Corps Propre.' *J. de Psychol.* Paris, 1931. Vol. XXVIII.
—— *L'Enfant Turbulent.* Alcan, Paris, 1925.
—— *Les Origines du Charactère chez l'Enfant.* Paris, 1934.
WALSHE, F. M. R. *Diseases of the Nervous System.* Livingstone, Edinburgh. Third edition, 1943. Pp. 1–60, 114–23, 192–6 and 320–3.
WILLEMSE, W. A. 'Constitution Types in Delinquency.' Practical Application and Bio-Physiological Foundation of Kretschmer's Types. *Character and Personality.* London, 1932. Vol. I, No. 1.
WOLFF, CH. *The Human Hand.* Methuen, London, 1942.
—— and ROLLON, H. R. 'The Hands of Mongolian Imbeciles in Relation to their three Personality Groups.' *Journ. Ment. Sci.,* Vol. LXXXVIII, No. 372. 1942.
—— 'The Hand of the Mental Defective.' *Brit. Journ. Med. Psychol.* Vol. XX, Part 2, 1944, pp. 147–60.
WOLFF, W. 'Ueber Factoren der Charakterologischen Urteilsbildung.' *Zschr. f. ang. Psychol.* 1930. Vol. 35.
—— 'The Experimental Study of Forms of Expressions.' *Character and Personality.* 1932–3. Vol. II.
—— 'Involuntary Self-Expression in Gait and Other Movements.' *Character and Personality.* 1934–5. Vol. II, No. 4.
WUNDT, W. *Grundzuege der Physiologischen Psychologie.* 6 Auflage. Leipzig, 1908.
ZOEPFFEL, H. 'Ein Versuch zur Experimentellen Feststellung der Persoenlichkeit im Saeuglingsalter.' *Zschr. f. Psychol.* 1929. Vol. III, pp. 273–306.

TABLE I

FREQUENCY OF CERTAIN PSYCHO-MOTOR REACTION IN 27 MENTAL PATIENTS AT WORK

(13 Schizophrenics ; 8 Paraphrenics ; 5 Manic Depressives)

	Schizo-phrenics	Para-phrenics	Manic Depressives
1 Autistic gestures	13	8	3
2 Persevering gestures	12	5	1
3 Stereotyped gestures	11	6	4
4 Reflex movements only	11	4	2
5 Arrhythmic gestures	10	6	4
6 Forward impulses entirely inhibited	9	4	0
7 Many unnecessary movements	9	4	1
8 Slow motor speed	7	4	3
9 Hair gestures	5	1	1
10 Non-emphatic gestures	5	1	0
11 Mask-like expressions	5	2	2
12 Sniffing, smelling, giggling	5	1	0
13 Writhing movements	4	1	0
14 Impulsive gestures	4	7	3
15 General motor unrest	4	5	1
16 Hypermobility of face	4	5	3
17 Quiet facial expressions	4	0	1
18 Facial tics	4	1	1
19 Wringing, pressing, interlocking of hands	3	3	3
20 Fast motor speed	3	2	4
21 Centrifugal gestures	3	4	2
22 Hiding gestures	3	3	3
23 Mouth and Tongue gestures	3	1	0
24 Emphatic gestures	3	8	5
25 Aggressive facial expressions	2	5	3
26 Rolling eyes	2	1	0
27 Index finger raised	2	2	0
28 Expansive gestures	1	7	3
29 Pulling hair, plucking eye-brows, &c.	1	1	1
30 Ambivalent motor speed	1	5	0
31 Opening and closing of fists	0	1	0
32 Hyper- (or hypo-) metric gestures	0	4	1
33 Thumb in palm	0	0	1

TABLE II

FREQUENCY OF CERTAIN PSYCHO-MOTOR REACTIONS IN
36 MENTAL PATIENTS AT MEALS

(7 Schizophrenics ; 3 Hypomaniacs ; 3 Depressed Phase ; 6 Melancholics who were treated with Electrical Shock Treatment ; 7 Melancholics not treated and 10 Epileptics)

	7 Schizo-phrenics	3 Hypo-maniacs	3 Depressed phase	6 Melancholics (treated)	7 Melancholics (not treated)	10 Epileptics
1 Autistic gestures	7	2	3	1	7	10
2 Persevering gestures	7	0	3	3	7	8
3 Stereotyped gestures	7	3	3	2	7	8
4 Reflex movements only	7	0	3	1	7	8
5 Arrhythmic gestures	7	0	3	1	7	10
6 Forward impulses entirely inhibited	7	0	2	1	7	8
7 Slow motor speed	7	3	3	6	5	8
8 Many unnecessary movements	7	3	1	0	2	10
9 Hair gestures	4	2	0	0	2	0
10 Non-emphatic gestures	0	0	2	6	5	2
11 Mask-like expressions	3	0	2	1	5	0
12 Sniffing, smelling, giggling	4	0	0	1	0	0
13 Writhing movements	4	0	0	0	0	0
14 Impulsive gestures	7	0	1	0	2	10
15 General motor unrest	7	0	1	0	2	8
16 Hypermobility of face	4	3	1	0	2	10
17 Quiet facial expressions	0	0	0	4	0	0
18 Facial tics	0	0	0	1	0	1
19 Wringing, pressing, interlocking of hands	0	0	1	1	2	6
20 Fast motor speed	0	0	0	0	2	2
21 Centrifugal gestures	0	3	0	0	1	1
22 Hiding gestures	0	0	2	5	4	6
23 Mouth and Tongue gestures	4	0	0	1	0	1
24 Emphatic gestures	0	0	1	0	2	10
25 Aggressive facial expressions	0	0	1	0	0	0
26 Rolling eyes	0	0	0	0	2	10
27 Index finger raised	0	0	0	0	0	0
28 Expansive gestures	0	3	0	1	0	2
29 Pulling hair, plucking eye-brows, &c.	0	0	0	0	2	0
30 Ambivalent motor speed	0	0	0	0	0	2
31 Opening and closing of fists	0	0	0	0	0	0
32 Hyper- or hypometric gestures	0	3	0	0	0	10
33 Thumb-up gestures	0	1	0	0	0	0
34 Thumb in palm	0	0	1	0	0	0
35 Affected or precious gestures	0	3	0	0	0	2
36 Fifth Finger held apart	1	2	0	0	0	2
37 Stretching hand gestures	0	0	0	0	0	10

TABLE III

ILLUSTRATES THE CORRELATION BETWEEN PSYCHO-MOTOR
PATTERNS AND HAND-TYPES IN MENTAL PATIENTS

Number of Cases	Psycho-Motor Patterns	Hand-type	Illness
6	I	4 Long sensitive 2 Small sensitive, narrow with regressive features	Schizophrenia 5 Catatonic 1 Paranoiac
3	I and II	3 Long sensitive of which 2 have regressive traits	1 Manic-depressive psychosis 2 Paraphrenics (paranoiac)
3	I and V	3 Small sensitive, broad with regressive traits	3 Schizophrenia and mental deficiency
2	I and IV	1 Elementary regressive 1 Small sensitive, narrow	Schizophrenia 1 Catatonic 2 Paranoiac
3	V	2 Fleshy motor 1 Elementary	3 Paraphrenia 2 With mental deficiency
4	V and III	2 Bony motor, one with regressive traits 2 Elementary regressive	3 Manic-depressives 1 Paraphrenia
3	V and IV	1 Fleshy motor 2 Elementary All 3 symptoms of hypothyroidism	1 Manic-depressive 1 Paraphrenia 1 Schizophrenia (hebephrenic)
24 Cases			

TABLE IV

ILLUSTRATES THE CORRELATION BETWEEN PSYCHO–MOTOR
PATTERNS AND HAND–TYPES IN MENTAL PATIENTS

Number of Cases	Psycho–Motor Patterns	Hand-type	Illness
5	I only	4 Long sensitive (2 of them with regressive traits) 1 Small sensitive, narrow	Schizophrenia (catatonic)
3	I and II	2 Long sensitive 1 Small sensitive, narrow	Paraphrenia (melancholia)
4	I and V	1 Elementary regressive 3 Small sensitive, broad	Schizophrenia with mental deficiency Schizophrenia (paranoiac type)
5	V	2 Bony motor 2 Fleshy motor 1 Elementary	Paraphrenia (paranoia)
4	V and III	2 Small sensitive, broad 2 Elementary regressive	Paraphrenia (hypomania) Schizophrenia (hebephrenic)
4	I and III	2 Bony motor 2 Sensitive small, broad	Paraphrenia (hypomania and megalomania)
25 Cases			

INDEX

THE THANET PRESS. MARGATE.

BODY MOVEMENT
Perspectives in Research
An Arno Press Collection

Christiansen, Bjørn
Thus Speaks the Body: Attempts Toward a Personology from the Point of View of Respiration and Postures. Oslo, Norway, 1963

Dewey, Evelyn
Behavior Development in Infants: A Survey of the Literature on Prenatal and Postnatal Activity 1920–1934. New York, 1935

Evolution of Facial Expression: Two Accounts
    a. Andrew, R. J.
        The Origin and Evolution of the Calls and Facial Expressions of the Primates (Reprinted from *Behaviour,* Vol. 20, Leiden, Netherlands, 1963)
    b. Huber, Ernst
        Evolution of Facial Musculature and Facial Expression. Baltimore, 1931

Facial Expression in Children: Three Studies
    a. Washburn, Ruth Wendell
        A Study of the Smiling and Laughing of Infants in the First Year of Life (Reprinted from *Genetic Psychology Monographs,* Vol. 6, Nos. 5 & 6, Worcester, Mass., 1929) November-December, 1929
    b. Spitz, René A., with the Assistance of K. M. Wolf
        The Smiling Response: A Contribution to the Ontogenesis of Social Relations (Reprinted from *Genetic Psychology Monographs,* Vol. 34, Provincetown, Mass., 1946) August, 1946
    c. Goodenough, Florence L.
        Expression of the Emotions in a Blind-Deaf Child (Reprinted from *Journal of Abnormal and Social Psychology,* Vol. 27, Lancaster, Pa., 1932)

Research Approaches to Movement and Personality
    a. Eisenberg, Philip
        Expressive Movements Related to Feeling of Dominance (Reprinted from *Archives of Psychology,* Vol. 30, No. 211, New York, 1937) May, 1937
    b. Bartenieff, Irmgard and Martha Davis
        Effort-Shape Analysis of Movement: The Unity of Expression and Function. New York, 1965
    c. Takala, Martti
        Studies of Psychomotor Personality Tests I. Helsinki, Finland, 1953

Wolff, Charlotte
A Psychology of Gesture. Translated from the French Manuscript by Anne Tennant. 2nd edition. London, 1948